Thor

&

More

By Jay Reed

The Legendary Outdoor Writer
of the *Milwaukee Journal Sentinel*

Editor: Mike Beno

Art Director: Gary Cox

Associate Editors: Christine Reed, Therese Safford

1

DEDICATION

This book is dedicated to Jay's friends and faithful readers…

To the flights of wild ducks that thrilled him every autumn…

To the loyal dogs he loved…

And to the Mighty Mississippi, where his life and love of
the outdoors began.

May you enjoy the adventures, the laughter and the tears
once again. That's why this book came to be. Special thanks
to Mike Beno for making it happen.

— Christine Reed, 2009, Whitefish Bay, Wisconsin

In These Pages, Jay Reed's Words Live On

He was our tie to the wood smoke, the loon calls, the frosty cackle of an early morning October rooster, the red plaid jackets and the camaraderie of the old deer camps.

He was our Sunday ritual. Trek to the paper box, coffee in hand. Pull out "the Journal," open to the outdoor pages before you even get back to the front porch. Settle in for the best read of the week.

He was our eyes and ears. He knew (so we knew) what was happening in the Wisconsin Department of Natural Resources, the State Legislature, and in the Northwoods.

He was our catalyst for change. When my colleagues and I planned the first Becoming an Outdoors Woman workshop, registration was lagging. We sent Jay a press release and the article he published in the *Milwaukee Journal* filled the workshop in one day. That first successful workshop introduced women to hunting, fishing, trapping and other outdoor skills in a supportive and fun atmosphere. Today, 20,000 women a year across North America learn to enjoy what Jay knew they would enjoy.

He is our bridge to the future. When Jay passed away, his friends and family set up a scholarship endowment at the UW-Stevens Point College of Natural Resources. This fund helps promising young resource managers move into careers where they can contribute to a world where fish and wildlife thrive. Proceeds from the sales of this book will be donated to the scholarship fund.

He was never my fishing partner…something I really regret. I first met Jay in the 1980s when I interviewed him about the Natural Resources Board for my doctoral dissertation. I know he would have been proud of me when I was appointed to the

Board just a few months after he passed away. Over the years fishing with my favorite guide, Milt Dieckman, we talked about getting Jay to come up to Hayward to fish with us. We did not get it done.

He was an icon in the Wisconsin outdoors. I have looked forward to this book for a long time. We can laugh and cry with him over the adventures of his yellow Lab, Thor. We can relearn the old lessons, relive the old adventures, and savor his ability to conjure up visions with words.

When my copy arrives, I plan to stoke up the woodstove, brew a cup of coffee and settle in for the best read of the year. And...I am going to fish with Jay Reed.

It is an honor to have been asked by Christine Reed to be a part of this.

Christine L. Thomas, PhD
Dean and Professor of Resource Management
College of Natural Resources
University of Wisconsin – Stevens Point

Jay Reed:
An Unforgettable Character
Who Lived an Action-Packed Life

The mourners were packed into Gesu Church in Milwaukee, Wisconsin on November 13, 2002. During the funeral, they heard the sharp bark of a Marine Corps drill sergeant from outside the front doors of the stone church. Then came three loud cracks from the rifles in a 21-gun salute.

In dress blues, the color guard marched down the center aisle, and, with an amazing display of grace, discipline and integrity, took the flag from the casket of Jay Reed, folded it, and presented it to his wife, Christine.

There wasn't a dry eye in the place. War veterans and bearded old hunters, people who hadn't cried in decades, were bawling like babies. "It made you want to be a Marine just so you could go out like that," recalls George Stanley, managing editor of the *Milwaukee Journal Sentinel*. Reed's longtime co-worker and hunting pal Don Bluhm remarked, "When it comes to ceremony, you can't beat the U.S. Marines and the Catholic Church."

The group had gathered to celebrate an unforgettable friend, a man widely known across Wisconsin. For some 40 years, Jay Reed's outdoor stories appeared in the pages of the state's largest newspaper. A soft-spoken and humble man, Reed had called himself "the scribbler," "a country boy," and an "old swamp rat."

He surely looked the part. Starting in 1963, two generations of outdoor enthusiasts saw Reed's bearded visage atop his columns on Thursdays and Sundays.

Late in his career, Reed allowed himself a little credit when he reflected, "I have been around the world on assignments. I have covered a war, a presidential debate, a South American rain forest, a World Series, the Kentucky Derby and more. Twice I damned near won Pulitzer Prizes. That ain't bad for a poor, unschooled boy from Nelson."

Jay Reed was born in Nelson, Wisconsin on November 20, 1928. He grew up in this rough-cut river town of 150 souls on the banks of the Mississippi. Reed's father died when the youngster was four, so Jay was raised by his mother, a sister, and his brother, Huck Siefert.

Huck was 10 years older than Jay, and the youngster wanted to do nothing but hunt, fish and trap with him. Jay would run a trap line in the morning, hide his shotgun and other gear under a bridge, then go to school. In the afternoon he'd retrieve his gear and continue hunting and trapping.

This was during the Depression years of the 1930s. The family was poor, so if Huck and Jay could kill something with meat on its back, it became dinner. If it had fur on its back, it was sold for pocket money.

Education was never high on Jay Reed's list. He didn't like school, struggled in his classes and rarely attended, much to the frustration of his mother who was a teacher.

In 1943, at age 15, Reed quit school altogether. He lied about his age, joined the Marines and shipped out for the western Pacific. There he made the World War II invasion landings on treacherous coral atolls like Peleliu.

After the war, Reed returned to Nelson, but became restless. Huck, the commercial fisherman, couldn't understand why Jay didn't stay forever, trapping turtles, netting catfish and shooting ducks.

Wanting a steady job, Reed went to Rockford, Illinois, where he poured iron in a foundry. At night he tended bar in a hotel. The owner must have seen something in the kid behind his bar, because he mentioned to Reed that the local newspaper was hiring.

That sounded better than pouring iron, so he applied at *The Rockford Register-Republic*, where he was hired

RATS! December 14, 1940, was a successful day afield for Jay Reed. Here, the 12-year old proudly displays two muskrats he bagged with his brother, Huck, who shot this photo near Nelson, Wisconsin.

DECORATED VETERAN. Jay Reed pictured at age 17. This photo was taken upon his return to the States at the end of World War II.

SWEATIN' DEADLINES. Jay Reed works the phones in the newsroom at *The Appleton Post-Crescent*, where he served as a reporter during the late 1950s and early '60s.

as a copy kid. He swept the floors and emptied the trash until the editor gave him some briefs to write.

Reed's first feature story won a writing award. It was about a women's golf tournament. By 1950, he was listed as a sportswriter, and soon had a column called, "Keeping Posted, With J.L. Reed."

Thus began Reed's long career in journalism without a formal education. He covered high school sports in Rockford, as well as the American Girls Baseball League and amateur boxing. At one memorable card he met the referee—Jack Dempsey.

In the early 1950s, Reed was called back to service in Korea. After his return, he found a job at *The Appleton Post-Crescent*. He wrote the police beat, county government stories, and even did some editing for the women's pages. Here his writing turned toward the outdoors, including features on deer hunting, trout fishing, and the 1957 state pheasant hunting outlook.

In 1963, Reed was recruited by the *Milwaukee Journal* as an outdoor writer. He'd remain in that job for the next 39 years, filing stories principally from Wisconsin, but also from such exotic places as Cuba, Panama...and Vietnam.

In 1967 and '68, he covered the Vietnam War, attached to combat units of the Marine Corps and the Army. Because of his service in two previous wars, Reed was given clearance to work on the front lines where he accompanied pilots on combat sorties and helped pick up the battle dead.

In 1989, Reed would return to Vietnam to file a series of reflective stories about that country after the war. That series, as well as the one he did in 1968, made Jay Reed a finalist for the Pulitzer Prize.

The broad body of Jay Reed's work, of course, dealt with hunting and fishing, which amounted to his dream job. He got paid to be a swamp rat, which was his first love and an image he loved to cultivate.

Through many years of wading the duck marshes, busting through grouse covers and tramping the pheasant fields, Reed set aside his favorite columns with the thought they'd be collected in a book some day. The result is in your hands, though Jay Reed didn't live to see it.

In the fall of 2002, while walking to his duck blind, Reed didn't feel quite right. His doctor later told him why. Cancer had spread from his lungs throughout his bones. Within a week of the diagnosis, he'd be hospitalized.

From his hospital bed, the lifelong smoker told his friend and newsroom colleague, Bill Janz, "If I got cancer, I figured it to be the lungs. I sure as hell asked for that." But Reed added, "Don't feel sorry for me, Billy. I've had a good run."

During that run, Reed hunted with countless companions. The most famous sidekick of all was Thor, his yellow Labrador retriever. Thousands of readers followed their adventures from puppyhood through 13 action-filled hunting seasons. It was not uncommon for Reed to pull into a gas station in some tiny rural town and hear a stranger call out to the dog by name.

In 1993, Reed wrote, "A late October day, deep in the swamps of the Chippewa River, the wind curling and snapping out of the northeast, the temperature dropping. That was the day my old dog told me he was going to die soon. He knew it and I knew it. If you own an old dog and if you work with him and play with him and forgive him his shortcomings and beg more time from him, you will understand why I wept that night in the duck swamp."

Reed buried Thor near his hunting camp. And nine years later, as he himself was dying, Reed asked his wife, Christine, and hunting companion, Don Bluhm, to sprinkle some of his ashes on the old dog's grave.

Christine saw to that...just as she saw to the posthumous publication of this book. Between its covers you'll once again enjoy the very best writings of Jay Reed... as chosen by the Old Swamp Rat himself.

A BATTERED JONES CAP became Jay Reed's trademark through 40 years of outdoor writing. The swamp rat image was something Reed loved to cultivate, yet, he was deeply familiar with Shakespeare and often quoted his work.

Thinking of an Old Friend on Opening Day

D eep in a forest way up north it's cold and clear a half hour before the opening of the 2008 gun deer season. Above me shine more stars than you can count or even imagine. Orion stretches his bow.

I'm sitting on a bucket in the woods of Washburn County, Wisconsin, waiting for the pre-dawn candle, listening to ghosts in the woods and thinking about Jay Reed.

How many times had he brought us to places like this when we couldn't get there ourselves? Where wings whistle as mallards spill into the decoys. Where we can smell the smoke, taste the coffee and hear the laughter of old friends.

Jay could bring us back to those sacred moments and places. He did it, like everything in his life, in his own way, his own style.

We first met as reporters working for arch-rival newsrooms—he for the *Milwaukee Journal*, me for the *Milwaukee Sentinel*. Jay was the dean of Wisconsin outdoor writers, a living legend some 30 years my senior. We each had been assigned to cover the loud and nasty boat-landing protests against Chippewa tribal spear-fishing, which happened every spring in the Northwoods during the late 1980s and early '90s.

Jay had little taste for the assignment. He tried not to suffer fools whenever he could avoid it and fools were drawn to these boat landing circuses like insects to a bright light.

What Jay did have a taste for was a good thick steak. He led a little crew of us to the best steak joint in Vilas County—a cozy place where the cook knew the difference between rare and medium rare.

Jay listened more than he talked. He gave compliments better than he received them. He could tell a good joke when he felt like it, but would much rather laugh at yours. At least once in the newsroom he was laughing so hard that he had to split his laughter in two, literally taking a breather in between.

He had just invited his new boss, Garry Howard, to go deer hunting so that he could "get to know the real Wisconsin."

Calling the *Milwaukee Journal's* new sports editor a city slicker was akin to calling Jay Reed a marsh rat—both were pretty dramatic understatements. Garry grew up in the projects of the South Bronx and had come to the Journal by way of the *Philadelphia Inquirer*.

"So you want to take me out in the woods," Garry said, "where there will be 600,000 good old boys with loaded guns?"

"I hadn't really thought of it that way, but...yeah," Jay said.

"Jay," Garry replied. "There ain't enough blaze orange in the *entire world* to cover my black ass."

The laughter started slowly, deep down in Jay's belly, as he realized Garry saw things from a somewhat different perspective. Soon he was laughing so hard he was gasping for air and his face started turning color. He wiped his eyes and paused, calming himself until he could breathe. Then the whole cycle started over again.

A good sense of humor ranked near the top of the list when it came to things Jay Reed appreciated. Honesty was another. I believe the fundamental honesty of Jay Reed's written work is why his readers appreciated him – and why they want to keep his words alive.

"I love lots of things," he wrote. "Our country. Sunrises. Sunsets. Cloudy days during duck season. I love a little coffee in the morning. A cold beer, after a hunt."

I miss his warm greeting. "Hello, my friend," he would say and then, as you reached to shake his hand, he would clasp it with both of his big mitts and look you straight in the eyes.

I miss the notes he used to send me when I was a young writer on the other side of the bridge that separated the fourth floor newsroom of the *Journal* Building at 333 W. State Street from the fourth floor newsroom of the adjacent *Sentinel* Building at 918 N. 4th Street.

Before the two newsrooms became one in 1995, notes of friendship crossed that bridge about as often as they did between the leaders of Israel and Palestine. But Jay sent several kind and generous messages across the border, knowing exactly how much the words would mean to me, having come from him.

I'll never forget the feeling of opening up an envelope and seeing the first sentence of one of those notes after some investigative reporting had garnered results. "George, I am so proud of you."

This collection of stories, which Jay had started to organize before he died in 2002, is his final gift to all who loved him and his work – one last note from Jay across the bridge.

I, for one, will treasure it.

George Stanley
Managing Editor
Milwaukee Journal Sentinel

CONTENTS

CHAPTER 1

Days of Thunder

INTRODUCTION

Thor, Jay Reed's yellow Labrador retriever, became a legendary name with the sportsmen of Wisconsin. From 1980 to 1993, Thor was regularly featured in Jay's outdoor columns and photos.

During those years, a bond developed between Thor and Jay Reed, but also, between Thor and Jay's readers. They came to know the dog and frequently wrote to inquire about him. In fact, Thor generated more mail than any other subject at the *Milwaukee Journal*'s outdoors department. Three sitting governors wrote Reed about Thor, who likely became the best-known dog in Wisconsin sporting history.

A columnist's job is a plum position at any newspaper, reserved for those who write most creatively and descriptively, with thought and humor. Those attributes in Jay Reed were recognized in 1963, when he was named outdoor columnist for the *Milwaukee Journal*. But a column is only as good as the columnist's story ideas...a weak idea results in a bad patch of words, no matter how adept a writer may be.

This was the first reason Thor became so important in Jay's work. On one level, Thor represented an ingenious journalistic device...a rich well of lively story ideas.

But Thor became far more than that, to Jay Reed, to his wife, Christine, and to the many thousands of readers across the Midwest who loved to follow tales of Thor's life and times, as woven with creativity and love by Jay Reed.

You'll see—and feel—the many reasons why in the touching stories that follow.

You'll Be Hearing a Lot About This Little Guy

Step right up, folks, and be introduced today to Candlewood's Thor of River Road.

He's a seven-week-old yellow Labrador retriever. He's got sultry fire in his eyes and love in his heart and he's just now figuring out how to get all four of his legs working together at the same time.

He lives in a world of giants where a chair is big as a mountain. He does not know, yet, that he should lift his rear leg if he is to go to the toilet with any degree of male dignity, but he mostly understands that whatever you do, you don't do it in the house.

Thor will travel with me to those places the *Milwaukee Journal* sends me. And when fall comes, we'll hunt together in every field and swamp I can find. He will prowl trout streams this spring and ride boats on the good fishing lakes of the state. He will find out what motel living is all about.

We should talk a little about lineage here because, by breeding at least, Thor is not your everyday, egg sucking, back-alley, garbage-grabber.

He came to us from Mary Howley's Candlewood Kennel near Madison. His grandfather, River Oaks Corky, was one of the most distinguished dogs in American field trialing, having won the national amateur field trial championship five times. In 1967, he won the national derby championship.

A HUNTING BUDDY. Jay Reed picked up Thor in mid-January, 1980. In this photo shot near Madison, the pup is seven weeks old.

His grandmother is Candlewood's Nellie-B-Good, a litter mate of Euroclydon, the 1977 national field champion.

Other big names in his line of breeding include Super Chief, a three-time national amateur field champion, Del-Tone Buck and Miss Cherokee Chief.

Thor's sire is Candlewood's Nifty Nick, a beautiful, deep-chested yellow Lab. The dam is Jamested's Tarbaby of Trieven, the mother of the 1979 Minnesota state derby champion.

Pedigrees mean more to professional dog people than they do to me, mostly because I really don't understand it all. But I figure any pup who has a sire named Nifty Nick can't be all bad.

This introduction of Thor to Journal readers is calculated. It is only the first of a number of stories that will be written about him in the days, months and years yet to come.

Those who read this page and are interested in such things will be able to follow his growth from puppyhood to adult. His training progress, whatever it is, will become a part of the public record.

And when golden fall comes, readers will be able to hunt with Thor through the stories and pictures that will appear here. And the record will show the peaks and the valleys, the wins and the losses, the tears and the triumphs.

> **"Readers will be able to follow his growth from puppyhood to adult..."**

Right now, though, what we've got is a little puppy, appealing as only puppies can be, whose world is just beginning to open. He does not know, yet, the course that has been charted for him.

And he really does not care.

What he knows right now is that a duck wing feels good in his mouth, that it's hard work to walk the edge of a frozen swamp and that nights are long and dark and not intended to be spent alone.

For Thor, the days of thunder are yet a long way down the road.

Thor is Getting His Legs Under Him

S ince he was introduced to Journal readers last January, Candlewood's Thor (of River Road) has been building muscle and learning about living up among the pine trees and pheasant fields of Suring in Oconto County.

In case you missed the first story or in case you have forgotten it or, even, if you don't really give a damn, Thor is a yellow Labrador retriever puppy. In writing about Thor the first time, I said that his growth from puppyhood to adult, and his training progress, whatever it is, will become a part of the public record.

The first installment of that record begins today.

Thor was seven weeks old when the first story appeared. Now he is 15 weeks. His age has more than doubled and so has his weight. He weighed about eight pounds back then. Now he is 25 pounds.

His legs have lengthened, his body has deepened, his face has become more angular. His color is soft, light yellow.

The only thing that has not changed about him physically are his eyes. They remain now, as they were in the beginning, deep, dark, luminous pools that reflect his moods.

It was part of our plan to have Thor travel with me as much as possible. And that has been the case. He has prowled the banks of the Peshtigo River. He has raced across the ice on Lake Winnebago and Shawano Lake and White Potato Lake. He has seen sturgeon and walleyes and northern pike flopping on the ice.

LONG AND LEGGY. Thor grew quickly, as Labradors do, through his first year in 1980. In this photo, shot by Jay Reed, he's starting to crowd the tailgate on Jay's Suburban.

He got tangled in a gill net at the Department of Natural Resources fish camp at Pipe. He has slept in motels at Gillett and Crivitz and Oshkosh and Abrams. He has romped through the cemetery at Hickory and he has collided with a tree at the public park at Kelly Lake when his puppy legs did not stop him in time.

18

He has proven to be an outstanding traveler. He has ridden hundreds of miles in my truck so far, and has never once gotten car sick.

As young as he is, Thor has already entered into the first phases of training. He has not been kenneled. Nor will he be.

By his 12th week, Thor understood the command to sit. By his 13th week, he understood the command to sit and stay.

If I hide a duck wing in a motel room, Thor can find it. It has become a constant game with us.

If I put a piece of steak on the floor in front of him and tell him to sit and stay, Thor will do that until told to pick it up.

If I walk him beside a river or in the woods and if I watch him closely, I can see the doors open to a new and fascinating world. An oak leaf rolling in the wind becomes something to chase; a stick becomes something to grab; a dried weed becomes something to bite at.

If I see him charge through a drift of snow I marvel at the fact that Thor knows nothing, yet, but winter. He does not

"An oak leaf rolling in the wind becomes something to chase..."

understand that there will be days of sun and heat and bugs that will swarm at his ears.

And if, when the day is over and I should doze in a motel room chair, he'll lick my hand and let me know that the world is a better place than I could have ever believed it could be.

For Thor, the time of thunder is not yet here. But the days, and nights, of love and learning are.

Thor is Growing, Learning …and Ready to Hunt

It is nearly dark outside now as I check the dog for ticks in the pale, yellow light of the one-room cabin here in Berry Lake, Wisconsin.

There's the low rumble of thunder in the distance and I hear the first of the rain snapping off the screened window. There's wind in the pines, moaning low and sad like a train.

My back is wet with sweat and I feel a chill settling in around my gut. There's a tightening of the mind. My skin creeps and crawls and I don't know why.

Thor sits obediently, silently, patiently, at my feet. I run my hands around his ears and down his neck looking to the tender underside. My fingers feel the rippling muscles along his back and the velvet smoothness of his flanks.

He's clean, the dog is, of ticks. The ugly pests would burrow into his skin and suck his blood and balloon to the size of a quarter, filled with sick, purple pus. But not this night.

Thor looks to me, then, to see if the job is done. I motion to him that it is. He stands, stretches, yawns and sits again to accept the dog biscuit I offer.

His black, liquid eyes smile back at me. His jaws snap through the crisp stuff and, when finished, he slides smoothly full length upon the floor.

With another stretch, another yawn he falls swiftly asleep, his rib cage moving softly, his legs twitching in cadence with his dreams.

I pull long and hard at another beer, feeling the liquid burn its way down my throat, cooling as it goes, but bringing warmth way down deep where it finally settles.

And the questions come flooding back, the ones that haunt me, sometimes, when I watch this dog in the quiet times.

Candlewood's Thor of River Road. Yellow Labrador. Five months old now. Fifty pounds and growing. His papers say he's half mine, half Bob Olson's of Suring.

Tell me, Thor, what strange powers you possess. Tell me how it is with you and Chris, the one who gave you your name; the one who can think clearly and sharply on any other subject, but who is reduced to tears when she has to say goodbye to you. You slept on her lap when you weighed less than 10 pounds. And you still do now that you are more than half grown.

20

Tell me, too, Thor, how you worked your way into the affections of Olson, a professional dog trainer, a hard man with animals because he has to be. How the heck did you do it?

And what about Cookie, his wife? She's been around dogs most of her life. She's seen them come and go. But you've got her, you know, and that's why I wonder about your power.

I can understand your thing with Roy and Russ, the Olson offspring. Puppies and little boys were made for each other.

I wonder about you, Thor. Are you really a gifted dog, as it would appear? Why do you make perfect water retrieves at a time when most other pups only know about water as something to drink?

Why didn't the sound of the shotgun bother you the first time we shot a bird over you at four months? Why were you not frightened of the crippled bird? Why did you know enough to put a paw on it, hold it down, get a good mouth grip on it, and bring it back?

> **"Puppies are supposed to tire after a few minutes of work, but you never do..."**

And tell me, Thor, about this thing you have with water. You never were afraid of it. You never did walk around a puddle. You always walked through it. We were not going to force you into the water this spring when it was cold. But remember the day up at Crivitz when, on your own, you simply jumped into the farm pond and started to swim?

And I wonder, too, about your attitude toward training. Puppies are supposed to tire after a few minutes of working out, but you never do. You want to keep going, keep driving. It's almost like a contest with you. And you most always are the winner. Why?

You are not even half a year old yet and already you are a celebrity, of sorts. Your picture has been in the newspaper. And you've appeared on television, performing flawlessly. People tend to know you when you ride into town. Motel owners often dislike dogs, but they welcome you. You've got a reputation and you haven't even started yet.

I sit here now in this cabin at Berry Lake and watch you sleep. You are innocence personified. Your heart is still too young to harbor hatred. Even the downed birds you retrieve you hold so gently that not even a feather is ruffled when you bring them back.

You are something, little Lab. You appear to have most all of the rudiments of hunting down pat at an age when other pups are just starting.

You've smelled the smell of the swamps and of cordite burning in the air.

You've seen pheasants bursting into the sky off the tip of your nose. You've heard the pounding wingbeat of a grouse when it flushes. You've had a number of shackled mallards in the firm grip of your mouth.

You know about the wind and the stories it can tell you through the magic of your nose. You can pick up a scent in the air as easily as you can from the wet marsh grass.

But these are mostly grownup things, grownup things for both men and dogs. And as I watch you sleeping now, I know that, most of all, you are still a puppy.

I know that from the way you chase your tail, from the way you play with your blanket or your tennis ball or the bone made of rawhide.

I know you are a puppy from the way you trust those who are closest to you. I know you are a puppy from the way you crawl close to Chris on her lap.

But I look at you now, here in the fading light with the rain coming down and I confess to thinking about October. I see a nice, little dog asleep at my feet, but I think about a killer who will stalk the swamps.

I think about a dog who will hunt with hate in his heart for those things the shotgun seeks. I think about a dog who will bust brush and ignore the cold and shake off the rain and revel in the mud and the blood.

Maybe that's why, Thor, as we share this cabin at Berry Lake tonight, my skin creeps and crawls and there's this cold feeling deep in my gut.

I believe you are going to be all of those things and more.

But I also know that dogs are, really, fragile things. Like crystal bubbles and dreams, they are made to break and disappear, to be with us only for a little while.

Thor Passes Final Exam...
But Not Cum Laude

T he days of thunder have at last arrived for Thor, the 10-month-old yellow Labrador retriever about whom much has been made, written and said since last January.

It is necessary now to make the promised public accounting of Thor's progress, or lack of it, since the dog has had a week of hunting under his choker chain.

As might be expected of a young dog, there have been peaks and valleys, successes and failures, tears and pride.

I will not fault the dog, now, for his errors. How can you fault a young dog for being overeager? But being a proud half-owner—with Bob Olson of Suring—I will praise Thor for the things he did well. What he needs more than anything else at the moment is additional hunting experience, and he's getting that. Already he is showing signs of overcoming the mistakes he made early in the hunt. But, let's start from the beginning:

DUCK DOG. Thor's first duck hunt set the stage for many more. Both he, and his master, loved waterfowling above all other field sports.

Thor came to the Mississippi River duck country to hunt with me. Did he ever come to hunt.

As it turned out, he hunted ducks with me, with the two guys across the lake, the two guys down the lake and anyone else who fired a shotgun within hearing range of our blind in the Upper Mississippi Wildlife Area near Alma.

Steady to shot through his entire training period, Thor forgot all about that once the guns of October started blazing.

It was something he had never heard before, a crescendo of gunfire erupting all around him. He forgot about obedience. He forgot about the command of the whistle, the command of the voice.

He wanted, purely and simply, to hunt. And that's what he did. When the people across the lake fired, he took off for them. I spent the first hour of this year's duck season retrieving my dog and returning a duck decoy he brought back to me from a party hunting down the lake.

When the first burst of gunfire had subsided, I moved Thor to a different blind. It was from there that he made his first retrieve for me under natural hunting conditions.

I dropped a wood duck across some open water along the edge of some marsh grass. Thor marked the bird, I sent him out. He followed the line, found the bird, brought it back on command, heeled and sat. It was beautiful.

> ## "I spent the first hour of duck season retrieving my dog..."

But his next chance was something else. I dropped a woody out across some open water. It fell into some willows and marsh grass. Thor marked the fall and went out on a line. I couldn't see him, then, but I could hear him for a time. Then nothing.

He responded neither to voice nor whistle command. So I walked out to where the duck had gone down. There was my dog sitting happily on a muskrat house, chewing the duck. Since this is a family newspaper I will say only that I got on him for that. He never did it again.

The next day, I hunted Thor in the same general area, only this time I had him leashed on a 10-foot length of rope. I spent most of the morning telling him to sit and stay every time a shot was fired.

By noon I released him and he had learned, finally, to stay at least fairly close. There were few birds flying, so when I got a crack at a hen mallard I took it and Thor made a good retrieve.

Thor did well, for the most part, hunting woodcock and grouse. He worked mostly within shooting range.

The first woodcock he saw in his life he picked up with a full grab. Then he dropped it. But he retrieved it by holding onto a wing tip.

Few dogs are willing to retrieve a woodcock. It is either because the consistency of the bird's feathers make them uncomfortable in a dog's mouth, or because of an odor, or a combination of both.

In any case, Thor picked up the first one. He failed, however, to find two others that were down, either because the day was hot and dry or because he simply didn't like the birds.

He had no problem with grouse.

He was good, generally, in hunting camp although he remains leery of strangers.

Thor has done some good things on the hunt so far. As has been pointed out, however, he has made a number of mistakes. And that proves something to me that I've believed from the beginning anyway.

What the heck. He's only human.

Dog vs. Bird in Duel of Death

They played their game of death on a stage bathed in golden sunshine. The air, still crackling from overnight frost, smelled sweetly of dried buckwheat, marsh hay, thistles and swamp water.

The wind was soft as a mother's kiss and the world around was strangely silent, as if all the other wild things there were watching.

The place was the Eldorado Public Hunting Area, a sprawling swatch of state-owned land a couple of gunshots west of Fond du Lac off Highway 23. The time was midweek.

And the players: There was this gaudy, regal ringneck pheasant. Its tail feathers were nearly as long as a man's arm. Its spurs were big enough and sharp enough to slice steak.

Born wild and free to this cover, the rooster was a survivor. That means he was tougher, smarter, meaner and luckier than the men and dogs who had hunted him before; than the foxes that had tried to kill him, than the winters that had tried to wipe him out.

And there was the dog, a rookie for sure, but something special. A yellow Lab still less than a year old, he had learned quickly about ringnecks and three had died off the end of his nose before.

Now the fires flamed in his heart when he caught the hot, sweet scent of pheasant. He was ready to play the game of death.

And there was the hunter, the man from Milwaukee. His was a bit part, to be sure, but he was there to see it all and feel it and know it and record it here for those interested.

There's this you should know about ringnecks, especially the ones with long tails and razor spurs. They didn't get that way by being dumb. They hold master's degrees in survival, doctorates in living.

Nature gave them wings so that they could fly and wisdom enough not to do it except as a last resort. Old ringnecks love the ground. They drive men and dogs crazy by running on it.

So there was this sun-drenched morning. The man from Milwaukee and his dog had hunted hard for about three hours. Eldorado wasn't exactly deserted that day. There were other hunters with dogs working the fields, but the big crowds were gone and there was about as much solitude as you could expect on public land toward the southern end of the state.

A half dozen times the dog "got hot" on pheasant scent, but it had petered out, evidence that a bird had been there but was gone.

26

So when the Lab got to working one more line, there was no reason for the hunter to think it was any different. But it was. The dog stuck to it, working more quickly, moving faster, becoming more excited.

After awhile, it became apparent to the hunter that the dog was working on a running bird. And it was clear that the pheasant was not one of those fresh from the game farm. The ringneck took the dog on a line off through thick weeds and grass along a line of trees.

Once, the Lab came back, tongue hanging out and panting, fooled by the bird that had circled on the ground and doubled back. But he cut the track again, only this time he did something that only a good dog could explain.

He worked away from the track this time and began driving hard toward the line of trees. The Lab had outfoxed the ringneck. He had worked the bird into a corner where it either had to come out in the open in the trees or flush from the heavy cover. There was no place else to go.

If you've never seen a dog hot with scent at that critical second just before the flush, you've missed something.

The Lab's tail was wagging 90 miles an hour. The hair on his neck and back bristled. His eyes were intent. There was no speed now. He moved carefully, slowly. And then the ringneck flushed, breaking from cover into the bright sunlight.

The bird hung in the air for a brief, glorious, spellbinding moment. Its head glistened blue-green and the white ring on its throat was virgin pure. Its body was coppery and rust and brown. Its tail was magnificent in length, spread gallantly like the proudest of crests. It cackled obscenities at both dog and man.

So that was it. The ringneck and the dog had played the game of death to the hilt. Each had done it well. Each deserved to win.

What had started as a simple hunting exercise had climaxed in a burst of beauty so compelling that the man from Milwaukee thought he had never, ever, seen anything quite like it before.

I know all about this, you see, because the dog in the game was mine, Candlewood's Thor of River Road. And I was the hunter.

Happy endings are nice, and maybe it should be that the bird was allowed to live and the dog was praised for a job well done. But in this game, you don't get two winners.

I killed the ringneck with one shot and the dog made a beautiful retrieve. The bird's tail feathers seemed to stick a mile out of my hunting coat as we walked back to the truck.

The game of death was over.

Ready for His Second Season, Thor is Growing Up

He is stretched full length at my feet now, this light, lemon-colored shadow.

His feet, that leave wolf-sized pad prints in the sand, twitch endlessly. And from deep within the great cavern of his chest, the growls rumble forth like thunder across the trees.

He sleeps on the edge of sleep, never drifting off so completely that the present isn't here but always deep enough so that the dreams are real and the blood is salty warm upon the tongue and the smell of gunpowder is hot and sweet to the nose.

This is Thor, no longer a pup but possessed of a puppy's heart.

This is Thor. Velvet soft to the touch, perfume sweet to the senses, obedient, mostly, to the command, and always rock hard and fiercely independent of the vagaries of life as presented to him these changing days.

This is Thor, the yellow Labrador retriever that came into my life and the lives of readers a year and a half ago. He is, now, a new page in a new book.

He's different than when you first met him as a seven-week-old puppy, unsure of the world, unsure of how to make all four legs work together at the same time.

READY FOR ACTION. Entering his second season, Thor was mostly grown and obviously growing on his master, who writes of him here with warmth.

He's different from the time when he was 10 months old and hunting ducks on the Mississippi River.

He's different from the time he met an old cock pheasant on the Eldorado Public Hunting Grounds and hounded the bird to its death.

He's different, for sure, but not complete. Maybe he never will be.

Even as time has brought physical changes to Thor, so have the events of his life.

He no longer is a two-owner dog. Thor lives now within the shadow of the city. He lives, full-time, with me and Chris on a little patch of green that has weeping willows and aspen and lilacs and room enough for him to run full speed.

He lives in a two story, half-brick, colonial dog house that is both prison and paradise. When we are all together it's heaven. When he's alone, it's hell.

He adjusted, with dignity, if not perfection, from the life of a kennel dog to the life of a house dog. I don't know what it would take to make him foul the house, just as he never fouls the motel rooms where he sometimes stays when on the road with me.

But he does not take kindly to being left alone, which is sometimes necessary. He accepts it now but he does not like it and he lets us know about it.

Mostly he observes the invisible fences that mark the property line. Mostly he understands where he can go and where he can't. But when Meg, the little female from

> **"He doesn't want Chris to mess with any other dog. He doesn't want me to mess with Chris..."**

next door or Stevie, the sheltie that lives in the house in back, are outside, temptation gets the best of him and, of course, he pays the price. But he's learning about life in the city, life outside the kennel. He knows, for instance, that roads are for cars, not for him.

His obedience to command reflects the fine training given him by Bob Olson, Thor's co-owner until this past April.

His inclination to sometimes cut a corner or break command or to go his own way reflects my own informal, less-than-precise manner of dealing with the dog.

Thor's color has not changed much from puppyhood. He remains essentially an extremely light yellow, almost white. He never did reach the weight or size we thought he might in the beginning. He weighs 65 pounds right now. He is stocky, as retrievers should be, but he edges toward the lanky side.

The only thing about Thor that has not changed are his eyes. Everything about him is reflected there. I see the fires of hell burning in them. I see the rock-hard glitter of diamonds or sunshine gleaming on a trout stream. And then there is the smoky softness of a dim café. And the tears brimming over

29

even as earth can fill a grave and make a mound. When my dog stares at me and I stare back, his eyes burn holes in my soul and I can feel the hair curl at the back of my neck and I am convinced, then, that he knows something about tomorrow that I will never know.

So what we've got right now, Chris and I, is a basically good, obedient dog, a fine companion, great company. He's adaptable. He's socially adept. But he's possessive. He does not want Chris to mess with any other dog. He does not want me to mess with Chris. He thinks the truck I drive belongs to him, not The Journal Company.

But he's got love in his heart enough to share equally.

Not to be forgotten in all this, however, is the wild game. After a rocky start, he got very good at that last fall.

And if he will begin this next hunting season doing as well as he was when the last one ended, I'll be satisfied.

So that's the update on Thor. He's not perfection, that's for sure.

But, by golly, he's close enough. 🐕

Happy Landings!
(Wonder Dog Meets a Musky)

This has to do with a musky, a dog and how life sometimes is when you spend much of it on the road.

In the pale, yellow glow of the single overhead light in cabin No. 6 at the Rustic Roost Motel here in Iron River, Wisconsin, I picked my dog clean of wood ticks, brushed him, fed him and sucked at a can of beer while he ate.

It had been some kind of day.

It had been, in fact, a day in which I discovered that my yellow Labrador, Thor, had all the inclinations of a greedy musky fisherman. And now I'm certain that he's going to make a basket case of me yet.

We came to Iron River, me and Thor, to do a number on the Brule River, which we had done. But there had been time for a little musky fishing farther south and west, and anybody who knows my habits will understand that if there is time for musky fishing, any time at all, I will usually take it.

NO DUMMY! A musky plug can look suspiciously like a dog-training dummy, especially to a Labrador retriever that is as perpetually eager as Thor.

Now my dog and I have been fishing together before. He has seen walleyes and bluegills and crappies and perch brought to boat. And it has excited him to no end. These are easy fish, though, and the situation has always been more or less controllable.

But we have never had to deal with a genuine musky together before.

I had rented a boat and motor from Bill and Barb McMahon at the Golden Fawn Resort on the Chippewa Flowage and headed out from there.

31

My dog rides a boat as if he were born in one. He sits up front, ears flapping in the wind. He knows he must stay centered. He knows he can't move from one side to the other. He knows he has to stay down. The first place we went was Clutcher's Bar, which produces a number of muskies every year. Besides, it's close and we didn't have all that much time. I read the wind, picked a drift line, cut the outboard and got ready to fish.

Now the thing about Thor is that he is a retriever. He is trained to bring back whatever I throw out. So when I am casting a musky plug that is nearly as big as the training dummy we use in working sessions each day, you can understand the problem that develops.

Every time I made a cast, Thor thought he should leap into the water and bring it back. He kept sitting, looking up at me, waiting for the command that never came. It had to be hard for him to figure out that this was fishing and not training. I'm not sure he ever did, in fact.

I did a lot of explaining and Thor heard as many cuss words as I know and some others I made up. But, after a while, we got the situation somewhat under control.

> **"Every time I cast, Thor thought he should leap in and bring it back..."**

That held until I got this musky on. Then it fell apart.

Somewhere near the end of the first drift across the bar, I got a hit, a strike. The musky broke water right away, and while it was nothing you'd put on the wall, it looked like it might measure 30 inches, which would make it legal.

Since I needed the makings for a fish fry, I decided right then that if I could boat it and if it was legal I would keep it. So I was a little serious in dealing with the fish.

Thor, as it turned out, was serious, too.

I played the fish as carefully as I could and finally worked it up to the side of the boat. When I reached down for the landing net, I saw that Thor was standing on the middle boat seat, ears up and hair bristling along his neck and back.

I don't remember if I told him to stay or get down. What I do know is that, in the next instant, the musky rolled and my dog was out of the boat in the water going for the fish.

As the old saying goes, I was as busy, then, as a one-armed paper hanger.

I dropped the net and the rod. I grabbed Thor by the skin on the back of his neck and his rump and hauled him back into the boat. Amazingly, the musky was still on. I brought it back to the boat and netted it. It measured out to a light 30 inches…too light, I figured, so I removed the hooks while it was still in the net and put it back in the lake.

And that was that.

I reached for a cigarette and discovered that the pack had dropped in the water. I was wet to my shoulders and when the dog shook himself I was wet to the waist.

I couldn't even cuss anymore. I could fault the dog a little, but not much. I could fault me a lot because I had let things get out of hand.

I beached the boat and the dog ran himself tired and then we went back to the Golden Fawn.

That night, here in Iron River, we ate at the Deep Lake Lodge and we talked with owner Ron Pezze and then we went back to the cabin where I picked the dog clean of ticks and brushed him and fed him and sucked a goodnight beer, which is where this story started.

I was beat. There is more to fishing, sometimes, than meets the eye.

Cruelty?
Now Wait Just a Minute

A fter I described in print not long ago the physical condition of my dog, Thor, after a week of hard hunting, at least two readers would like to hang me from the highest game rack.

Dorothy McCarty of Chicago writes, in part:

"I have never been so repulsed by the writings of another human. How dare you proclaim your cruelty and insensitive treatment of an animal that you insist treat you as his God? How can you live with yourself?

"I cannot believe a human can display such cruelty to a being that possesses all the kind, magnificent qualities you lack.

"I ask no reply to this letter. I'm sure one of your ilk would not be capable of any defense of your sad and unacceptable actions."

And Robert J. Kraemer of Fond du Lac writes, also in part:

"After reading an article titled, 'Duck Hunt is Rough on Both Man and Dog,' my opinion of Reed is that of an inhuman, sadistic misfit in modern society."

Well, what can I say? And the same to you, Sir and Madam? No. That's not the way to go.

The thing is, when you buy a newspaper you also buy the right to find fault with, or dispute with, the authors published therein. For the price of a stamp, stationery and some of your time you can rip 'em any way you want. You are entitled.

I've been ripped before and will be again. Or at least I hope I will be. What that means is I'm being read, and in my business, that's what counts.

Okay, readers McCarty and Kraemer charge me with cruelty to my dog because, in the course of hunting, his nose got cut, his feet grew sore and he developed wear spots on both front legs. But we continued to hunt anyway. That's what sent them out looking for rope.

The way to be really cruel to a gundog, the way to hurt it, the way to cut it deeply, is to go hunting without it. That's the way it is with Thor. If readers McCarty and Kraemer knew my dog, they'd understand that.

Hell, Thor whimpers when I take out the garbage without him. When I'm going on a trip and he can't, I have to load my luggage the night before to save his feelings. I have to sneak my guns out of the house without him seeing or he goes crazy.

What readers McCarty and Kraemer will never understand is the last thing I would do in this world is be cruel to my dog. And further, I submit, they have a misguided opinion of what constitutes cruelty.

There isn't a good gundog that doesn't hunt hurt. There isn't a good gundog owner who doesn't recognize the limits to which you can put your dog at any given time. And there isn't a good gun dog that wouldn't prefer the hunt to staying at home, no matter what its physical condition.

Thor, you have to understand, was born to hunt. I know it and he knows it. He's not one of those fluffy, fancy, four-legged, hothouse plants that kiss us on cue and do nothing more energetic than lick the hand of the one who feeds it. He is not so helpless as to be my robot. He's no innocent. He's not virginal. You should know how independent he can be.

He's big, he's young, he's strong and he's tough. He lives in a world of violence. Violence, in fact, is his business. He knows what blood tastes like, his and mine and that of the birds and animals we've killed together.

> ## "Thor, you have to understand, was born to hunt..."

His mouth is soft enough to retrieve a duck without ruffling its feathers. But it is strong enough to crush the head of a raccoon in one crunch.

He could run all day on three legs if he had to. The hurts he had after that first week of hunting didn't slow him or harm him. I wouldn't have allowed that to happen.

There has been a lot of hunting since the story that aroused the readers appeared. And Thor has been in on most of it. The old hurts have healed and there are some new ones.

I can assure readers McCarty and Kraemer that if Thor is ever in serious trouble, I won't hunt him, and he'll have the best care that love and money can provide.

And I can assure Thor that I won't leave him behind just because some people think I'm being cruel to him.

In fact, I checked with him just the other day to see if he'd rather stay home than go on a one-day duck hunt over at Grand River.

He responded with two growls and a snarl, and then he spilled my beer.

Now that's cruelty.

Thor Champs at the Bit
As the Hunt Winds Down

Prompted by many letters from interested readers plus a memorandum from my boss, there is offered today a year-end update on Thor, my yellow Labrador retriever, who has turned out to be neither supermutt nor wonderdog, but just a heck of a good guy.

Except for a couple of uninspired pheasant hunts at the Bong Recreational Area near Burlington and at the Eldorado Public Hunting Grounds near Fond du Lac, Thor has been mostly laying around the house since the last week of October.

That's because I spent two weeks in Montana trying to shoot an elk. And that's because there was a Wisconsin deer hunting season in there and that's because there was some vacation time to use up and that's because I have been mostly burned out from a steady diet of recreational hunting since early September.

Thor has not taken kindly to all of this. With dogs, even as it is with men, too much down time is not a good thing.

What he forgets already is that the two of us spent nearly two months in the woods and swamps together. We trained and hunted as hard as it is possible for a man and a dog to train and hunt.

And I can report, with no more than an owner's normal pride, that Thor hunted very, very well.

EYES TO THE SKY. It's the only place you'll find the ducks, and Thor quickly learned to help his master scan the air for flocks of them.

It started, the real thing did, up in Ladysmith when grouse season opened. Thor did what he is supposed to do. He worked within gun range and he flushed a lot of birds. Most of the flushes were not into the gun, but that was not the fault of the dog.

He brought some grouse into shooting range and he found every bird that went down, not only for me but for others with whom we hunted.

Because Thor is just over two years old now, I know my dog well enough to say, in truth, that he is a good grouse and pheasant hunter.

But where he does his best work is with ducks. And that is as it should be for a retriever. He did not lose a duck this fall, either for me or for those others who were in my hunting party from time to time. And, let me tell you, he retrieved a mound of meat.

He understands now, as he did not the season before, that he must stay close to our blind. No longer does he want to hunt for everybody else in the field. He is steady to shot, as the field trial people say, and he marks the downed birds as they fall.

He spends as much time looking into the sky as I do. In fact, I have the feeling that I would not have to look up at all. If I just watched my dog, I would know whenever there was one or more birds approaching because you never saw such excitement.

> **"He spends as much time looking into the sky as I do..."**

I learned this fall while hunting ducks with Thor to trust his judgment. Several times I marked the fall of downed birds only to see Thor work off into different directions. He always found the birds, though, and after a while I just quit worrying and let the dog work.

Thor made blind retrieves, too. Those are the ones where the bird goes down but the dog, for various reasons, does not see where it fell.

With Thor, all I had to do was send him out in the right direction. He rarely looked back for further help. His method was to hunt in wide circles working the wind. Once he scented the downed bird it was all over.

I found a couple of times that Thor uses his nose much more than his eyes. I don't know if this is good or bad. Once when Donald Bluhm and I were hunting together, Thor ignored a wood duck that was downed in plain sight out in the middle of a pothole. Thor worked around the edge, instead, until he winded the bird and then made the retrieve. He gave no indication that he saw it in the first place.

Thor broke ice this fall for the first time in his young life. He didn't like it at first. But once he got used to it, there was no problem.

And the dog hunted hurt, as was reported earlier in the *Milwaukee Journal*. His front legs and nose were worn bleeding raw. Beyond that, he sustained a deep cut across the top of the tip of his nose on the first day of grouse season. He ripped that cut open a half dozen times through the rest of October.

His feet were so sore when we returned from one trip that he limped around the house as if on hot coals.

He is not a deer chaser, for which I am greatly thankful. He eyeballs them when he sees them but he does not pursue. He has not yet run afoul of a porcupine, a skunk or raccoon. Those glorious moments await down the road.

Around the house, Thor, generally, is a joy. He is a chow hound of the first order, yet he knows enough to stay away from the dinner table.

He is developing that which passes for a personality in dogs. He generally likes people. He is overpoweringly friendly at first meeting, but it cools after a short time.

Although he is now removed from puppyhood, he retains many puppy instincts. He likes to play with a tennis ball or rawhide chew bone. But when you get out the retrieving dummies with which we train, it is all business with this dog who seems to know the difference between work and play.

There are other things he seems to understand without being told. For example, everyone knows about dogs and trees. Take Thor for a walk and he'll lift his leg on every tree in sight. I mean every one.

The other day, when we put up a Christmas tree, you know what I thought he'd do, even though he's a most reliably housebroken dog.

As it turns out, he didn't and hasn't and probably won't. He seems to know that this tree, even though of the kind he has lifted his leg against a thousand times, is for looking at and enjoying.

Thor is bored with his current inactivity. At one point, in fact, he got the idea that he was in command. It was our fault. We had gotten out of the training routine. Now we try to work with him at least a little every day. And we try to run him hard a couple of times a week.

Thor was born to hunt and he was very good at it this fall. And he'll be even better next year because we'll do all the things to be done in Wisconsin and, on top of that, the pheasant fields of South Dakota and the duck swamps of Louisiana are in our plans.

Beyond that, though, he's a fixture around the house. Whether he's underfoot or driving you crazy wanting to go out or come in or if he's trying to con you out of something to eat, he's a good guy to have around.

And when night comes and you watch him sleep on a pair of old boots in the corner of the den, you wonder how you ever made it before he came along and you die inside when you think about how it would be if he were gone.

So Thor is doing okay, you see. He sure as heck gets my vote.

This Pup Has Become a Hunter

They were nothing more than specks in the sky; two periods dangling at the end of a sentence of distant trees on the far side of the flat, sprawling Mississippi River marsh.

My dog saw them first.

I knew it when his tail wagged faster, when the hair bristled along his back, when he did a little jig step in the muck along the high bank where we stood.

I picked them out and watched. They were coming our way. Directly at us, in fact.

So I crouched down and my dog, as is his habit, did the same. When I get down, he gets down. His eyes were polished-glass bright and they were fixed on the approaching birds. I could hear a low growl rumbling in his chest like far-away thunder.

We were hidden by an overhanging tree and a stand of thick marsh grass out in front.

We waited.

They were wood ducks. I could tell that for certain. And they were up just a little over treetop height. Good shooting range if they kept their course.

RELIABLE RETRIEVER. It didn't take Thor long to get the hang of duck hunting—and a big part of that is to dependably make retrieves from water, land, and thick marshes that amount to a mixture of both.

We, my dog and I, sank deeper in the muck. The birds were coming just right.

At the precise moment that only a shooter's instinct can select, I swung my shotgun to the bird on the left and when the bead on the barrel reached the tip of its bill I squeezed the trigger.

Then there was the 12-gauge thunder of the hunt and the wood duck collapsed in mid-air, dropping across some open water into a head-high stand of marsh grass.

I gave my dog the command to hunt and he literally flew into the open water and started swimming toward the edge of the marsh grass on line with the spot where the bird dropped because he, too, had marked its fall. Across the water he disappeared into the tall marsh grass. I couldn't see him anymore, but I marked his progress by sound and by the movement of the grass.

He was, it seemed, about the length of a football field away. I waited and watched and listened and then I knew he had found the bird because his motions slowed. Several moments went by and, at last, he emerged from the marsh grass, wood duck grasped in classic hold.

He completed the retrieve, accepted my praise and immediately began scanning the sky for more action.

What is important about all that is there is no way in this world I would have ever found that duck by myself. What is also important is that I no longer worry about where a duck falls once I shoot it, because I know my dog will find it. He always does.

Thor, the yellow Labrador, no longer is the excited, frantic, wild-as-the-wind rookie hunter

> **"I no longer worry about where a duck falls once I shoot. I know my dog will find it..."**

I wrote about several years ago. The cuddly pup that hundreds of readers wrote to the Journal about is four years old and has developed into a cool, calculating, but endlessly enthusiastic hunter of ducks.

He has harnessed his own boundless energy and he has learned to wait for the action to come to him — unlike early on when he tried to cover every hunter and every gun and every corner of every swamp.

He makes some mistakes, never doubt that. But, then, so do I and so do other people with whom we hunt. But one thing you can be absolutely certain about is that when you down a duck and Thor marks the fall or, sometimes even when he does not mark it, the bird is yours just as certain as tomorrow's sunrise because he will find it.

Duck hunters talk for hours about the relative merits of various shotguns and types of ammunition best for killing. Theories abound about decoys and how they should be set up. Some men practice for hours on duck calls to get the tone and phrasing just right.

Others spend hundreds upon hundreds of dollars to obtain the best equipment, the best boots, the best waders, the best boats, the best of everything with which to enter the duck swamps.

But I'll tell you true: It all means not one single, solitary thing if you can't find the duck once you shoot it. And to do that, plainly and simply you need a dog. A good dog.

Pheasant hunters, once in awhile, will lose a bird they have downed. So will grouse hunters. Even deer hunters sometimes fail to find a buck or doe they have shot. It happens. It's sad, but it happens.

But there is no form of recreational hunting in which more game is lost, and, thus, wasted, than duck hunting. There are two reasons for that.

One has to do with the type of terrain most duck hunting takes place in. By and large it is wet, mucky, weedy. It is thick, sometimes to the point where a man just can't walk through it. Finding a duck that drops into it, sometimes at distances of a hundred yards or more, is most often all but impossible.

The second reason is that a majority of waterfowl hunters do not use retrieving dogs to find that game.

I'll tell you one thing. I've always hated to waste game and that goes back a very long time to when we shot it and ate it because it was the only meat we could afford. I haven't changed one bit since then. I still hate to waste it.

I'm glad I've got my dog, Thor, for more reasons than you can count. Next to my wife, he is the best, most loyal living being I know.

And out in the duck swamps during the days of thunder I know I will not waste any game because he is there. He is the most efficient piece of hunting equipment I have ever had.

There are a lot of other Thors out in the state. I know that.

The thing is, there should be more. 🐕

41

Call of the Brule

The calling…

Maybe you know about it. For some it's the priesthood or the convent.

For some it's the streets where the wine is neon red, where tomorrow never means that much, where dreams shatter like waves upon some lonely beach.

For others it's the mountains and the restless winds that blow there.

For me, though, it's always been the river here in Douglas County that men call The Brule. It has been calling to me for more than two decades. Sometimes I'd hear that river in the dead of night and sometimes its voice would rise above the jukebox and the laughter. And sometimes I'd hear it even over and above the sweet smell of perfume and soft touches in the dark. But no matter when and no matter where and no matter what the circumstance I'd hear it and respond.

The thing about all this is that while I knew I had the calling, I never knew until just recently that my dog, Thor, did too.

It started with a short, simple trip up to Eureka on the Fox River designed to air the dog after a long winter, do a little fishing and, perhaps, pick up a story in the process.

We did all that, Thor and I, except the story part, but I could tell right away that something was different. There was a little touch of warmth to the air and the sun came

WATER DOG. Whether he was on a hunting trip, fishing excursion or a training session, Thor loved his days on the water.

out and you could smell the excitement. And I could see it in my dog.

He ran harder, swam faster and responded to command better than at any time since last duck season. When it was time to go he climbed into the truck and sat straight up in the front seat instead of curling up in the back to tongue himself dry.

Clearly, he wanted more and so did I but, at that moment, I didn't know what or why. So instead of going south toward home, we headed north.

"We'll go to Lake Winnebago," I told him. "We'll look around and then

42

go home." But we didn't. By the time we got to Highway 21 in Oshkosh I knew what was going on and so did my dog. We headed west. And north.

The Brule, you see, was calling.

I don't know how it can be that dogs understand things that happened before they were born, but that's when my love affair with the Brule began—long before the yellow Lab came into my life.

The Brule, once to me, was everything. It was the beginning. It was the start of a dream come true. It was the foundation upon which memories were built. It was very, very special.

The first of all the fishing seasons began at the Brule. And because the Brule has never been easy to fish, it was the pain that had to be endured, the ticket you had to buy with money made of blood and tears that would entitle you to all the other joys of summer.

But all that changed when a law was written that said you could fish the Brule any time of the year. That's when, for me, at least, they took away the magic from the river. With one swipe of the pen they turned it into the equal of any other carp-filled river system in the state. I hated it.

> **"My dog was showing me something, telling me something..."**

The Brule was worth more than that, I thought. And what about the ghosts and the memories? Would they wipe them out with a law that has no feeling, a law that could never cry or laugh, a law that could never remember how things used to be?

They could and did, of course.

But old loves, like sweet dreams and memories, never really die.

We moved north and west across the state, Thor and I did, stopping only for lunch and gasoline. My dog, never once, did lie down. He kept looking out the windshield, his nose in the same general direction as pointed by the dashboard compass.

We arrived in Brule country by mid-afternoon, rented a cabin and headed for the Co-op Park bridge.

I fished downstream from there, using a single salmon egg on a small hook weighted with split shot. Thor stalked the banks and scented nearly every log and tree along the way with at least a drop or two, which is some kind of an accomplishment unless you have a mile-long bladder.

We kept it up for two hours.

I didn't catch a fish, which was no big deal in itself because that has happened to me here before. Many times.

So, because I was still living in yesterday, I did what I always used to do. I looked to the ghost of Walley Neimuth for help. But the ghost was gone. And I looked for the ghost of Thad Grady and it, too, was gone. And then I wondered what Mel Ellis would do or Burt Dahlberg and some of the others who worked the Brule with skill and love.

But there was nothing. Only silence and the river and the fading glow of yesterday.

Thor couldn't help either but, God, he was having a time. It was his first trip to the Brule and he couldn't know about yesterday. He couldn't know how it used to be. He couldn't know about how it was that the river, in our time together, had taken me to the top of the mountain and down again.

Thor didn't care about yesterday. He was running new ground, feeling new feelings, smelling new smells. He felt the strength of the river's current because he swam in it even as I stood in it to fish. He felt the chill of the water and the smell of its foam and he discovered the cut of the knife-edged rocks.

Before my eyes, my dog was feeling all the joys and the hurts of the Brule as I had so many years before. The difference was that he was enjoying as I hadn't for so long.

My dog was showing me something, telling me something, about how now is now and yesterday was yesterday and, finally, I got it.

For the first time in more than 20 years I was actually fishing the Brule River alone, except for my dog.

The ghosts were gone. The memories were pale. Yesterday was finally over. And there really would be a meaningful tomorrow.

And there was no pain.

So, with some daylight left, my dog and I drove up to Lake Superior at the mouth of the Brule. Thor ran with the wind and played tag with the surf and rolled in the golden sand. And the spirit of a man named Reed was able, finally, to soar above the trees of the valley of the Brule.

That night, back in the cabin after dinner, while Thor snored softly at my feet, I felt strangely, wonderfully good.

The Brule would call again and I would answer. I knew that for certain. But I also knew it would never, ever be the same again. It would be better.

I was finally free of the ghostly shackles that had held me for so long.

And the big, yellow dog, twitching and growling now in his sleep had been the key. Dogs, like the Man Upstairs, work in mysterious ways.

Don't Fret, Thor,
The Ducks Will Fly Once More

What we have here today is a letter to my dog, Thor, who can't really read but who will get the message because he works in mysterious ways.

Dear Thor:
I am standing here beside a pothole at a place called Crex Meadows, which you know about because you've hunted ducks here before.

Among the things I want to know is, why are you here? I left you at home 300 miles away. You've got no business here. It's summer. It's hot. The ducks have just brought off their broods.

You can't hunt. Not now. That's why I didn't bring you along.

But you are here anyway. I know it. I can sense it. I can feel your hot breath on my hand and I can see your tail waving in the marsh grass.

Hell, I can even smell you because wet dogs have an odor all their own.

But listen, pal. You are screwing things up. You are messing with the timetable.

Remember I made a deal with you last

PRECIOUS DAYS AFIELD. Hunting season happens but part of the year. Even when Thor was not at his side hunting, Jay Reed had a habit of ruminating about those golden autumn days and eagerly anticipating their arrival next season.

summer that, this summer, I would not wish the days away like I did then? It was late in June, you'll recall, or early July, when I told you I wished duck hunting season would open the next day. And you jumped around and ran

45

over to the closet where we keep the shotguns.

Well, that summer sped by and the first thing we knew we were up to our eyeballs in marsh grass and river mud waiting for the mallards to come in.

Trouble was, you became a year older and so did I and between the two of us we had wished away some valuable time. And I told you, damn it, we would not do that again.

I mean we made a deal and you are not holding up your end of it.

I know that's true because I'm supposed to be alone standing here in Crex and I'm not. You are here. You are right beside me. I can feel your body pushing against my left leg, urging me to move on out into the muck and mud.

Right now, this minute, you are looking up at me and your eyes are drilling holes into me. They are bright and shiny like you are high on something and, every once in awhile, you look out toward that point of grass which you know damned well will be a good place to stand once the birds begin flying.

> "The days of thunder, Thor. That's what living is all about..."

Oh, I know you are here all right. I know it because when I look out into the marsh now I see the green grass turn brown and brittle before my eyes.

The sky is lowering and becoming gray and the wind is switching to the north and it's got a cold edge to it. The leaves are stripping away from the willows and there are muskrat houses and the water's got a wicked chop to it.

I know you are here because, all of a sudden, I'm wearing hip boots and a hunting coat. I can feel the weight of the shotgun in my right hand and I can smell the smells of cordite and rotting leaves and swamp water.

God, I can see my hands turn red with duck blood as we pull the guts from that which we kill. I can hear you gag and cough when a duck feather gets down your throat. I can feel you tremble and crouch down low when, off in the distance, you see the spots that will turn out to be ducks winging in low over the trees.

I can hear the growl that starts as a rumble way down deep in your chest when you sense action.

All of this tells me that you are here, Thor. You are with me right now. And you were with me last night in the motel.

Remember how it is in duck camp each fall when you beat the alarm clock? You come to me and nudge my arm and blow hot breath in my face and get me out of the sack while the stars are still out and the frost is still thick on the ground.

You did it again to me, only it wasn't duck camp and it wasn't fall and there was no frost. It was summer and the air was hot and there were no stars and you were supposed to be 300 miles away.

Thor, I've got no business being up at that hour of the day when there is no duck hunting, no marsh to go to, no hip boots to pull on, no shotgun to check.

So stop already. Will you?

Okay, buddy. I know you won't. And to tell the truth, I really don't want you to.

So walk with me here this day in Crex Meadows. Stay with me in the motels at night. Shake me out of the sack before the night turns into day.

It's okay. It's the way it should be. The days of thunder, Thor. That's what living is all about. You know it. You were born to it. And so was I. Maybe we are wishing our lives away, yours and mine. Well, what the hell.

I wish duck season opened tomorrow.

Like Father, Like Son

There was a family reunion, of sorts, here in Madison this recent blazing-hot August afternoon.

And while it wasn't exactly a history-making event, it did mark the first-time-ever meeting of two of Wisconsin's best-known yellow Labrador retrievers: Candlewood's Nifty Nick and Candlewood's Thor of River Road.

Nick, a state field-trial champion and one of the Midwest's most valuable and sought-after stud dogs, is owned by Mary Howley of the Candlewood Kennels.

Thor, as faithful readers know, belongs to me. Or is it the other way around?

In any case, Nick is Thor's sire, which of course makes them father and son.

As reunions go, this one was something short on sentiment. Dogs save that for people. There was a little whining, a little growling, a little sniffing and a little scratching at the ground.

Hackles rose in the beginning, but only for a short time. And that was about it. After that the two behaved the way you'd expect two trained, adult, male dogs would behave.

I wanted to see Nick more than you can imagine. You can't be even on the fringe of the dog business without knowing about that animal. For knowledgeable people in the world of field dogs, Nick is the standard of excellence by which yellow Lab retrievers are measured.

HOT DOGS. Thor and his sire, Nifty Nick (left), helped Jay Reed to commemorate their reunion by posing for Jay's camera on the tailgate of his Chevy Suburban during August.

The fact that his characteristics tend to show up in the pups he sires makes him nearly invaluable at stud.

Being possessed of more than just a little pride in my own dog, I wanted to see Nick and Thor together. I wanted to have them both at hand to see and feel and look and touch and compare.

I was not disappointed.

At eight years old, Nifty Nick is, to my eye, everything I expected him to be: Deep chested, straight backed, lean flanked, with a powerful neck, a handsome head, big feet and luminous eyes.

A social animal, he displayed his fondness for playing, his intense interest in people. At the same time, though, his split-second response to command reflected the fine-tuned training so deeply ingrained within him.

I was happy to discover that Thor, at five years old, is a Xerox copy of his sire in most respects. Physically, they are nearly identical, except that Thor tends to be a bit more leggy than Nick and Nick is a bit deeper in color.

Their mannerisms are the same. So is their response to people, including strangers.

The main differences I could see reflected the age gap between the two and the fact that Nick is exposed to the professional training of Mary Howley, while Thor must contend with my far-less-than-professional approach.

> **"Thor, at five years old, is a Xerox copy of his sire in most respects..."**

Nick is laid back, cool, as they say. His experience with people and places, with times and events, is evident.

Thor, on the other hand, is more on the edge of his chair, in a manner of speaking. His exuberance, his anxiety to get at things, the excitement that boils within him gives him away as a younger dog.

Nick has learned to wait, in other words. Thor has not.

The dogs displayed only nominal interest in each other. While they did their thing in the kennel area, and while I watched, I wondered about another dog, long since gone.

River Oaks Corky. Sire to Nick, Grandsire to Thor. He was, perhaps, the most gifted, the most distinguished dog ever in American field trialing history. How much of him did I see in the two dogs? What would he have done had he been here? Would they have all acted the same way?

And I saw another Lab from out of the misty past, a yellow named Pax upon whose grave the snows of a dozen winters have fallen. You'd never have mistaken him for either Thor or Nick.

Pax limped to his grave, as he did through most of his years, on a foot that once was sliced nearly in half by barbed wire. And he wasn't as pretty as these two dogs, either.

But, God, he was a hunter.

Now there is one more thing to tell about this reunion.

I wanted some pictures of Nick and Thor. Since Thor was seven weeks old, I have photographed him for official pictures while he sits on the tailgate of my company truck.

So why not for this reunion?

I lowered the gate and Mary commanded Nick to a sitting position there and I did the same with Thor. The two sat as they were told, but were jumpy.

After a couple of commands to each dog, they finally sat still long enough for pictures. But they wouldn't raise their ears, wouldn't look alert. They sat with tongues hanging out and panting in the heat of the day.

It was only after they had returned to the kennel area that I discovered that the tailgate was fiery hot from the sun. Which accounts, of course, for their reluctance to sit still.

Sometimes, you see, it is not only dogs that require training.

Even at reunions.

The Mad Cackle

Rhapsody...An ecstatic or highly emotional utterance... –Webster's New Collegiate Dictionary

Old hunting hands call it a ringneck rhapsody.

If you've had any experience at all in hunting pheasants, you've heard it: The cackle of a male bird forced to fly.

It cuts the air like a knife and it rings in the ears like something lean and mean.

It is pretty, but it ain't nice.

At least it isn't to those of us who have learned to interpret what the pheasant is really saying as it climbs into the sky.

Have you ever heard sailors swear? They are pretty good at it. But merchant seamen are the world champs. And what a ringneck pheasant says when it is pushed into the air would make those guys blush.

Of all the sounds in the outdoors, the cackle of a ringneck pheasant has the sharpest edge to it.

The honking of wild geese in flight tends to bring tears to the eyes and a tug to the heart strings.

BIRD UP! Flushed by Thor, this cock pheasant claws to gain air. Now it's all up to the shooter.

The howl of a timber wolf sets the hair to curling at the back of your neck.

The grunt of a bear or the snort of a buck deer gets your pulse to pounding, as does the strident sounds of a mouthy mallard hen.

But once a ringneck gives you a piece of its mind when it takes to the air, you know you've been told off by the best of them.

That is why I have no intention of sharing with you what a ringneck cackled at me and my dog, Thor, the other day, near Centerville, Wisconsin, in a field turned the color of Fort Knox gold. If I did, they'd have to call this the blue sheet. You'd have to hide the page from the kids. You'd wash out your ears with soap.

We didn't really need to hunt for pheasants that day. We'd had a good trip into the duck swamps farther north. Four mallard drakes, greenheads, were already in repose on a bed of ice in a freezer chest in the truck.

And Thor and I were on our way back to Milwaukee. It was, after all, time for a clean shirt.

But there is this rolling country north of LaCrosse where pheasants live, some wild and some planted. And there was time to hunt because it was still daylight and we had no schedule.

"He jumped with both front legs into a clump of grass and a pheasant clawed its way into the sky…"

So we pulled off the highway north of Centerville and followed the narrow road back to the place where we had been in other years; back to the field where the ghosts of other ringnecks scamper along the fence rows.

We started our pheasant hunt at a time of day when early darkness stood out on the edges waiting to close in. It was cloudy to begin with and that accentuated the deepening gloom.

But we headed off across the cutover field, quartering into what little wind there was.

I will tell you now that Thor is not the greatest pheasant dog that ever came down the pike. Waterfowl, after all, are his bag. But he ain't bad on dry land. He hunts close, and if you know about pheasants you'll understand that is good.

He's got a nose that won't quit. And he was already sharpened on pheasants by a couple of trips to Leo Scallon's hunting preserve at Waupun, plus some fair, but thin, action at the Eldorado Public Hunting Grounds near Fond du Lac.

In any case, we quartered across that field to a fence row and worked down it, still pretty much into the wind. Like most flushing dogs, Thor is easy to read once he gets on pheasant scent.

He gets "birdy" in other words. His tail whips back and forth and the hackles rise on his neck and back. We were working into a little stand of willows and canary grass when he began to show all those signs.

The pheasant burst into the air right off the end of the dog's nose. It was a hen, though, so I didn't shoot. My dog, who has little or no regard for hunting laws, was incredulous.

And how do you explain?

So we kept working and walking, reaching the end of the fence row and circling back toward the truck. It was growing darker. Our day was about done.

It was out in the middle of the field where the cover was thin that Thor cut pheasant scent. Even a dummy could have read the dog's actions. I did.

He whipped around in mid-stride 20 yards or so in front of me. His tail was a blur of motion. He jumped with both front legs into a clump of grass and a ringneck pheasant, its long tail tapering off into the wind, clawed its way into the sky.

It cackled. Lord, how it cackled. It cussed us out in the finest pheasant profanity you have ever heard.

The sight of the bird, and the sound of it, froze in my mind as one of the outdoor world's most beautiful scenarios.

I pulled up on the bird and squeezed the trigger, afraid for an instant, that I might miss the shot.

But I didn't. Thor made the retrieve.

Our hunt was over.

Only a Duck Hunter
And His Dog Understand

Like gentle swirls of bridal veil, the fog tumbled down to fold itself around, and almost hide, the demure face of the swamps.

The air was wet without rain, chill without cold, but teardrops trembled on oaken eyelashes.

There was no wind, but the leaves were aquiver and they sang a song of silence that the hunter could plainly hear.

And so could his dog. It must have been.

Why else would the deep-chested animal, its rich, yellow coat mottled with mud stains, allow its hackles to bristle? Why else did the softly ominous rumble of a growl build in its throat?

Thor could hear something. Or he could see something. Or he could sense something.

It was out there somewhere, hidden in the fog. The dog knew it. The hunter knew it. But what, really, was it? A dream, maybe?

There are circumstances here that need explaining.

It was nearly mid-morning and Thor and the hunter were deep in the swamps that are fed and nurtured by water from the Chippewa River.

GENTLE TO THE TOUCH. Hunting along the river, Thor finishes off one of his countless retrieves, delivering a duck to his master.

It is a tangled jungle of a place, with deep-running sloughs and high, dry oak ridges and beaver flowages and potholes. Not many people know it well enough to do much more than hunt its edges.

But a long time ago, when life was just beginning for the hunter, it had been his playground, his yard. He had come to know it and love it.

And because there was no evil there, because it was a place without

54

sorrow, a place without tears, a place without regret, he had returned to it, as often as he could down through the years because it, alone, had never really changed.

So when the weather turned dirty and the ducks began to fly, he came back one more time, with his dog, to do it all again.

And that's why they were huddled there in the buck brush beside a beaver flowage in the fog looking for something they could not see, listening for something they could not hear, feeling for something they could not touch.

Two ducks, one a mallard drake with an emerald head and pumpkin-orange legs and a full-curl tail, the other a mallard hen, brown as the dry marsh grass, nestled in the game bag of the hunter's coat.

He had killed them early on, before the fog dropped. Thor had retrieved them. The two birds represented a daily bag limit. The hunter could kill no more. That's why his shotgun, unloaded now, leaned against a nearby tree.

> **"The fog closed in tighter, shutting off the light, and the day became as night..."**

He could have been out of the swamps two hours ago. He could have been back at camp, comfortably dry, comfortably warm. And Thor could have been sleeping in the corner, dreaming dreams that dogs dream when their world is right.

But the hunter couldn't go. He couldn't leave. The fog closed in tighter, shutting off the light, and the day became as night and shadows fell across the fog, giving dimension and substance to this mysterious world where only the hunter and the dog existed.

And then the questions came, the ones that haunt the heart, the ones that dig and twist and grind and pull.

Why? What is there about this acreage of trees and muck and water that so fascinate, so mesmerize? What is there in the sound of rushing wings that make a man's legs tremble, his heart stand still?

For the hunter and the dog, are the duck marshes really a prison cell in which to do hard time for as long as breath feeds life?

Or are the swamps really a grave to be buried in once October comes and the nights grow long and the days grow short and the wind takes on a cutting edge?

Maybe it isn't that. Maybe it isn't that at all.

Maybe the swamps are a mother's breast from which those of us who hunt suck the milk of the only life we really know or care about.

Or maybe the swamp is a womb where both man and dog, at the same time, can curl into position and know the comfort and protection of it and be fed by its fluids forevermore.

Or maybe, too, these swamps are the only place on earth where the hunter and his dog, unalterably linked by an umbilical leash, can go to live with memories from another time that can never be again.

Something was there, all right. But it was in the heart of the hunter and of the dog.

Later on the sun burned the fog away and there was the beaver flowage and the oak ridge and the deep-running sloughs. The house was in order.

And all that remained was the long walk back to where the other life begins.

If you are a duck hunter, you will understand all this. If you are not, forget it.

Walk, Run and Retrieve

This is for the Old Pals of Wisconsin.

And the Smokies and Beasts and Belles and Ladies and Tramps and Champs and Thors and Thunders and Nifty Nicks.

It is for the faithful family pets who, when fall rolls around, double as premier hunters. They never squeeze a trigger, but they do more for the success of any given hunt than the two-legged folks who do the bragging once the sun goes down.

We are dealing with dogs here, of course. Hunting dogs. The ones who beat the brush and leap fences and climb windfalls and swim through marsh scum and follow invisible signs in the wind that only they can read.

If you own such a dog and if you intend to hunt him this fall and if you haven't already started, now is the time to do Old Rover an immense favor.

Now is the time, you see, to launch into a conditioning program for your dog. He needs it, you know. And he's entitled to it. And if you want the best out of him this fall, it is your responsibility to get on with it.

FETCH! Pre-season training and conditioning work is important for any retriever.

It makes sense, when you think about it. What's your dog been doing all summer? Slinking around his kennel? Or lying around if he is a house and yard dog? Snapping at flies? Digging holes in the yard to beat the heat?

No matter what his age, how do you figure that animal will be able to go full bore once the hunt begins? He won't, of course. He'll poop out in an hour, especially if the weather is hot. And he'll hurt so much on the second day he'll be no good to you then, either.

What you should do, starting right now, is set aside a minimum of a half hour every day. Get him moving. Get him running. Work him on a retrieving dummy. Do it every day until the hunt begins.

And, on weekends if that is when your time is free, take him to a public hunting ground or, at least, someplace in the field where he can run free.

Give him his head for 10 minutes or so. Let him run the edge off. Then bring him to check. Simulate a hunt. Work a field of heavy cover. Or work a cornfield or a stand of marsh grass.

Make him stay within gun range. Whistle him close and lean on him if he strays. Work in 15- or 20-minute bursts. Then ease up.

If the weather is hot and there is no natural water around, carry a container with you. He'll need a lot of water. Make certain he gets it.

After a rest period, move out again.

Journal photographer Carl Hoyt and I came here to the Eldorado Public Hunting Grounds—about 10 miles west of Fond du Lac—with my dog, Thor, to get some pictures to illustrate this plea for dog conditioning.

Thor has been working, more or less regularly, for about a month now. And I understand that my job gives me more opportunity to work my dog than is the case with most others.

But what I'm saying here is that whatever conditioning you can do with your dog will help him once the hunts begin.

Being a Labrador retriever, Thor is mostly a waterfowl dog, but I also use him on grouse, pheasants and woodcock. That being the case, I condition him in water and on dry land. When I can't get him into the field, I throw a retrieving dummy for him in the backyard.

At seven years old, he is beyond the intense training stage. So what we do is simply repeat those things that have become second nature to him, like retrieving on command, sitting, staying and quartering within gun range.

The exercise is what really counts. The work tends to toughen his foot pads. His nose always takes a terrible beating from the cutting edge of marsh grass as do the corners of his eyes and the underside of his chest where his hair is thin.

The work we do now gradually toughens those trouble spots and when the actual hunt begins, he won't suffer the hurts he would otherwise.

One thing to remember, though, is not to overdo it. You can't get your dog in shape in one trip afield or in one backyard session. Go at it a little at a time.

You owe at least that much to your dog. I know I owe it to mine.

So, walk a country road with your dog these days. Better yet, walk a country mile. He will be better for it and so will you.

He is, after all, only human. Right?

Skunked Again

An Iowa skunk with super scent glands and unerring aim turned our pheasant hunt into nostril-searing, gut-grinding confusion scant hours after it started here, near the town of Williamsburg.

My yellow Labrador retriever, Thor, who hunts anything that moves except deer, got squirted, head on and dead center at short range, when his nose took him into a little circle of thick cover out behind a barn where we were hunting.

Anyone who owns an aggressive hunting dog runs the risk of this happening. Anyone who has gone through it will appreciate the rest of this account...

We had worked a field of milo early on and popped three birds while flushing uncounted numbers of hens.

Thor was working as well as he has ever worked on pheasants. He stayed close and ranged in front of, and between, the four of us who were driving. He put up an enormous number of pheasants, most within shooting range.

Then we moved to a different farm, expecting more of the same.

LABS ARE LOVABLE, until the day they tangle with a skunk...then need to ride in your vehicle alongside you or sleep next to your bed in a tiny motel room.

We were only minutes into the field and Thor had already flushed a hen. He was working just ahead of me and to the right, generally in the direction where Rick Anderson, of Hayward, Wisconsin, was hunting.

I saw Thor get "birdy," as hunters say, with tail whipping and back hair bristling. He disappeared into the cover and I expected a pheasant to come busting out.

Instead, I heard Thor give a sharp yelp and watched him come stagger-

59

ing out of the weed patch. He was shaking his head violently from side to side and white foam oozed and bubbled from his mouth.

The left side of his head from his nose to eye to ear and down his neck and upper shoulder was awash and glistening with a yellowish stain that dripped and widened as he stumbled toward me.

My eyes told me what had happened. My nose confirmed it.

The moments that followed immediately thereafter are a bit hazy. I tried to comfort my dog as best I could as he became violently sick to his stomach.

His sides heaved as he retched. He gagged on the foam that filled his mouth. I scraped a handful of mud from the ground and plastered it on the area where he had been hit. I used weeds to try to wipe it away. More mud. More weeds.

All the while Thor continued to retch and gag and by this time, the odor was so overwhelming that I felt like doing the same thing. The rest of the hunting party gathered around, albeit at a respectful distance: Anderson

> **"My eyes told me what had happened. My nose confirmed it..."**

and Ward Willliamson and Milt Dieckman, all of Hayward, and Merle Huedepohl of Williamsburg and Journal photographer Sherman Gessert.

I suggested that the rest of them continue hunting until I could get a handle on how Thor was doing. They disappeared quickly.

Thor finally stopped retching, but his legs were staggering weak. He rubbed the side of his head and neck.

So the party gathered at our vehicles, Huedepohl's pickup and my Journal truck. Since there was no way to clean up the dog on the spot and since it was obvious that he was in no shape to hunt, I decided to take him back to the motel.

It would not have been prudent to put the dog in the Journal vehicle at that point since the truck was enclosed and Thor stank to high heaven. So did I, by this time.

So we got in the back of Huedepohl's pickup and settled in between and among a three-wheeler, some broken two-by-fours, a batch of empty aluminum cans and a bag of dead pheasants.

Because he was sick, Thor climbed on my lap and put his head on my shoulder. Now we smelled one and the same.

At a small store in the motel complex, Gessert found four cans of tomato juice and some baby shampoo. Then he and the others returned to the hunt, leaving Thor and me alone.

I thought I should explain all this to the motel operators, but I got only as far as the door when the woman at the desk waved me away. This had obviously happened here before.

I took Thor out behind the motel and soaked his scented area with two cans of tomato juice. Stained with red, he looked as if I had cut his throat.

Then I hustled him inside the motel and put him in the bathtub. I took off my own clothes, which smelled at least as ripe as the dog, put them in a garbage bag and put them in the hallway.

Then I washed the dog clean of tomato juice, lathered him with baby shampoo, and rinsed it away. Then I did it all again.

After putting on fresh clothes and cleaning up in the bathroom, we went outside and walked in the wind for an hour.

Let the record show that by next morning, Thor had recovered, although a fair scent of skunk, mingled with some of Gessert's after-shave, still clung to him. He hunted like a demon for the rest of our stay, although few cared to get close to him to tell him so.

The people at the motel were great about it. They closed off the hallway doors where our room was located.

And they asked me to take that bag of clothes outside.

I got a hunch that Room 128 at the Colony Haus Motor Inn here in Williamsburg will be out of use of a while. 🐾

Dog Owner With Delicate Problem Needs Your Help

The subject matter contained herein is of a "delicate nature," but not to worry.

You won't have to hide it from the kids or disappear into the john to read it. There's no need for a plain brown wrapper. It can be sent through the mail without fear.

With disclaimers in place, then, let us push on to the central theme, which has to do with how best to obtain a sample of your dog's urine when called upon to do so by your veterinarian.

Maybe this is not at the top of the priority list when it comes to throbbing conservation issues of the day but it is important, let me tell you, when you think your dog might have a serious physical problem.

I've read a lot of pet columns in my life and every once in a while they allude to the need for doing this.

They have always stopped short, though, of telling us exactly how to go about it, especially when you are dealing with a big, completely house-broken animal that has lifted his leg in the wild places of a half dozen states and Canada.

My yellow Lab, Thor, is currently undergoing a series of tests for severe weight loss experienced this fall and winter. Getting a blood sample from him was easy. So was the stool sample.

The urine thing was something else and you should know about it, if you have a dog, because your turn may come.

CAN DO! Retrieve, that is. Thor and his master certainly enjoyed pheasant hunting better than visits to the vet—and the sometimes undignified necessities that go with such trips.

My dog does a lot of things on command, but relieving himself is not one of them. Thus it wasn't hard to figure out that to obtain a sample of his urine I would have to follow him around, container in hand, and trap it whenever the dog's spirit, and bladder, moved.

Remembering the olden days in the Marine Corps when a medic would, on occasion, put a bottle in my hand with orders to fill it up, I reasoned that, with Thor, I'd need something with a rather large opening since he has demonstrated time and again that his aim is, at best, uncertain.

A clean coffee can was the best idea I could come up with.

Morning seemed to be the obvious time to make the collection, since it is then that the dog's need for relief is most acute. The routine has been the same for nearly seven years. We get up, I open the door. Thor goes out to do his thing. No problem. Ever.

Thus it came to pass this recent dark, cold and windy morning that we went through the same routine, with one difference. This time I went with my dog, step for step, trot for trot, coffee can in hand.

> **"My dog does a lot of things on command, but relieving himself is not one of them..."**

Thor's no dummy. This was different and he knew it. First thing he did was stop and look at me. If he could speak he would have said: "What the hell is going on here? Go back in the house and drink coffee like you usually do."

But I stuck with him. Finally he hit the dogwood bushes, a favorite spot of his, I knew, because he kills the grass there every summer.

Sure enough. Thor lifted his leg. I put the can in position. As the stream sprayed the bottom of the can, with only a little hitting my wrist, it made a metallic sound and Thor shut it off. Just like that. I had collected about 16 drops. Not enough. Remember the old sign that says, "Don't do it in the lake"? Thor must have seen one that said, "Don't do it in the can."

So I followed him to his next spot near a giant willow tree. Same thing. A few drops. Still not enough.

By this time, the dog was wise to what was happening. So he stared trotting ahead of me. I trotted after him. Then he actually ran. And so did I, realizing all the while how silly this must have looked to anyone who might be watching.

By the time I collected enough for the sample bottle, Thor was ready to take my hand off up to the elbow. And the people who live next door were certain that I had finally snapped, that my next stop, for sure, would be the funny farm.

The good thing, in the end, is that my dog has cleared all the tests and is responding to a revised feeding program. Things are looking good again.

Awhile back, it will be remembered, I wrote a story about Thor getting skunked while hunting in Iowa. After that, I got all kinds of free advice through the mail from caring readers who had dealt with the same problem.

Maybe some of those kind readers, or others, could let me know if there is a way to collect, with at least some degree of dignity, a urine sample from a dog.

If there is I'd like to know about it. So would Thor. He still ain't speaking to me.

A Dog Provides Bragging Rights

There are many reasons to own a hunting dog, not the least of which is the right to brag about it when the situation calls for bragging.

That situation for me, is right now.

So if you don't want to listen to me brag about my dog, you should stop reading this and turn to other sections of this newspaper where you can, I am sure, read about welfare or housing or taxes or other grinding issues of the day.

My dog's name is Thor. He is a yellow Labrador retriever. If you are a long-time reader of this space, you already know about him. Stories about him, and pictures of him, have appeared here, too frequently for some and not often enough for many others. What must be said today is that Thor has had a heck of a good fall at hunting, and there still remains a trip to the pheasant fields of Iowa. This means, of course, that I have had a heck of a good fall at hunting because this dog and I are a team. He hunts when I hunt and I hunt when he hunts except for deer season, in which they don't allow dogs.

Thor is eight years old now. He first appeared on these pages when he was less than a year of age. That was when he tried to hunt with everyone in the woods, when he ate a wood duck while sitting atop a muskrat house, when he retrieved a decoy, when he wouldn't listen to any command once the shooting started.

Between then and now, Thor has hunted from Saskatchewan and Alberta to South Dakota to Iowa and Nebraska plus Wisconsin and some places in between.

This fall, this year of 1987, this yellow Labrador has hunted better, more efficiently, more obediently, more effectively than he ever has before in his lifetime.

He is smooth. He is polished. He rarely needs commands because he knows what his job is and knows what he has to do. If he is not perfection to you, he is to me and that's all that really matters.

Take that from an owner who likes to brag about his dog. The thing about it, though, is that it is true. No bull. No lip service. No fakery.

Circumstances dictate that Thor and I frequently must hunt with other people. Mostly there are other folks and other dogs around, and so what Thor does or does not do, is pretty much there for the world to see. Those who have seen him work know what I'm talking about.

Between the ducks and grouse and pheasants I shot over him and those shot by others hunting with us, Thor made a hundred or more routine retrieves this fall. There were two, however, on ducks, that were far from routine.

These were miracle jobs, the kind you wouldn't expect the best dog you've ever seen complete. But Thor made them both. And there were witnesses each time. And I was so proud I thought I'd bust.

While we had company on many of our hunts this fall, there was a day in late October when just the two of us went to Horicon Marsh to fill our goose tag.

It was cool and cloudy and the air was full of rain mist and I had to pinch myself because it was just the kind of day I like best.

Our old friend of a hundred years, John O'Donovan, Jr. of Waupun, had offered us the use of his blind and so that's where we were shortly after daylight.

For the first hour we just watched the geese coming out of the marsh. Thor, an old hand at this business by now, couldn't understand why I didn't shoot. He'd hunker down under every flight in range and look at me with puzzled eyes.

Finally, when a flock of seven or eight winged down within perfect range, I picked out a bird and killed it.

Thor marked the fall and made the retrieve but with some difficulty because it was a big bird, more than a mouthful even for a 70-pound Lab.

After that, we watched more geese and when we left the blind, the birds were still flying and there was no way to tell that the one we carried was missing from the sky.

Anyone who has a good dog, or has had one, knows about what I'm writing here and why I am writing it. The thing is, this fall, and its attendant pleasures of the field, made me realize some things appropriate to Thor that were not always that clear before.

You see, I don't have to look for rainbows anymore or thunderheads or beams of moonlight or rays of sunshine.

I don't need to look to the sky for the glitter of stars or to the lakes for the sparkle of sunlight.

I don't need to search for justice or love or loyalty or sympathy or pride or truth or joy.

I no longer need to seek out examples of dignity and class and honor and courage.

All of these, you see, are mirrored in my dog's eyes and in his heart.

I'll bet they are in yours, too.

Sage Advice From a Tired Old Hunter

M e and my dog, Thor, are walking basket cases these fading days of October, here in Buffalo City, Wisconsin.

We are second-hand rejects. We've spent more time with muskrats than people.

We are wind-whipped, sun-broiled, rain-soaked and now, snow stung. We ache in the joints. We limp along on legs stiffened by cold water. My feet are sore from too many humid hours inside wet waders and hip boots.

Thor has grown lean and mean since the hunt began. He has tasted the blood of ducks and grouse and geese and pheasants. He has hunted hard and well. But he, like me, has a shopworn look.

There's a spot on his belly that is rubbed raw. It is leather tough but beads of blood still ooze from it at times.

We look ratty and we smell of the swamps. We are so used to searching the skies by day that, now, we do it at night, even in the cafes where we eat. We are jerky, in other words, and there are

READY TO HUNT. Jay and Thor appear ready for any kind of hunting action when they posed for this newspaper shot. In this story, you'll see they found plenty of action most any time they took to the fields or marshes.

folks here who think we should be locked up. And maybe we should.

We are cold and tired and humped at the shoulders, and we want to go home but we can't because there are more swamps to hunt and the geese are flying down at Mather and we've got a Horicon tag yet to fill and there is a score to settle with several foul-mouthed ringnecks and we

67

are running out of time.

Thus, we are in need of aid and comfort this sweet Sunday morning so, if you will please, tell us a story about the olden days when there were no bag limits and a man and his dog could rub their backs against any fence post.

But before you do that, offer a solution, if you can, to the mystery of why it is a man can, some days, seemingly shoot the eyes out of speeding mallards at 40 yards and, the next day, can't hit the broad side of a barn at 10 paces.

Why is that true? I'd like to know. So would my dog.

We came here from the north, where the duck season is continuous, to these big river flats at midweek because the second half of the hunting season in the south opened.

And it was a good opener by most accounts. It was my purpose to shoot selectively,

"There's something about the back of a hunter's head that tends to attract flying ducks..."

taking only mallard drakes, those seductive, heavy breasted greenheads with feet orange as Halloween pumpkins.

Now I ain't the best shot that ever came down the pike. I'll admit to that. But humility has its limits. The truth is, I can usually pretty much make it hum with a shotgun.

But not Wednesday. Not the day the second half of the southern zone duck hunting season opened.

I'd be ashamed to tell you how many shots I fired that day to kill two birds, which wasn't even a bag limit. There was no crippling involved. I mean I wasn't even close.

My dog, Thor, who has seen me miss a variety of shots over the years, knows that something will not drop every time I fire the gun. But this day was ridiculous. Pass shots, jump shots, flare shots. I missed them all.

The next morning, though, was different. I only had a couple of hours because it was traveling time and I was due in Wisconsin Rapids that night. I fired three shots and killed two greenheads. I had to use a second round on one of them because it had a lot of life left on the way down.

With faith restored, I left the swamps and took to the road but I thought about it all the way down and across the state. Why? I stunk up the swamps one day and was right on the next. Give me a clue, if you have one.

And now there is this: It is expected of people in my business, from time to time, to offer some sure-fire tips on how better to engage in this enterprise of duck hunting. So here come a couple, field tested this very week.

You want a lot of ducks to fly over your blind, right? You want them in good shooting range, you want them in number and you want them to be of the species you are selectively shooting.

No problem.

To make sure this will happen, what you must do is leave your blind. Walk away a couple of hundred yards. Make certain you are well beyond shooting range.

Then look back and observe. As sure as you're born, the ducks will move over your blind. They'll dive bomb it. They may even land in front of it. You will discover that as long as you stay clear of your blind, the ducks will work over it. This happened a number of times to me this month so I know it will work for you, too. It does, however, tend to frustrate.

Here's another: Because of the physical layout of the place you have selected to hunt, you'd like, for best results, to have the ducks fly at your position from one particular direction, right?

To make certain this will happen, all you have to do is turn your back toward the direction from which you want or expect the ducks to come. If you do that, the proper approach is guaranteed.

There is something about the back of a hunter's head that tends to attract flying ducks. When they come in from behind you, of course, they tend to move beyond shooting range before you can raise your shotgun.

To test the validity of this tip, once you've got the birds coming in from behind you, just turn around. Soon they will be working from the opposite direction.

I know for a fact that this tip will work for you just as it has for me this very week.

Be careful, though, that the swamps don't burn your mind. That may be my problem right now.

The Dog Days Are the Best Days

He is asleep now, Thor is, stretched full length and growling intermittently, within the circle of those things he knows and loves the best.

The waders are there, of course, and the hip boots and the bag of decoys and the ammunition box and the shooting vest and the hunting coat and the boat cushions and the two shotguns, freshly cleaned and scenting of fine oil.

We have spent the evening, my yellow Labrador and I, assembling those things required for the opening of another duck hunting season.

My God, It's the seventh, for me and him. Can you believe it?

I wrote so very much about Thor when he was a puppy and so very little about him after that.

So now we are going into our seventh time around and you should know about this animal, about how he is now, about how he has developed, about what he is and what he does.

And in knowing that, you will come to understand the days of thunder and what they mean to those of us who care.

Thor has a zest for life unequaled by any other living thing I've ever known. And his first love, beyond the two people he lives with, is to hunt.

He observes the passage of time between hunting seasons with a sort of calculated reserve, always displaying interest in everything going on about

UNBREAKABLE BOND. Dog and master were never happier than they were while pursuing game in the field. Together.

him but holding back something of himself, it seems, for the golden days of fall.

I believe, in fact, that Thor would hunt himself to death if I would let him.

Thor is not a big dog as Labs sometimes go. He cuts in a couple marks

70

under 70 pounds. He is wide and deep at the chest and lean at the shanks. You can't count his ribs by looking at him but you can feel them just under his thick skin.

His feet are big, like those of a wolf, his neck is full and his head and ears are the way the book says they should be. His tail is thick and powerful.

At bottom line, Thor is what he was bred and born to be, a hunter.

Beyond that his temperament is even. He is extremely social. He is not a fighter unless provoked.

He accepts most every person, most every dog, at face value. But he will turn, fangs bared and back hair bristling, at those who would try to dominate him.

To me, Thor is the perfect hunter, the perfect companion. And that's the way it should be. But he would not be for you, or you, or you. He is not, for example, steady to shot, which is my fault, not his. He holds only until he can mark the fall of the bird and then he is gone, commands to the contrary.

> ## "Thor is what he was born and bred to be, a hunter..."

After that, he hunts, mostly on his own, until he finds the bird he is looking for.

I simply do not lose ducks with Thor. That's it. Plain and simple.

He is , for the most part, responsive to command. But not always. What I know is that he will come, mostly, when he is called. He will sit and stay when told.

Except under unusual conditions, he rarely needs to be commanded, either in the field or in the house. He seems to know the right thing to do without being told.

In his seventh hunting year, Thor knows that he must stay close to me. In the city. In the woods. He worries when we get out of sight of each other, even as I do. And so we work it out. Together.

Ever since he was three years old, Thor has developed a firm mouth. Notice that I said firm, not hard.

Back then, he was slapped and slashed by a crippled Canada goose at the Horicon Marsh. Ever since, any bird he has retrieved has not been alive when he presented it to my hand.

But the flesh of those birds has never been marked or abused. I have yet to find the first teeth marks on birds he has retrieved.

Thor is big enough and strong enough to retrieve geese with the same classic breast hold he puts on mallards or teal.

He is a good pheasant dog, but not a great one. He hunts close when we are in heavy cover but he tends to range when we work open areas. His habit of working close in heavy cover also makes him a good grouse dog, although I am not certain that he knows what we are doing when we hunt for them. But since he has never lost a downed grouse, I have to believe he has an idea of what is going on.

Maybe you knew Thor, through these writings, when he was a puppy.

If you did, the only thing about him that has not changed are his eyes. They remain deep brown, liquid mirrors that reflect his pain, his joy, his needs, his wants.

And for me, because I love him more than anyone should ever love a dog, they penetrate my soul and set my mind to wondering why a man should care so much for an animal that all else becomes inconsequential.

And so I watch my dog sleeping within the circle of those things that announce the approach of the days of thunder.

And I see the gray building around his muzzle.

We have so little time left.

And that's when I begin to cry.

At Age 10, Thor Lives for the Hunt

Because of special assignments and some vacation time that needed to be burned, my dog Thor has been aced out of a week of grouse hunting. And the yellow Lab does not take kindly to that.

He has come, over the years, to understand that if he is not at Black River Falls or Necedah or Winter or Park Falls when the bird season opens, the world will come to an end.

Since he can't read regulations pamphlets, and no doubt wouldn't if he could, Thor takes to other means for determining the seasons.

He can sniff a turn in the wind quicker than we can smell a steak on the grill. He hears the wild geese at night and I, in turn, hear the deep rumbling growl that builds within him.

Thor turns restless this time of year. He patrols the backyard as if it were a patch of bird cover. His nose is always in the air, reading the wind as if it were a best seller.

After a summer of snapping at flies, digging holes to find cool dirt, and being generally disagreeable to anything except a full dish, he is ready to hunt.

With nine years behind him and the 10th ready to go on the books in November, Thor does not yet realize that he has attained that level of life humans sometimes refer to as the golden years.

It is the time, we are told, to stop and smell the flowers. It is the time to feed from the storeroom of accomplishment, to walk instead of run, to laugh instead of cry, to linger over sunsets as if they were rich wine.

Thor knows nothing of that, at least in his mind and heart. He knows only the creed of going full bore. Hunt till you drop, has been his theory, and then get up and hunt some more.

As faithful readers know, Thor has hunted hurt many times. He has hunted bloody from assorted cuts and slices on feet, legs and nose. He has hunted limping. He has hunted smelling mighty like a skunk, throwing up every 100 yards from the nausea of it.

He has hunted so long and so hard on certain days and in certain places that he needed help to get out of the truck when his muscles stiffened on the ride back home.

To hunt, really, is the only thing he knows or cares about. Time spent between hunts, between seasons, has no meaning.

I think about all of that these days, more than I should. It's because I saw some things in Thor last year that even he does not realize.

Maybe it is partly because of all the hunts that have gone before, the ice he broke, the cold water he swam in, the snow he plowed through to flush a bird or make a retrieve, or maybe it is simply because of his age, but Thor's body is beginning to betray him.

He looks better than he ever has. There's not an ounce of fat on him. He's sleek and trim and as finely honed as a fillet knife.

But he no longer has the strength to go all day. He does not run out of the woods or swamps anymore. He walks. And, when we hunt, especially for ducks, you can see him saving himself because he waits patiently for the action instead of prowling around looking for it.

No longer do I have to worry about him moving out of gun range when we hunt for pheasants. There was a time when I had to run him for an hour before we got to the good cover just to take the edge off him. No more.

> **"He looks better than he ever has. But he no longer has the strength to go all day..."**

When Thor was younger, I had a heck of a time getting him out of the woods or swamps. He always wanted to stay longer. He wanted one more flush, one more bird, one more swing through the toughest cover.

Now, though, after several hours of hard hunting, he returns to the car without argument. He's still eager to get to the hunt before daylight, but the comforts of camp call to him with a compelling voice and he listens.

At this point, we have yet to flush our first bird. And duck season won't open for another couple of weeks. And we don't hunt geese until later in October.

So, I don't know how this fall hunting season of 1989 will shake down. I got a hunch, though, that it will be different.

For years, my dog, Thor, has been the crutch I've leaned upon for hunting success. And he has rarely failed.

This fall, maybe, he'll have to lean on me. At least a little. I hope I can return the favor.

Precious Days for Old Partners

Show me a duck hunt in this year of 1990 and I will show you this:

Happiness: An old dog courses the swamps and finds the fountain of youth there. He becomes a pup again, and he works the water and the wind and the cover and the birds the way he did when he was at the top of his game.

Sadness: The old dog has been fed and he has slept and now it is morning and you have to lift him off the couch where he has spent the night because his muscles have tightened and his feet are sore and he is old, with only heart and wanting left to pump the engine. The fountain of youth was false, or was it?

With each step after that he loosens up, and when he sees you put the shotgun in the truck his eyes glisten and his tail wags.

He is ready. He wants to go. He will go. Which is why you want to cry because you know time is running out for the dog and so the hot tears roll down your cheek on a frosty dawn when only the stars can see.

Then you lift him into the truck, an assist that his eyes and a gentle growl tell you he does not want. But you do it and he accepts it because both of you know that is how it has to be.

And then you drive to the hunting grounds and the old dog tries to stand in the back of the truck but he can't because his legs won't let him. His heart tells him, though, that these are the good times.

Maybe he knows his days are numbered. Maybe he knows there are not that many more retrieves for him to make. Maybe he knows that for him, one day soon, the sunset will write a final chapter to this business called duck hunting, this business called life.

Maybe that's why he puts so much effort into it now. Maybe that's why he works so hard, although he's always been a hard worker.

But then you drop this mallard drake into a stand of tall marsh grass and mud and water. The dog marks the fall and, on command, goes to fetch.

He works it exactly right and, finally, he emerges, bird in mouth, but instead of coming directly to you, he detours across the lumpy weed growth to a strip of high land. You can see him all the way and he can see you.

But the whole operation takes minutes longer than it should have. Finally, he comes to heel, bird in mouth, and you take it from him and praise him.

Why, though, did he take the long route? Was he, perhaps, squeezing one more moment of ecstasy out of a time, for him, rapidly diminishing?

The dog responds to call. Always has. But we are in this place where we can see ducks dropping into a pothole beyond the line of trees that stand just before us.

We have our limit, two drake mallards and a wood duck. There is nothing left for the two of us to do except watch the movement of birds and take pleasure from it.

The dog stands out at the edge of the marsh grass, belly deep in water. He stares across the trees and he watches the birds and his tail wags and his eyes glisten and his body trembles.

He is wet and he is muddy and he shivers along the length of his back and into his flanks. The sun is dropping and darkness is about to cover the swamps and we have to get back to the boat because there is yet a long way to go to get back to camp.

But he does not respond, this time, to my call. He stands and he looks and he watches. And so you walk up to your dog on this evening of evenings and you kneel beside him and you watch what he is watching.

And then you know.

The dog is smarter than you. These sights do not come that often in a lifetime. You see them, early on, but you don't really appreciate them. You have to get old, you have to get close to death, to see sunsets as they really are.

That's why my dog did not respond to call, I am sure now. He was taking one more look. He was sipping from the cup one more time.

I know all about that. Only I was not capable of putting it all together at that place, at that time.

We get back to the boat and he jumps in. He does not look his age, or act it, until later.

We get back to camp. After he eats, I have to lift him up on the couch where he will spend the night. I will lift him down in the morning.

Show me a duck season and I will show you happiness. Show me a duck season and I will show you sadness.

My dog's name is Thor. He is 11 years old. You have read about him in this space before.

If you own an old dog and if you work with him and play with him and live with him and forgive him his shortcomings and beg more time for him, you'll understand why I am sad this night.

There never were enough years for Thor and me to start with. Now the time we had, most of it, at least, has all but ticked away. 🐾

Duck Hunt Opens with Perfection

Except for a couple of basics, it is not yet known what historians will say about the opening weekend of Wisconsin's 1991 duck hunting season.

Like old dogs and creeks with no current, the keepers of waterfowl ledgers are slow to the point and languid as leaves without a breeze to make them dance.

The basics, though, of the early days of the duck hunting season this year are clear as the air of a cold October morning.

The weather here in Durand, Wisconsin was nearly perfect.

And the state appeared to have a reasonable population of wild ducks.

Beyond that, the success, or failure, of the opening weekend will be told in the stories circulating now around the duck camps of the state and the hard statistics to be gathered by the researchers and biologists and game managers whose job it is to separate fact from fiction.

So this part is certain:

The opening weekend weather, at least here in the land of the Chippewa River, was as close to perfect as you can get.

It was, in fact, beautiful.

There were clouds and there was rain and there was snow and there was wind, generally from the northwest, that had a knife's edge to it.

And there were ducks to be had.

Woodies, mostly, and some teal and a few widgeon and bluebills. Mallards, the state's bread-and-butter duck, may or may not have been available in number depending upon whom you asked.

In any case, there appeared to be no shortage of shooting opportunities in this part of the state.

Our party of three had seven birds in the bag, six wood ducks and one mallard, when we hung it up and left the swamps. It was enough to eat and that's all we wanted.

Had our guns been more accurate, we'd have scored with bag limits. To some, that's important. To us, it was not. What was important had to do with the conditions under which we hunted.

For more openings than we cared to count, the weather had been bright, clear, warm and sunny, circumstances better suited for picnics than duck hunting.

This opening weekend, weather-wise, gave us everything. There were clouds but, once in a while, the sun would come out, look around and then hustle back to cover.

Occasionally, there was fallout from the sky. Much of it was rain, drops of which had the goal of becoming snow. It under achieved at times but, at others, it turned our world temporarily white.

We worked a beaver-deep pothole in the state-owned Tiffany Public Hunting Grounds south of here. We had a spread of 23 decoys out about a half hour before the noon starting time. No other hunters were near.

The first bird to die was a wood duck, dropped by Dave Van Wormer, of Wisconsin Rapids.

Donald Bluhm, of Whitefish Bay, scored with a couple of wood ducks during that first flurry of action.

There was more action after that. Had our guns been perfect, we'd have hit limits. But that was never the idea.

So, when we had met the demands of the roasting pan, we bagged the decoys and headed back for camp.

"In his 12th year of doing duck business, Thor hunted with style and class and dignity..."

It should also be noted here for the record, if nothing else, that an old dog, a yellow Labrador retriever named Thor, now in his 12th year of doing duck business in the swamps, hunted with style and class and dignity.

He found and retrieved those birds he was expected to find and retrieve. Having done it for so many years, that was a given.

But, beyond that, he provided proof positive to the hunting party that there is renewed life to be found out in the swamps where rain and snow and a sharp northwest wind are precious commodities to be treasured like diamonds and pearls and memories of yesterday.

Duck hunting openings are times to be savored. So I don't really care what the historians say.

This one, here, was a dandy.

Duck Hunting's Best
When Snowflakes Fly

L ike promises made at closing time, November snowstorms along the
  Mississippi River are not to be taken lightly.
         They can be dangerous.

There are those here in Nelson, Wisconsin, who still remember the historic Armistice Day storm of 1940, when the winds of hell roiled the big river and they stacked the frozen dead on docks and railroad rights-of-way from Winona to Alma and beyond.

And any swamp rat, young or old, worth his hip boots can tell you of storms that swept in quickly, leaving them joyless and fearful for the moment that there might never be another tomorrow.

The thing about these storms, though, coming as they tend to in early November, is that they almost always provide duck hunting opportunity beyond compare.

And those of us born with a compulsion to seek out ducks in any place, under any conditions and at any time it is legal to do so, are rarely able to resist temptation's call.

COLD DUCK. Cold snowy days keep most sane people indoors. But avid duck hunters are not often accused of being sane. They know that snow squalls produce some of the finest waterfowl shooting of the season.

Which is why my dog, Thor, and I were deep in the Mississippi/Chippewa River swamps this day in 1991, when the most recent November storm raged through our world.

The story of that storm has already been told. It dumped a ton of snow on places in Wisconsin and Minnesota. It whipped the region with angry wind. It coated the countryside with a thick glaze of ice. And it ushered in a spate of bone-chilling weather.

Tragically, it also took some lives.

But just so the record is clear, I never once felt threatened or in danger because of the storm. Except for the discomfort of being cold and wet and wind-whipped, there was never a problem.

In truth, we got out of the woods before the brunt of the storm hit. Had it been a mountain, we were hunting in the foothills of it.

You should know about all this because it represents, at the same time, both the best and worst of what duck hunting in Wisconsin sometimes offers.

We knew the storm was on its way. The radio told us that. So did television. And here, at least, its beginning consisted of steady rain, strengthening wind and falling temperatures.

In the minds of duck hunters, it was nothing more than opportunity presenting itself. Nobody thought less, or

> **"By the time the decoys were in place, the freezing rain turned to snow..."**

more, of it than that, which is why we were not alone in the swamps that day and why I launched my boat about an hour before noon.

Water levels were up slightly but it would still take my outboard about an hour to reach the place I intended to hunt. In addition to my dog and shotgun, I had a bag containing seven decoys, a Thermos of coffee, a sandwich and an extra parka packed in plastic to keep it dry.

Soon the rain turned to freezing sleet and by the time I reached the place we were to hunt, my boat looked exactly like a 14-foot, flat-bottomed diamond.

The moisture hit and froze, turning the front cowling so slippery my dog had to abandon it in favor of the carpeted deck. The canvas case containing my shotgun froze stiff as did the decoy bag. Slivers of ice extended from my dog's belly

By the time the decoys were in place, the freezing rain had turned to snow. It switched my world into a cold, gray place where the only living things seemed to be me, my dog, and the mallards that fought to land on the little pothole.

As a duck hunter, you want to make moments like this last. They do not come your way very often. But as a prudent human, you sense the need to get the business over with and move out.

I killed one mallard drake out of a flock of five that dipped low over my decoys. I took another greenhead from a trio that did the same. The dog made both retrieves easily, but with unusual style.

Had the law allowed it, the killing could have gone on because the ducks kept coming. But we didn't pause, after that, for lengthy speeches. I collected the decoys, slurped some coffee, shared the sandwich with the dog and headed back to the boat which, by then, held an ankle-deep collection of snow.

On the way out, the snow continued to fall, the wind picking up some of it, making it do a devil's dance across the water. Were they really squalls? Or were they the spirits of yesterday come to ride along with me this day?

Duck season is over now in the northern half of the state and it ends today in the southern zone.

For me, though, it ended there that day in the snow and wind. Nothing more could top it. All of the dimensions that mark the outside scope of the hunt had been achieved.

Duck hunters will understand that.

Beautiful is the word that comes to mind.

This Lab Won't Beg for Attention

American Kennel Club registration statistics for 1991 show that the Labrador retriever was the most popular among registered breeds, topping the cocker spaniel, which had been top dog since 1982.

Waving a copy of the news story like it was a flag at a parade, I hunted down my dog, Thor, who was sleeping in the hallway, his head resting on a pair of hip boots.

"Look alive, old buddy," I said. "You are at the top of the list, the peak of the mountain. Labs are the most popular dogs in the country, if not the world and the entire universe. It says so right here."

Thor raised his head slightly, stretched and yawned.

"Give me a break," he snarled. "Can't you see I'm resting up for duck season?"

"Get serious," I said to him, "and stop growling. It says in this story that Labs have a wonderful temperament. That's one of the things that make them so appealing."

Thor curled his lips displaying a full set of ivories.

"Big deal," he growled derisively. "Those Labs with good temperament never had to put up with you. And, anyway, dog food is still dog food if you are a prince or a pauper. I mean, what's in it for us Labs? You going to walk me on a golden leash from now on, or what?"

BELOVED BREED. According to the American Kennel Club, the Labrador retriever has been the most popular dog in the United States for many years.

"You miss the point," I said, handing him a dog biscuit. "This is an honor. It's like an award, a prize...recognition. It sets you apart."

Thor chomped on the biscuit for awhile, looking me straight in the eye.

"An honor?" he snarled. "An honor? Think about it, dummy. How many ducks will honor retrieve for you next fall? How many pheasants will it flush? Honor ain't going to pay the kennel rent or the vet's bill."

"You are right about that," I said, scratching his ears. "But I still think this is something pretty special. Being the most popular is really something."

Thor looked at me, this time with a little sympathy.

"Coming from you, I understand that," he said. "I forget that you could have the only boat in a flood and still be unpopular."

"That was an unkind cut," I said to him. "Watch your tongue or you'll find yourself on the world's shortest leash."

Thor actually smiled at that.

"I forget my place, oh revered master," he said sarcastically. "Let me bring you your smelly slippers or retrieve the newspaper for you and get newsprint all over my lips. Let me curl uncomfortably at your feet while you smoke that God-awful pipe or a cigarette or whatever vile weed you choose to contaminate the air with."

"What the heck has gotten into you?" I asked. "The Labradors of this world, of which you are one, have just been accorded a place in canine history, and all you can do is snarl invectives. I can assume, I suppose, that you are unimpressed with it all."

"You've got that right," Thor said. "And there's more. My guess is that you intend to take this conversation we've had and blab in all over the state in your newspaper. Well, let me tell you that if anybody ever asks, I'll deny that you and I talk."

"No need to be mean now, old fella," I said. "Ever since you were a puppy, you and I have talked more than politicians at a parade."

Thor looked at me, smiling.

"I know that, and you know that," he said. "But you know what society would have to say about somebody who claims to talk with his dog, right? Well, just cause you are a quart shy of a full gallon, is no reason for people to think I am.

"After all, I'm a Labrador, the most popular dog in the land. So go talk to a cocker spaniel or a poodle after this. See how far you get. And don't ever forget that I sure as heck ain't Mr. Ed."

After that, I went to see Kate, Max Harter's marvelous Chessy up in Grantsburg.

She wouldn't give me the time of day, either. She did, though, ask for a recount. I heard her say it. I did. 🐾

Hunting Won't Be the Same Without Old Thor

Consider this an update on my dog, Thor.

It will, I think, answer a number of questions from readers who have called or written the Outdoor Department.

If you've never loved an animal, turn to some other section, because you will have no interest in what follows here.

It is for believers and those who came aboard more than a decade ago to read about a seven-week-old puppy who, at the time, couldn't make all four of his feet work together. It is for those who have followed him.

For the first time in 13 years, I am hunting ducks without Thor. The deep-chested yellow Lab with soul-searching eyes is at home, sleeping in the sun, snapping at flies and softly growling, every now and then, when he is disturbed.

He is OK, at least as much as a retriever of his years and mileage can be. He knows no pain, so far as we can tell, and he displays, from time to time, bursts of puppy-like energy.

But the years have taken a toll on my dog. He is paying, now, for every time he broke ice to retrieve a duck; for every time the snow built up on his back and flanks; for every time the wind cut at him as we sat, shivering together and soaked to the skin, waiting for one more shot, one more flight, one more thrill from whistling wings.

His eyes are as bright as they ever were. But Thor has lost his hearing, or most of it.

IN HIS YOUNGER YEARS, Thor could retrieve pheasants and ducks all day long. He slowed up, of course, during his later days. Waterfowling became too much for him then, but Jay made sure he enjoyed some upland bird hunting in his last season.

And his hindquarters, once powerful enough to propel him through the deepest mud and thickest marsh grass for endless hours, are withered now and weakened, devoid of sufficient strength to handle anything save the thinnest, easiest, driest cover. And that only for short runs.

There was a meeting not long ago at Miserak's Kennels on Highway 175, between Richfield and Slinger. Mary and Joe Miserak were there because it is their place. They are two of Wisconsin's finest Labrador breeders, trainers and handlers, and the dearest of friends, to boot.

They have taken care of Thor, over the years, when he could not be at home or traveling with us. They have watched over him. They have tended to his hurts and to his cares. They know him.

My wife, Christine, was at that meeting, too. She holds a love for Thor so deep and so all-consuming as to be immeasurable in scope.

And, of course, there was Thor and me.

What came out of it was a decision, mutually reached, that Thor should not be out in a duck swamp anymore. It was agreed that I should hunt him, in short bursts, only on dry land for pheasants or grouse.

It would be in the dog's best interests.

> **"That sharing — everything from bologna to bag limits — is what I'll miss the most..."**

And that, of course, is the way it will be.

So much for the practical aspects.

In truth, I would not care if my dog would die while hunting ducks. In fact, I'd be envious of him if he did because there is no better way to go.

The problem is, though, that I would need to recover him and if you've ever hunted for ducks with a good dog in the deepest marshes, you know that is not always possible.

So Thor's days as a duck dog, that activity for which he was born in the first place, are over.

These words are being written on a Thursday. They won't hit the streets until Sunday and, by then, I will have had a day or so of duck hunting without him.

Right now, I don't know how it will all shake down. I've hunted ducks without a dog before, so I have an idea. But it's been a long time. And memory tends to fade.

I know it won't be the same kind of ballgame. I know I'll have to change my way of doing business. For 13 years, I've never worried about where a duck might drop because I knew Thor would find it. Old habits are hard to break.

That, though, is really the least of it. The act of hunting with Thor, being with him, sharing the best and worst of it, from Saskatchewan to Nebraska to the Dakotas and Iowa and every swamp in Wisconsin, has been, for me, what the outdoor experience is really all about.

That sharing—everything from bologna to bag limits, from misery to miracles—is what I think I'll miss the most.

By the time you read these words, I will have had a crash course in reality.

And I will know, among other things, whether or not it is possible to shoot well, or even at all, through eyes veiled by a curtain of tears.

It is said that all good things must one day end. For me and for Thor and the ducks we once pursued together, it has.

Like dragons and dreams and frosty dawns, the days of thunder never were intended to last forever. And that's a sad thing.

So now let me go to cry alone.

Thor is Game in His Last Hunt

Step right up, folks, and be introduced to Candlewood's Thor of River Road. He is a seven-week-old yellow Labrador retriever. – The Milwaukee Journal, January 20, 1980

So what can you do for an old hunting dog whose days are clearly numbered, whose hearing is gone, whose eyes have faded, whose once endless strength has evaporated like swamp fog before the sun?

My old friend, Bob Voit, of Brookfield, who owns the Burnett Shooting Preserve and Game Farm, gave me a partial answer.

"Why don't you bring Thor up here and we'll give him one more hunt?" he said in a recent telephone conversation.

You have to understand about Bob Voit. He's an old friend. He saw Thor hunt when the dog was at the top of his game. And he said at the time that the Lab was a miracle. He said I should count my blessings for having him.

And, over the years, he followed Thor, through the words and pictures that have appeared on this page. Bob Voit, please understand, has a heart as large as the outdoors and all of the marvelous things the outdoors contain.

GOLDEN DAYS and olden days were called to mind by Thor's last hunt. Those happiest years enjoyed by a dog and his master will live on in the pages of this book.

Which is why he called me after reading the story about Thor's retirement.

"Bring him up here," Voit said. "We'll salt an easy field with ringnecks. We'll give him one more shot. We'll fill his nose with hot pheasant scent. He deserves it."

Voit was right, of course. Only I wasn't certain. The thing is, Thor is in reasonably good shape, considering his years, but his strength is mostly gone as is his hearing. His nose isn't what it once was, either.

In the end, though, I took my dog to Voit's game farm in Burnett. And it was as Voit said it would be: A salted field of ringnecks, one more shot at yesterday when the hot scent of birds burned the nose and when the wind ruffled the marsh grass and today was today because tomorrow didn't matter.

Some good people who care about Thor were there.

Don Bluhm, of Whitefish Bay, was on hand. He has hunted over Thor since the beginning.

Stan Thieman, who owns the Spirit of 76 Veterinary Clinic, in West Allis, was there. Out of respect for Thor, he had left behind his yellow Labrador, Katie.

Steve Gutknecht, a teacher at Milwaukee's Juneau High School, came up for the day because he, too, had hunted over Thor in earlier days.

Bob Voit's son, Jim, came over from Beaver Dam, where

> **"His tail pumped wildly...and he pushed that ringneck out the way he would have years earlier..."**

he operates Voit's Victory Kennels. A breeder and trainer of pointing dogs, Jim Voit had seen Thor hunt before.

And so that was the hunting party that formed this late December day at the Burnett Shooting Preserve. It was raining, believe it or not, and the moisture soaked through the snow that lathered the field where Thor would hunt.

The ringnecks were down, planted by Jim Voit and Dr. Stan.

I helped Thor from the Journal's truck, lifted the leash and turned him free.

On the first bird, but only the first bird, he worked as if it were yesterday. He quartered across the line of hunters and went into the wind for the ringneck.

The hair bristled along his back and his tail pumped wildly back and forth and he pushed that ringneck out the way he would have years earlier.

But he used it all up in that effort. After that, he mostly walked. Sometimes he trotted. He worked right by two more birds and never did flush them until directed to the exact spots.

Two more ringnecks ran on him. He plodded on the tracks but had no chance of putting them up.

And, finally he came back to the line of hunters and walked with them.

The whole episode lasted about an hour. And Thor had had it. He knew it. I knew it. He walked with me, later, as two young pointers strutted their stuff. But he had no interest.

So I helped him into my truck. He stretched out and went to sleep.

I knew it was Thor's last hunt. I think he did, as well. But no matter. And now there is this:

For all of you who have followed Thor through the years, you will read no more about him here, at least by my hand.

It's over you see, and done with. He will die someday soon or, if necessary, I will have him put down.

In any case the Thor story ends here.

He was the subject of more mail and telephone calls than any other topic about which I have ever written.

But the days of thunder, you see, never last forever.

So let them end now, once and for all, with dignity, at Christmas time.

Thor has earned that. And more.

Thor's Days of Thunder Are Sadly Over

By Bob Riepenhoff, Journal Outdoor Editor

H ow's Thor?"
That was the one question asked more often than any other, through the years, of *Milwaukee Journal* outdoor writer Jay Reed.

It was asked in more letters, telephone calls and casual conversations than anyone could ever hope to count.

Clearly, the people who read these pages each week care very deeply about Thor.

Through the years, the answers to inquiries about Thor—his growth, his progress as a hunter and his latest adventures—came easily.

But now the words are harder to find. And for Jay, understandably, there are no more words at all to say about his beloved companion.

> **"Thor seemed most alive when he was scanning the skies or lunging to make another retrieve..."**

So the unpleasant duty of reporting the bad news about Thor falls to me.

Thor—perhaps the best-known hunting dog in the state of Wisconsin—died on July 3, 1993. He was buried the same day on a gentle knoll on the edge of the Mississippi River swamps.

He was 13 years old when he was diagnosed with bone cancer last month. Within weeks, his condition had deteriorated to the point where Jay and his wife, Christine, were left with no alternative but to have Thor put down.

It's hard to measure the impact Thor's life had on so many readers, or the way he touched so many hearts.

Thor literally grew up, from puppy to working retriever, before our eyes on the outdoor pages of the *Milwaukee Journal*.

Readers were introduced to Candlewood's Thor of River Road—the official name on the puppy's registration papers—on January 20, 1980. From that point on, Thor was a regular presence in these pages.

"Thor will travel with me to those places the *Journal* sends me," Jay wrote in that first story. "And when fall comes, we'll hunt together in every field and swamp I can find."

Jay kept that promise—not only that fall, but for 12 more autumns after that.

Thor had a distinguished hunting career that Jay recorded and celebrated in numerous columns and feature stories. There was a strong and deep bond of affection between the man and his dog that was present in every story. It was something to which any hunter—or anyone who ever loved a dog—could easily relate.

Among the many letters Jay received about his dog, three came to him from governors. For a while, Jay was even sending out pictures of Thor, complete with a paw print, to those who wrote.

Thor was happiest when he was doing the work he was born to do. Even after he passed his prime, Thor seemed most alive when he was scanning the skies or lunging to make another retrieve from a duck blind on the Mississippi River.

In the end, you could say that Thor was a fine companion and a dog who never tired of the hunt, who was never slowed down by the mud or the cold, and who coveted the swamps as the rest of us covet heaven.

And let's say one more thing, on behalf of all of us who have enjoyed reading about him for so many years:

We'll miss you, Thor.

Hunting Yarns

CHAPTER 2

INTRODUCTION

Thor lived to hunt and so did his master who wrote, "Hunting has always been the largest part of living for me. It was more than a hobby. It was the axis around which life revolved."

Jay Reed loved to hunt every kind of game in Wisconsin, including grouse, pheasant, woodcock and deer. But duck hunting, by far, was his deepest love.

Put Jay Reed in a rickety blind almost anywhere in November and you'd have one happy soul. Make sure the snow is spitting hard from leaden clouds in the northeast. A stiff wind, quartering over his shoulder, should roil the water with a wicked chop.

Form some ice on his boat, set a Thermos of hot coffee on the floor of the blind , throw in a stand of cattails, add a generous helping of smelly marsh muck, and you'd have placed Jay Reed in his own version of heaven.

In the stories that follow, he'll take you along.

Jackpine's Dancer Had a Pair

Mr. Terry Galvin, Sports Editor
the *Milwaukee Journal*

Dear Terry:
I am writing to you from Jackpine Joe's Saloon in Upnorth, Wisconsin, because I think I got a story here, only I'm not smart enough to know for sure.

You get an enormous salary (which you richly deserve, I hasten to add) to figure out things like this.

What happened was that me and Chilblain Charley and Mattress Mike were ice fishing all day and we had eight crappies in the bag by the time it got dark. Now I know that ain't much for three grown men, but times are tough here.

Anyways, we stopped at Jackpine's for a touch of brandy to chase the chill. Jackpine was there moving all the tables against the wall. That's as hard as we'd seen him work since he thought Paul Molitor was coming in for a Friday night fish fry.

Jackpine looked like he was about to bust.

"What's the matter?" Chilblain asked, powering his chew into a spittoon. "Did the Brewers get another one of them there big-name pitchers who's going to lead us all to the promised land next summer?"

Jackpine's face just got redder and his neck began to swell like a buck in rut.

"No, you damned old coot," Jackpine said. "I got some news. Some real news."

"Why are you moving the tables?" Chilblain asked. "You gonna have a dance, or something?"

"You got it right the first time," Jackpine said, dribbling brandy along the bar as he poured us each a shot.

Right then, Terry, I knew something big was afoot because Jackpine ain't spilled a drop of booze since they traded Gorman Thomas.

Anyways, he settled back with his head on the towel rack and a look on his face like he knowed the answer to all the world's problems.

"I want you boys to be the first to know," he said, his voice rising with emotion. "I've hired an exotic dancer to work this joint on Saturday nights."

Well, Terry. That was like a bombshell or a four bagger loaded. We were all stunned. Jackpine let it settle in on us for a while and then he said:

"You bet your Green Bay Packer tickets. An exotic dancer. And she's got the biggest pair of Spinones you've ever seen in your life."

"You've got to be kidding," said Chilblain Charley. Mattress Mike couldn't even speak. He tossed off his brandy and motioned for another.

"Not only that," said Jackpine, "they are the biggest ones I've ever seen in my life and, as you know, I've seen some Spinones."

"You mean you've already seen them?" Chilblain asked.

"You bet," Jackpine said. "She uses them in her act. They do tricks."

"I could have expected that," Chilblain said dryly.

"She was a smash at the Coyote's Den down in Green Bay," Jackpine said.

> **"They are the biggest ones I have ever seen in my life..."**

Well, I can tell you, Terry, we were all shaken down to our very foundations. Jackpine said the dancer's stage name was Golden Glorious but that her friends, of which he was one, called her Goldie.

"I'll bet," Jackpine said, keeping the conversation going, "that you guys would like to see Goldie's Spinones. I mean, I bet you'd really like to see them. Like right now."

Terry, I've never seen Chilblain and Mattress in such a state. But you'll be happy to know I kept my cool, more or less.

"You mean she's here right now?" Chilblain asked.

"You bet," Jackpine told him. "She's back in the dressing room."

"Now just a goldarn minute," Mattress Mike said. "You ain't got no dressing room in this place."

Jackpine looked at him as you would look at a child who had just said something dumb.

"Well of course there's a dressing room. She is using that room where we keep the beer cool in summer."

"Ain't that a trifle cold this time of year?" Chilblain asked.

"Naw," said Jackpine. "Goldie likes it on the cool side. Says it is good for her Spinones."

"Tell you what," Jackpine continued. "Since you guys are my best customers, if you are willing to put up $10 each, I'll take you back to the dressing room, introduce you to Goldie and she'll show you her Spinones. Guaranteed."

Terry, I've never seen money appear on a bar so fast since the time…
well, no need to go into that now.

We put our money down and Jackpine folded it neatly and stuck it in
his shirt pocket and then he took us to the back room where he knocked on
the door.

"Is that you, Jackpine?" a voice asked.

"It's me, Goldie. I got some friends with me. They want to come in. Is
it OK?"

"I suppose they want to see my Spinones," the voice said, and Jackpine
answered that was true.

"Well, sure. Come in. You know how proud I am of them."

And so we entered and Jackpine made introductions all around.
We stood there rather awkwardly for a while. And then Goldie showed us
her Spinones.

I'm telling you, Terry, Jackpine was right. They were big. And they
were pretty.

She had them on one of those leashes that hold two dogs at the
same time.

When I looked at Goldie's Spinones all I saw were teeth and curled lips
as in snarl, even though the American Kennel Club book says they have
good dispositions.

There were two of the biggest Italian hunting dogs I have ever seen in
my life. I kid you not.

Chilblain Charley was speechless.

Mattress Mike said: "But Jackpine, I thought…I mean 10 bucks…
for this…"

"I know what you thought," said Jackpine. "You are a dirty old man
and you've been had along with Chilblain and the author from Milwaukee.
It does my heart good."

Well, that's all there is to it, Terry. I thought there might be a story here.
Goldie says she'll be working some clubs in Milwaukee this fall and, on
her off days, she intends to work her Spinones in the Theresa Marsh and
Horicon areas. They are outstanding hunters, as you know.

No More Mr. Nice Guy

Call this a formal declaration of war. Call it the line in the sand over which the enemy has now crossed.

Call it what you will, but the big guns are coming out now. It's Katie bar the door. All bets are off. No holds will be barred. Sucker punches will be the order of the day, and night. There will, in short, be hell to pay.

And what, you ask, prompts these violent intentions? What has riled the blood and jump-started the emotions to this extreme extent?

Just this: The mice that heretofore have peacefully inhabited my hunting and fishing camp here in Nelson, Wisconsin, have demolished The Camp Duck.

They've done this without provocation, without conscience, and with obvious malice. After coexisting peacefully with me and an assortment of hunters, fishermen and dogs, the mice have turned lawless. They have resorted to vandalism.

It should be noted that The Camp Duck is, more accurately was, a mounted greenhead mallard, a magnificent representative of the species with a triple curl and all of the feathered beauty know to man.

PROBLEMS MOUNTED. Ol' Jay encountered difficulties during the wintertime closure of his hunting camp in Nelson. Father time and various vermin took a toll on the taxidermy pieces displayed there.

It was shot a couple of years ago by my hunting partner, Don Bluhm, of Whitefish Bay. One of the state's most talented taxidermists, Jay Snopek, who has a place several 12-gauge shots down the railroad track from my camp, mounted it. Bluhm donated it to the camp.

The big mallard occupied a place of honor atop the refrigerator, where, with its wings cupped, it was lifelike enough to appear ready to land on the kitchen floor.

At first, the mice nibbled only a little at the mallard's orange feet. Then they stopped. The thought was that they would now respect the bird for what it was. So, when we closed the camp for winter, the duck was left in its place.

I made an unscheduled stop at camp a week or so ago. It was colder than a mausoleum inside. And the duck was in ruins.

So I now, officially, vow revenge.

I know from experience that the mice living in my camp are too smart to be trapped. And I refuse, for both personal and practical reasons, to use poison. That, of course, reduces the options to dangerously low levels.

So what, then, to do? I called a meeting of the board of directors, of which I am the only member. I concurrently hold the offices of president and chief executive officer. And I also pay the bills.

Luckily, I am blessed with more advisers than there are whiskers on the nose of a mouse. So some ideas were put on the table.

Why not, it was suggested, put up no trespassing signs? If the mice are smart enough to avoid traps, they might also be able to read.

It was thought that I might be able to receive legislative relief given the fact that I have been so liberal with free advice to the lawmakers.

Somebody said I should petition the Department of Natural Resources to conduct a study of the problem. We discarded that idea because the department is lacking in funds these days.

It was also suggested that I take a page from the notebooks of some governmental entities, those with deer problems, and consider hiring sharpshooters to come in at night and blast those mice over feeding stations.

Given the already pock-marked interior of the camp, my advisers couldn't decide what kind of guns the sharpshooters should use. The one pattern of fine shot on the north wall is already more than one would like to have in a camp that stresses gun safety, among other things. Somebody said we might be able to flood them out except for the fact that they probably live in the attic. And somebody else said I could put a bounty on them, much as the state used to do with beaver.

So, no decision has been reached as yet.

In the end, though, I think I'll just watch and see what the manager of the Milwaukee Brewers and the coach of the Milwaukee Bucks do to survive.

They are used to dealing with impossible situations.

A Hunter's Life: No Remorse

What we have here, by request, is a litany of death...and some thoughts about that, all deeply personal.

Just don't confuse it with confession, for I seek no forgiveness, nor approval, nor absolution from anybody.

I killed my first deer on the day of my 12th birthday 40 years ago. I killed my last one last season, in 1979. In between, a lot of bucks, and some does, have gone down off the end of my rifle. And moose. And bear. And there will be more.

I have killed every kind of bird and animal that is legally hunted in Wisconsin. In the beginning, I spent every day of every summer and fall killing something. Those were times when most everything carried a bounty. So I shot, clubbed or snared crows, woodchucks, gophers and rattlesnakes.

And I trapped back then, too, as well as later. So I've killed beaver, otter, fox, skunk, coyote, muskrat, mink and raccoon.

I've fished for both profit and recreation. That's killing too, although most people choose not to recognize it.

If it had wings, if it could swim, if it lived in the woods, if it was good to eat or sell and if it was a legal target, I killed it. To do that, I used guns, knives, traps, snares, clubs, the boots on my feet and the hands on my arms.

All of the above is noted only so you will understand that death and I have been on a first-name basis for a long time.

Now the questions before the house are these:

How do you feel when you point a rifle or a shotgun at some wild thing, pull the trigger and watch it die? And, how can you bring yourself to kill these beautiful, wild creatures?

OK. The answer to the first is this: If I've hunted within the rules, if I've shot well and if I've done everything right, I feel good.

And to the second: It's easy, if you understand yourself.

Know this, first. I've never felt remorse for anything I've killed. I have yet to shed my first tear over a wild bird or wild animal dead at my own hands.

And if I ever do, I'll hang up my guns and never hunt again.

This is why: The kill is only one part of the hunt. To me, perhaps, the least compelling part. But it is necessary. To hunt wild game without killing would be like playing a game of golf without a ball; like playing cards without a deck, like loving without someone to love.

To purposely inflict death on a wild creature is an intensely personal thing. It is right only if you believe, in your heart, that it is right.

I reached an accommodation with myself a long time ago. I never have killed just to watch something die. I never have killed for the sake of killing. I nearly wrecked a car once, avoiding a rabbit that ran across the road while I was on the way to, of all things, a rabbit hunt.

I have killed for money. I have killed for meat. But I have never killed for fun.

I like to hunt. I don't really know why. But that's the way it is and I accept it. And I have satisfied myself that killing is a necessary part of hunting.

And I believe this: Those who do not care to kill should not take a gun into the woods.

Beyond that, I believe that death is as equal to one as it is another. It is the same for a fish or a grouse or a pheasant as it is for a deer or a bear. Those who would kill one and say it is all right, but would not kill the other because it is wrong, are only deluding themselves.

The fish killed with a hook is no less dead than the deer killed by a rifle bullet.

And then there's this. It's important to me, if no one else.

I love and respect the wild game I hunt and kill. These birds, these animals, have more of my love and respect than do most of the people with whom I have to deal.

Wild creatures have class, dignity, loyalty and courage to a greater degree than most humans. When I hunt them and kill them within the rules of the game, I believe they understand. And that's why I shed no tears for them.

If I weep at all, it is for those who do not, and never will, have the answer.

I am aware that many who read these words won't like what I have to say. This will rub a lot of folks the wrong way.

That's understandable. It's never easy to discuss death, especially the kind that's inflicted in the name of recreation.

I'm not trying to change anybody's mind. You've got your thoughts. I've got mine. We're all entitled.

Just know this: Wisconsin's major hunting seasons are about to open, and you can bet I'll be out there somewhere.

I'll hunt and I'll shoot and if I do each well, I will kill. And there'll be no tears.

I'll do it, as I have from the beginning, with love.

Old Friends Are Best

It's old, the shotgun is. A relic.

It's not antique. Not that. It is just old. And used. Shopworn and consumed by time. But still useful.

It has been down the road. And it shows. Its stock is held together by duct tape and the bluing is mostly gone from its barrels.

If the gun were human its face would be wrinkled and its shoulders stooped. It would need a cane and a crutch. Its hair would be gray.

And if that gun could talk, what stories it would tell about yesterday.

It could talk about hunts all the way from Saskatchewan and Ontario and Manitoba to Iowa and Dakota and Nebraska and Michigan and Minnesota and all over Wisconsin.

It could tell of the big, long-tailed pheasants it has killed. It could tell of the mountain of

DOUBLE TROUBLE befell this buck as Jay Reed took aim with his old Stevens side-by-side shotgun.

ducks and geese and grouse that died and it wouldn't have to lie.

And the gun, you see, if it could talk, could tell about the failings of the man who carried it. They were, and are, many.

It is a side-by-side, double-barrel, 12-gauge shotgun. Stevens by make.

The man, now from Milwaukee, bought it new back in late 1945 for $50 because the only gun he had before that was an M1 rifle that the government took back when it had no more need for him to shoot it.

Even new, the shotgun wasn't much to look at. Actually, it was ugly.

It had a plastic stock and a plastic forearm because all the wood had been used up in the war effort. It had a double trigger and it kicked like an army mule.

It always was, and still is, a gun for country boys. You wouldn't show it off. You wouldn't brag about it. You wouldn't put it on the wall.

But, let me tell you, that gun can shoot. Lordy, how it can shoot. It gives extra range to whatever make of ammunition is put into it. It kills, sometimes, in spite of the failings of the man who shoots it.

And now there is this: Shotguns are for game birds, right? Pheasants, ducks, quail, geese and grouse. You bet. That's the way it was intended.

Well, back in those years when the state's deer herd was growing and spreading, hunting seasons were developed in agricultural areas where it was deemed that shotguns, with slugs, would be safer to use than high-powered rifles. It is still that way.

"Even new, the shotgun wasn't much to look at..."

And so it came to pass that the plastic-stocked shotgun would be used for deer hunting by the man, now from Milwaukee, for a very good reason. It was the only gun he owned.

The book on successful shooting says side-by-side doubles are not to be trusted with slugs. Maybe so. But this one can be trusted. Its right barrel, full choked and fired with the lead trigger, shoots a slug up to 70 yards as accurately as any rifle.

Its left barrel, choked modified, is something else. But when the two sight beads on its dividing rib are lined up properly, and held on target, there is seldom need to fire the other round anyway. The first one kills.

The man, now from Milwaukee, did not, sadly, keep a record of the number of deer killed with that shotgun. He guesses that it might be about 40, most by his hand but some by others who borrowed the gun.

Memory dims, of course, over time, but he remembers many of the bucks that dropped when the shotgun kicked and roared.

And one more memory was made a week ago Saturday when the current Wisconsin deer season opened.

He was in the swamps again, where he was born, where he has lived so much, and where, one day it will all end.

The double gun with the taped stock, the nicked, scratched, worn barrels, was cradled in his arms. It was about 8:30 a.m., give or take a tick of the clock, when he saw the buck step out of a willow thicket.

It was a big animal with a heavy rack. It did not follow the deer trail out in front of the hunter's stand. Instead it slipped slowly along the edge of a marsh where the grass was high and the brush thick.

It stopped, for the length of a heartbeat, near a windfall with only its head, neck and front shoulders visible to the hunter.

The old shotgun roared with its right barrel and the buck leaped into the tight brush and disappeared.

The hunter gathered his gear, reloaded the gun and walked to the spot. There was blood, enough that he knew the deer was his. He followed it for a hundred yards or so.

And there it was. The big buck. Stone cold dead on the ground. He looked it over carefully, making certain the last of its life was gone. Its antlers were proudly high and wide and thick at the base. They held nine full points.

First, he unloaded the shotgun. Then he placed it next to the buck. Then he sat on a nearby stump, staring at the gun and the deer.

They were alike. Both were old. Both were used. Both showed those signs that years bring.

In those moments that he sat alone there in the swamps that morning with the gun and the deer, something nagged at the man.

He should have been totally satisfied with the hunt and its outcome. He should have had that good feeling deep in his gut, the one he had known so many times before. But he didn't.

And then, suddenly, he knew why. An old deer and an old gun and an old hunter had crossed paths that day.

The man understood that he was just like, and a part of, the other two.

There's Only One Thing Dumber Than a Grouse

They say, mostly, that ruffed grouse are dumb. And maybe that is so.
It could be that they are simply trusting, which possibly is the same thing as being dumb.

Frequently, they'll sit beside a road or trail in full view of a car and allow time enough for a man to get out, remove his shotgun from a case, load it and shoot.

Sometimes they'll flutter straight up from ground to tree, feeling fully safe in that circumstance. They are not, of course.

Dogs tend to baffle grouse.

Pax, the yellow Labrador I hunted with a few years ago, was never famous for his skill as a grouse dog. Yet, he created a lot of easy grouse shots for me.

My dog often romped out of good shooting range when we were in the grouse woods, which is bad, but he was rarely out of sight. I couldn't begin to count the number of times grouse flushed and treed at the approach of my dog. There they would sit, looking down at the Lab, paying no attention whatever to my approach.

Those were easy kills.

All of the above is evidence for the side that holds that grouse are foolish birds with suicidal instincts.

Let me offer now, to the contrary, this account of a half day's grouse hunting near Fifield, in northern Wisconsin. Everything will show but the tears.

DUMB AND DUMBER? Jay Reed caught up with "Mr. Pa'tridge" on this day...which looks somewhat more successful than the hunting trip he describes in this column from October 22, 1978.

Start with the terrain. It was a triangular patch of woods, brush and windfalls about a mile and a half wide.

104

Loggers had crunched a sort of trail through it from one road to another, the distance being a bit over a mile. It was good grouse country. It had a "birdy" look to it, as the saying goes.

I should have seen the handwriting on the wall with the first bird I flushed. It came up behind me. I must have walked within feet of it. Yet, instead of flushing out in front where I might have had a poke at it, the bird waited until I had walked by.

Dumb, right?

Now I don't know what kind of equipment the loggers used when they were cutting, but the ruts left behind were deep and steep. And, after a wet summer and fall, they were full of water.

Let it be known that deep, water-filled ruts and 8-inch hunting boots are not compatible.

It came to pass, anyway, that when I slipped into the first rut, sinking nearly to my hips in muddy water, two grouse elected at that precise moment to flush immediately to my left.

Since I was using the butt of my shotgun to steady myself at the time, I failed to get off a shot.

> "My feet were wet, I was mud covered to the hips and sweat-soaked the rest of the way..."

Those birds are really dumb.

After removing boots, wringing out socks and putting boots back on again, I resumed the hunt. Having been burned by the water-filled ruts once, I moved off the trail and walked through the brush on the north side.

Two more birds elected to flush on the south side. No shots fired. Dumb, dumb, dumb. Right?

The prickly ash was honed sharp and most of it stood head high or better. In a short time the sides of my neck and the backs of my hands were bleeding. It was hot that day. Hot enough, at least, for mosquitoes to be out. They fed on me.

My feet were wet, I was mud covered to the hips and sweat-soaked the rest of the way. Blood had caked on my shirt collar. I wondered why I was there.

And then I came to this clearing. You should know about this because it illustrates again how really dumb grouse can be.

The clearing was about as big as an average living room. It held some scrubby brush and grass and not much else, except for one spike of popple that was maybe 10 feet high, no bigger around than two inches and skinny at the top with no growth at all.

When I stepped into the clearing, a grouse flushed near the base of that popple. It flew straight away from me and in a direct line with the tree. It was hidden, and I never did get off a shot.

Now, grouse are not the biggest birds in the world, but they are bigger than a two-inch popple, so one might wonder how it could remain hidden behind the tree.

I don't know the answer. But it did. Maybe it's something only dumb birds can do. Totally whipped by then, I returned to my truck and suffered the final indignity of the day.

I cased my shotgun, took off my wet boots and put on some dry shoes. I put down the tailgate of my truck, sat back on it, opened a can of beer and lit a cigarette. I sucked on each for a while and then, in order, put the empty beer can in the truck, snubbed out the cigarette and slammed the tailgate shut.

At that sound, a grouse flushed from the side of the road no more than six feet from where I rested.

Enough.

I know for sure there was something dumb out there in the woods that day. I also know, for sure, it didn't have feathers.

Hunting Habits
Need to Change

L et's get this down for the record right away so there will be no misunderstanding.

I am a deer hunter. I have hunted deer all my adult life, plus back far enough to those times when I was still learning how to lace my boots right.

Although it is not my favorite hunting season of the year (ducks hold that spot), I still look forward to it with more than a little enthusiasm.

Beyond that, I am in full accord with the purposes of the hunt and I have yet to shed my first tear for Bambi done-in legally during rifle season.

Having said that, I will tell you that there are a number of things that I don't like about the way deer hunting has evolved over the years. There are some things I don't like about the season. And there are some things I don't like about the people who take part in the hunt.

All of which may mean nothing to anybody, but I'm entitled to do one of these columns just for me, if nobody else.

AN ETHICAL HUNTER. In this gutsy piece from November 13, 1983, Jay described some of the hunting practices he particularly disliked, despite the fact that many of them were legal and commonly practiced by his readers.

So here goes: I don't like gang hunting. Never did. One of the most distasteful sights to me, in any deer season is to see a group of 15 to 20 hunters clustered around a half-dozen pickup trucks getting ready for their next drive.

There's something about it that ain't fittin'.

I don't like the common practice of hunting from tree stands by either riflemen or archers. I think the state should pass a law to ban it for both.

To me, there's something evil about crawling up into a tree like a squirrel and either blasting or sticking a deer on the ground. It is the most unfair of all unfair advantages and, somehow, I don't think that is the way the hunt was intended.

If you can't work it out to shoot a deer from the ground then, by God, I don't think you are entitled to shoot one at all. Man, I can hear the screams of the hotshot hunters already when they read that. I have never hunted from a tree stand and never will.

I don't like the way most deer are carried home from the hunt. To see a big buck lashed to the top or a car like a common suitcase degrades the animal.

Last year I saw a pickup camper with a doe and fawn swaying from neck ropes on the back. The eyes of the deer bulged and their tongues squirted out the sides of their mouths and it looked a lot like a mobile scaffold.

> "I don't like gang hunting...I don't like tree stands..."

If hunters ever wonder why they get so much heat from anti- and non-hunters, they should remember how a deer looks when it is trussed up like garbage and hung up on a car or truck for all the world to see.

I don't like hunters who, after having shot a buck and gutted it, refuse to wash the blood from their hands and arms until they've gone into town and had a beer or whatever.

I don't like hunters who wear their blaze-orange coats and pants like it was a Class A Uniform for everything from going to the toilet to eating out in a supper club.

These are suits for the woods and that's where they should be worn. There are people who think that blaze-orange getup makes them 10 feet tall and the envy of every female eye in the area, especially if they've got a knife big enough to cut pulp hanging from the belt. I think it's crazy.

I don't like regulations that permit a hunter to go back in the woods to hunt again even after that hunter has already killed a deer. There's no sense to it. The law says a license holder is entitled to kill one deer and that's the way it should be.

If that successful hunter wants to go back into the woods again to help his buddies, then he should do it without a rifle in his hands.

Of all the hypocritical acts of which hunters are guilty, that one right there is the most flagrant and the state should do something about it. And the Wisconsin Conservation Congress should lead the fight.

I don't like hunters who carry portable radios with them into the woods to listen to a football game. If you are going to hunt, then hunt. If you want to listen to football then get the hell out of the woods, where you are only in the way.

In the end, I guess, what I don't like most about deer hunting is what the public perception of the hunt has become. Shooting a deer has turned into a social attribute. Not shooting one tends to be a scar on your personal abilities.

Somebody was quoted in the Journal the other day as saying this about deer season: "It's all I live for, all I care about."

Well, OK. To each his own.

Here is one voice, though, that says it ain't a crusade. It ain't the end-all.

When done properly, legally, the deer hunt is nothing more than the honorable pursuit of an animal that, it its domain, exhibits more class, more dignity, more courage, more bravery, more strength in the face of death than its pursuers will ever know or even begin to understand.

Winter Wind Brings Cold, But It Also Brings Ducks

Ten miles above Winona we came to Fountain City, nestling sweetly at the feet of cliffs that lift their awful fronts, Jove-like, toward the blue depths of heaven, bathing them in virgin atmospheres that have known no other contact save that of angels' wings. – From Life on the Mississippi *by Mark Twain*

Some men who were there will remember it for a long time as the day winter came to Wisconsin in the year of '81.

Others, like me, will remember it as the time when the winds of hell blew in clouds of migratory stragglers from somewhere in the north, because the swamps were suddenly populated with heavy-breasted, thickly feathered mallards that hadn't been there the day before.

> **"By late afternoon, every child of the swamp knew something was afoot..."**

It was a day that was really two if you count the night before, and you should, because that's when it really started.

And you should know this: The man and his dog had come back to the river because, after searching the state, they were convinced that it remained, as it was in the beginning, the best place in all of Wisconsin to hunt ducks.

There was wind and there was rain the day before but nothing really unusual for mid-October. But by late afternoon, every child of the swamp knew something was afoot.

It started when the wind picked up enough to bend the trees and kick the clouds across the sky. The rain, which had been sweetly warm, turned suddenly cold. And the drops thickened.

The air developed a cutting edge. Clothing already wet with sweat and day-long rain became chilled bandages for bodies beginning to rebel against dropping temperatures.

You could sense something evil in it all, and so could the birds, because there came about some movement in the sky.

And when the hunter downed the last mallard to fill his bag limit he noted the swiftness of his dog in making the retrieve. The message clearly was to hurry and get out of there.

Then came the night when it really all began.

Safe in the cabin with the heat turned up to dry wet clothing and boots, the man and the dog listened to the wind drive sheets of rain against the walls and windows. It was coming straight out of the north and the drops made zinging, pinging sounds as they ricocheted into the depth of the night.

The cabin creaked against the force of the wind and that was the music that lulled both man and dog to sleep that night.

Somewhere, sometime during the small hours it had stopped because the first thing the man heard when he awoke at 4:30 a.m. was the silence. And it persisted while the man went about doing all those things you do at the beginning of the day in duck camp.

He put the dog out first and then he heated coffee water. Then he checked his boots to see if they were dry, and they were.

When he let the dog back inside and reached down to stroke the animal's ears, he realized what had happened. It had turned cold overnight. Really cold. The animal's coat was frigid to the touch.

He stepped outside the cabin and the grass crunched underfoot. It was frozen solid. The rain puddles, too, were sheets of glassy ice. And, in the light streaming from the cabin window, he saw the spits of snow as they glistened in the yellow shaft and then disappeared.

The chill was all the way through him and he went back inside to the warmth of the cabin and steaming coffee.

He dressed that day for winter. It was the first time for long underwear and two pairs of pants and an extra shirt. It was the first time for gloves, the first time for three pairs of socks.

By the time man and dog left the cabin, the wind was blowing once again and when they had reached the hunting grounds, it was whistling a small gale right out of the northwest.

It was still midnight black when they made their way down the sharp incline off the road, but the sky was beginning to turn a shade lighter.

They broke ice right away, a strange sensation for the young dog who'd never had to do that before. And they broke ice all the way down to their shooting blind, across the beaver flowages, around the potholes.

The marsh grass was brittle with ice. And there was wind, always the wind.

It was howling and sharp as a knife blade. It bent the willows and swayed the big elms. It ripped the leaves from the birches and sent them swirling across the lightening sky.

When the man and the dog reached their blind it was 10 minutes before shooting time. Particles of ice clung to the underside of the dog. At first the man could feel the heat worked up from the walk into the swamp; the beginnings of sweat ran down the middle of his back.

But that soon changed to a growing chill that seemed to reach all the way through him. He turned away from the wind and huddled, with the dog, behind the protecting ring of grass and willows and there they waited for the hunting day to begin.

As soon as it was light enough to see and shoot, the man knew this day would be different from all the rest. The storm had brought winter, for sure, but it had also brought ducks.

The birds were moving everywhere, it seemed. At first none came within his range but he could see them around the perimeter of the lake and he could hear the shooting of other guns.

And then the two mallards came from out of nowhere and he followed the flight of one and when the shotgun bellowed the bird crumpled and fell across the water into a swatch of marsh grass.

Now the dog had to break ice once again for it ringed the edge of the little lake. And he did so, tentatively at first, and then with more confidence until he reached open water.

He disappeared into the marsh grass and then, in moments, reappeared with the mallard firmly in his grasp. It was a picture retrieve and the man glowed with pride.

The man shot a limit of ducks, greenhead mallards all, that day in the wind and the cold and the ice. The work of the dog was without fault. And the man had shot well. It was the kind of day duck hunters dream about.

But it was even more than that.

Back at the cabin that night, the ducks cleaned and a steak on the stove, with dry socks and whisky warm, the man decided that when you put it all together — the ducks, the dog work, the shooting, the weather — it was the best day of duck hunting he'd ever had.

And that's something. 🐾

Lightning Flashed
And a Rifle Spoke

The man from Milwaukee couldn't believe it.

At 5:45 a.m. on the second day of the Wisconsin deer hunting season, he sat in his truck, parked along Highway 35 near Durand, looking out into the inky blackness. It was warm. He had the window on the driver's side rolled all the way down.

Overhead, thunder rumbled and roared and lightning flashed across the sky, bathing the world with spilt seconds of brilliant light. It was as if someone, somewhere, was standing at a light switch, flicking it on and off.

At 6:00 a.m. he snuffed out a final cigarette, stepped from the truck, locked it, grabbed his gun and headed into the woods. He felt the first splatter of raindrops then: big, oozing drops, the kind that fall in summer ahead of a really severe storm.

After 20 minutes of brisk walking during which he didn't once use the flashlight because the lightning showed him the way, the man from Milwaukee was at

KNOCKED DOWN, DRAGGED OUT. With the help of a hunting partner, Jay Reed drags this buck out of the woods—as he did the spike buck described in this column.

his pre-selected deer stand. It was, he firmly believed, one of the best stands in the woods. Except, that is, for one thing. He had hunted there through opening day and had seen nothing that even looked like a deer.

He had already decided he was going to give it about two hours more that morning. Then, if nothing happened, he would move.

At 6:30 a.m., the time when legal shooting opened, it was raining

113

steadily; there was enough light to see within shooting range, but that was about all.

By 7:30 a.m. the world of the woods was gray and misty and very wet. When you stand silently alone in the woods, in a rainstorm, you hear many sounds that you don't hear when there is no rain, no wind.

The forest that morning was alive with sounds, some of it gunfire from hunters who had found action, but most of it from the falling rain, which was increasing steadily.

At 8 a.m., the hunter was soaked. His deer hunting clothing, effective for ordinary November weather, was not designed to be worn in a heavy rainstorm.

So the man from Milwaukee left his pre-selected best stand in the woods and moved out generally in the direction of where he had heard the shooting.

When he came to a ridge of high ground, he walked along it for a while until he spotted a huge tree trunk rotted out hollow at the base. He inspected it closely. It was dry inside.

"He felt the first splatter of raindrops then... big, oozing drops..."

And maybe there would be enough room for him to fit. On hands and knees he crawled inside, then hunkered down, half sitting, half kneeling. It was uncomfortable. But it was dry.

He lit a damp cigarette and smoked slowly and contemplatively, watching the rain as if he were inside a building.

It was a steady, almost torrential downpour. The man from Milwaukee wondered if he had ever hunted for deer in such conditions before. He decided he hadn't.

Was this any way for a grown man to spend his birthday? That's what it was, that second day of the deer hunting season. But there he was, squeezed like a raccoon inside a hollow tree, deep in the swamps, with lightning flashing and thunder rumbling and rain pouring down.

Now there are rare times in the lives of all men who hunt deer, when, unaccountably, they do the right thing at exactly the right time.

The man from Milwaukee did such a thing just then.

There was no way he could use his gun while cramped inside that hollow tree. But that was of no great concern because he didn't believe a deer would be moving anyway with the storm blowing the way it was.

114

In any case, he decided to leave the shelter of the hollow tree. He crawled out, stretched his legs and arms and picked up his gun.

At that moment, he heard voices, and down the ridge a quarter of a mile or so he saw flashes of red, one or two hunters moving through the woods.

And a second later, he saw two deer coming ahead of the hunters directly toward the place where he was standing.

At times like that, things happen rapidly and in thinking about them afterwards, they tend to blur in the frailty of memory.

The man from Milwaukee glanced at both deer. Neither was big. Tiny spikes jutted from the head of one. He swung on it, placed the sight on its shoulder and fired. The deer was dead in mid-stride.

And that, as they say, was that.

He field dressed the animal, laying aside the liver and heart. In his expert preparation for the hunt he had forgotten a rope.

So the man from Milwaukee removed his belt and fastened it around the head and front legs of the little buck. Then he hoisted it up a tree limb so it could hang and cool.

For an hour he sat in the rain, smoking cigarettes, thinking about this hunt and all the hunts that had gone before.

When steam stopped rolling from the buck's body cavity, the man from Milwaukee lowered the animal to the ground and began dragging it to the truck.

The hunt was over and, in moments, the rain washed away the bloody line that showed the place where the buck went down.

Paradise is Another Name For Duck Hunting

This is how it was in the beginning, I think, when they made paradise on Earth.

It started with the river, the big river that flows between the rock-ribbed hills with their eternal cheeks of limestone.

They called it Mississippi.

There were swamps along its route made of mud and marsh grass and willows and alder. And there was backwater, some of it nothing more than stagnant pools. But there were cuts called sloughs, and some of them ran deep and swift while others were sluggish and shallow.

There were little bays and potholes hidden from eye-level view by screens of cattails, and there were narrow, dry-land ridges where trees grew. They were paths to somewhere or nowhere, depending on who trod them.

They left plenty of room for the wind to blow. The open spaces were fields upon which the breezes of autumn could exercise muscles grown fat and flabby over summer.

The sky was a giant window and they left it open so that when the sweet rain fell it could soak the land and ooze its way back to water, once again giving life to everything it touched along the way.

PARADISE IS A SWAMP. The backwaters of the Mississippi River had enormous pull on Jay Reed, seen here wading with a brace of ducks.

But with all this, it was yet paradise incomplete.

So they added wild birds called ducks and made them compatible with the swamps and marshes. Some were smart and some were dull. Some could fly faster than the wind. Others were slow.

But all of them, each and every one of them, were breathtakingly beautiful. They were works of finest art. They were miracles with wings.

They were more than that.

It must have been at the heart of the plan in the beginning that these swamps, these marshes, these ducks would do more than simply decorate paradise.

Indeed, down through the years, they would test man's skills. They would measure his endurance, his stamina, his mental and physical capabilities.

They would be the white-hot coals over which he would be required to walk. They would be the bed of nails upon which he would have to sleep. They would be the fire that would scorch his soul, the flame that would sear his heart.

They would be the fulcrum upon which man could test the lever of his ability to withstand abuse. They would be the mirror in which man could see the deepest, most secret reflections of himself.

But paradise, as planned, was still incomplete.

So they added weather. A full range of it. From death-dealing storms with wicked wind and freezing temperatures to soft, summer sunshine and delicate little breezes that titillate the senses. They mixed it all in with the swamps and the marshes and the ducks.

They made some days good and some days bad. And, sometimes, there would be fog thick and wet and cold enough to hide everything from everybody and turn paradise into a mysterious otherworld.

And they did more.

They added muskrats to the swamps. They would build houses in the fall so that the men who sought the ducks would have places to sit, to rest, to eat, to otherwise gather their senses about them while in the marshes.

And they gave these men dogs to share the burden of the quest of ducks, to add class and dignity to the effort, to provide grace and skill and comfort to it all.

And they created seasons, times for the quest so that there could be days in front to dream, to wish, to anticipate it all; and days after to remember.

They made good friends with which all of this might be shared and enjoyed. They added good food and sleep-filled nights to make it even better.

When they were done with that, paradise on Earth was, at last, complete. So they put a name to it.

They called it duck hunting season.

They Can't Take the Hunt Away

They say the party's over. They say deer season ends today.

The Department of Natural Resources and the conservation laws of Wisconsin are quite emphatic about that. So is society.

They say it's time to wash the glasses and put away our funny, blaze orange hats and coats and all the rest of the toys we play with for nine days every year.

What they want us deer hunters to do, you see, is start eating and sleeping regular again. They want us to take showers every day and put on clean socks every morning.

They don't want us to wear long underwear anymore. They don't want us to overdose on greasy eggs and bacon fat and pancakes. They want us to wear clean shirts and keep regular hours. They want us to use a bathroom instead of a log. They don't want us to carry toilet paper in our hip pockets anymore.

They don't want us lugging rifles wherever we go, and they certainly don't want us playing cards every night. They want us to clean up our language. They don't want us to laugh too loud or talk too much. And no more of those awful stories, either.

They want us to come back to reality. That's the real purpose for ending deer hunting season. They want us down from the mountain and back to the mainstream. Polite society can't tolerate the jackpine savages for any more than nine days.

MAGNIFICENT MEMORIES are made in the deer woods every autumn. In the mind of the devoted hunter, the magic of deer season never ends.

But for some of us, the party is never over. Not the deer hunting party. What we've got are memories. You've got yours, I've got mine.

I know that a hundred times, or maybe a thousand during the next 12 months when the demands of family, profession and society back me into what looks like an inescapable corner, I'm going to close my eyes and slip right into deer season.

I'm going to sit down and listen to Tony Bizjak of Crivitz and Hank Neuburg of Hubertus as they talk about the olden days of deer hunting. They've shared the joys of more than 40 hunts together and they've killed a mountain of deer meat along the way.

They've seen the good times and the bad. Like most of us in the middle or better years, they think the old times were best. I don't know if either of them got a deer this year because I lost track of them after opening weekend.

What I do know is that they enjoyed the hunt whether they bagged a deer or not. And I know I want to hear them talk again about deer hunting, and I will, in memory, if no other way.

And I'm going to visit with Jim Lane of Oconto Falls at his hunting shack at Silver Cliff, even though we couldn't actually bring it off this year. I know we would have talked and laughed and rekindled memories of fine

> "There is no animal in the woods more beautiful than a wild deer..."

hunting partners now gone, but not in spirit.

And I know I'll go back, more often than anywhere else, to that knoll in the woods where my buck went down. I'll walk the ridge again where there was a good trail and I'll prowl through the thick brush at the bottom where there was another runway.

And then I'll remember how I picked the knoll as a stand. It was halfway between the two trails, a little piece of high ground that offered fairly clear shooting for about 75 or 80 yards all the way around.

And I'll remember....

There was fresh, ankle-deep snow and not enough wind to make to make any real difference. I brushed the snow and the leaves away so I had about a three-foot circle in which to move without making a sound.

God, that morning was beautiful. I can't remember when the woods were ever softer, sweeter. It wasn't cold enough to be uncomfortable. And it wasn't warm enough to be too hot.

There were squirrels to watch and birds to listen to. And when the first deer came by, it was a doe. I realized again, as I had so many times before down through the years, that there is no animal in the woods more beautiful than a wild deer.

There were more deer after that, again all does, and more squirrels and more forest sounds. I felt like an audience of one at the greatest show on earth.

And then came the buck. Like a great, gray shadow he slipped out of the heavy brush and stopped, momentarily, in a stand of trees.

This was beauty as I never remembered seeing it before. This great animal, its every sense at highest pitch, its every movement calculated, was a picture of magnificence. This was his kingdom and there was no doubt he was king.

His antlers, highly polished, gleamed even in the dull light of that gray, November day. His eyes burned bright with hellfire.

He began to move, slowly at first, and then a bit faster, with a gait somewhere between a walk and a slow trot. Over the sights of my carbine, I could see his shoulder muscles ripple and flow.

The woods were deadly silent and when I cocked the rifle, the metallic click, soft, faint, was enough to cause the buck's ears to quiver and, for the briefest part of a second, he stopped.

In years before, at times like that, I could always feel heart-thumping excitement flowing through my body. But not this time. Not this moment. I was filled, instead, with the calming knowledge that I was sole witness to a scene of wild, untamed, haunting beauty.

The buck was now clearly lined up over the sights of my rifle. The front post rested just behind, and low, at his shoulder. I guessed the range at 80 yards or less.

Three more steps and he would be clear of the trees, clear of the brush. I waited, the picture of it all burning indelibly in my mind.

And then I squeezed the trigger.

The buck humped as I've seen them do before when mortally wounded. He ran to the top of the ridge and disappeared. I knew then my hunt was over. I knew the animal would be just over the rise. I knew it would be dead.

And it was.

I'll remember all of that, and much more. Much more.

This business about deer season ending today is just a formality. They can make me hang up my rifle and they can make me put away my blaze orange coat and they can make me come back to reality. But they can't close the deer season on me. Or you, either. Not really.

Simple Pleasures of A Grouse Hunter

The two grouse died 15 minutes, a modest oak knoll and a shallow valley apart.

They died because the leaves are down now, the trees are naked and there's no curtain for the birds to hide behind when they fly.

They died because the dog flushed them into gun range and because the hunter pulled the trigger at the right time.

Beyond all that, they died because it was the way the Lord intended.

The man from Milwaukee thought a lot about that as he knelt beneath the cabin's overhang here in Couderay, Wisconsin, pulling out the guts and stripping the grouse of their skin and feathers.

> **"Tomorrow the cabin would be filled with the aromas of grouse breast and wild rice..."**

Little more than a short cast away, the murky water of the Chippewa Flowage splashed softly against the shoreline. The wind had more muscle than you would expect of it at dusk. And dead, gray sky was dropping moisture too thick to be rain and too thin to be snow. The air had an icy edge to it. When the wind curled around the corner of the cabin, it picked up handfuls of wet leaves and plastered them with soft smacks against the window glass, papering it with sheets of yellow and rust and dull crimson.

When the dressing job was finished, the man from Milwaukee took the two birds down to the water line and washed them. Then he cleaned his hands of the blood and feathers and, back in the cabin, put the grouse to soak in a salt solution overnight.

For a fleeting moment, he thought of how it would be tomorrow when the cabin would be filled with the aromas of sautéed breast of grouse and wild rice.

After that, he fed the dog and removed his boots and socks and shirt. He slipped into a pair of soft moccasins, opened a can of beer, lit a cigarette and settled back into a chair.

God, how his legs ached. He could feel the beginning of muscle cramps that surely would get him overnight, and he almost envied the road hunters, the ones who ride the fire lanes and logging roads in search of grouse.

But he couldn't do that, not anymore; not with the young and eager dog whose only reason for living is to hunt. That's why he had been walking, more or less steadily, from daylight until just before dusk.

He and his dog had flushed a lot of birds that day. So many, in fact, that he had lost count. He had had some shots, but not really good ones; not until right down at the end. That's when he killed the two birds 15 minutes apart.

The man from Milwaukee opened another beer. The dog was sleeping now, snoring softly and growling in his dreams. The cabin was warm and the smells inside it were good—hunting-camp smells that you can fully appreciate only if you were born to it.

The grouse, he figured now, were bonuses provided by The Man Upstairs. They had to be. The man from Milwaukee and his dog had hunted hard that day. They had paid their dues, and the two grouse were their reward.

He closed his eyes, then, the man from Milwaukee did, and he dozed.

Maybe this day, this cabin, this time, this experience was really what heaven is all about. The dog must be part of it, for certain. And the grouse.

But the half-rain, half-snow was too. It had made him feel good and clean. His mind had been clear. And he didn't have to reach for the strength to walk.

One man's prison is another man's paradise, just like my pain is your pleasure. Or something like that.

And tomorrow's dawn would find him on a willow point, standing in the wind overlooking a set of decoys. Maybe the mallards and whistlers would be flying. And after that, he'd fish for muskies until an hour before dusk when he tried for grouse again.

He was awakened, then, by the nuzzling of his dog, who wanted to go out one last time.

It was raining and it was cold and the wind had lost none of its muscle.

The man from Milwaukee smiled, realizing for the first time that he had not had dinner. But what the heck? No man has to eat when his soul is full.

When the dog came back, he turned off the light and the little cabin lost its pale, yellow glow. And sleep came easily.

He would not have to do it again—until tomorrow.

The Wild Duck is a Guru for Hunters

Ａnd soon the dream will come to pass…

The wild duck is a smallish bird. Feathered, of course, its feet are webbed and its eyes are sharp and it feeds on a variety of things from fish to grass to acorns.

It decorates the sky with fall flights in perfect "V" formation or scraggly lines or individual periods between sentences of clouds.

It captivates the imaginations of poets.

It thrills bird watchers.

It drives retrieving dogs crazy.

And it motivates action in otherwise sedentary men.

That, though, is what the books say. It's what the technicians tell you. It is what is written in and on the minds of men.

If you really want to know about the wild duck, you have to look to the heart. You have to look to the soul. You have to look deep into those places where love and adoration and devotion and mindless worship begin.

And it's necessary to do this now because Wisconsin's duck hunting season opens at noon Friday and perhaps as many as 100,000 people will take part in it.

MALLARDS ON HIS MIND. This celebration of the opening day of duck season was printed on September 26, 1982.

The wild duck, you see, in all of its species, in all of its varieties, is a guru, a leader, a mystic symbol to which some hunters turn time and time again for renewed strength and vigor and reason for being.

The wild duck is an aphrodisiac for the soul.

Why else would men follow it, like disciples, to those places where mud sucks their legs hip-deep? Where razor marsh grass cuts their hands and frees their blood to flow outside the skin?

Why else would they leave warm bed and board to stand in darkness in the rain or fog? Why else would they forsake the comfort of home to fight the wind and endure the sting of snow pellets snapping off their brittle cheeks?

There are no written answers. There are no scientific explanations. There's nothing rational here. Nothing solid. Nothing you can point a finger at and say this is the reason why.

It's not like that. Not duck hunting. No way.

The duck hunter, you see, the real one, is something special.

He sees fire where there is no flame. He hears music where there is no melody. He senses comfort where there is only agony.

Duck hunting is, and always has been, a parade without bands, a circus without clowns, an orchestra without musicians. It is, and has been, an exercise in which men participate without really knowing why.

And the beauty of it is that there is no need for explanation. If you can hear a symphony in the whistle of wings in a sky still black with night; if your heart can throb to the beat of it; if you can feel warmth deep inside to the sound of it, that's all that matters.

If the smell of the swamp is sweet as perfume; if the whisper of the wind holds a promise of love yet to come; if the cut of the wind stimulates and excites, then there is no need for explanations.

What the hell. Nobody hunts ducks for food anymore. You hunt, instead, for a taste. You know what it's like to roll a sip of rich, red wine across your tongue? Well, duck hunting is the same way. What you get, though, is a glass instead of a carafe, a taste instead of a bottle.

That, of course, is what they've done to duck hunting, those people who make the rules. They've squeezed it and tightened it. They've shaved off the corners until there isn't much left except the heart of it which is you and me and the wild ducks and the smells and the feelings.

But it's enough. It holds us.

We are mesmerized, you see. Hypnotized.

That's because we hear the music while everybody else is stone deaf.

That's because we can feel the beat and smell the smells and know the beauty of it. We are lucky, don't you see.

Duck hunting starts Friday.

Ruffed Grouse Die,
But Not in Vain

Nine ruffed grouse came down to the old Clam Lake Tower Road to feed one recent evening. Three of them died, which was bad for the grouse but good for the hunter who shot them. It was his limit, and limits of partridge are hard to come by here and most everywhere else grouse hunters gather these early days of fall.

Of the six that survived, two were shot at and missed. They likely will live the rest of the season for now they are nervous. Partridge are fast learners and seldom err again once they have come within gun range.

"That's our brood stock," as local residents are fond of saying.

The other four probably will come out to the road again. If they come out often enough they will die for certain because men will be hunting there. Some will have quicker guns than did the man who was too slow to even snap off a shot at them.

DINNER CONVERSATION. Jay Reed recounted for his partners the details of bagging this ruffed grouse—which surely appeared on the hunting camp dinner table that evening.

Bird No. 1 in the hunter's bag was neck-deep in fresh green clover just before it died. When the hunter rounded a bend the bird hopped out of the roadbed into some thick briar. It huddled there among brown leaves, believing it had found safety. The hunter moved closer and the partridge panicked. It flushed to the gunner's right, broke into a clearing and was cut down in a cloud of fine shot.

Bird No. 2 showed no fear at all while the hunter walked toward it. It crouched in the dirt where it had been scratching for grit. But then, as the man kept walking toward it, the bird broke into the air as if to fly farther down the road. It was an easy kill.

Bird No. 3 nearly survived to live another day. It scurried off the road into some thick brush when the hunter approached. As the footsteps became louder the bird moved even farther back in the growth. When the footsteps stopped, the bird flushed. It was a long shot but a pellet or two broke the bird's wing and brought it down. The hunter had to search a while before he found the wounded grouse. When it tried vainly to get away, another spray of fine shot killed it on the ground.

Talk to half a dozen hunters and you get half a dozen different ideas about the state of the bird population here. If a man has a bird or two in the bag and, if he has seen others, chances are he will tell you the population is up and hunting will get better as fall takes a stronger grip on this land.

If a man has seen no birds at all, his view will be that there are no partridge this year, that the foxes or coyotes or owls have gotten them all, that a man might better spend his spare time fishing.

> **"Limits of partridge are hard to come by most everywhere..."**

The truth lies somewhere between those two extremes. There are birds here, probably more than a year ago. But there are not as many as in those lush seasons several years ago when a man could walk down any fire lane and have a good chance of filling out a limit.

It is of no consequence to the three grouse that died that evening along the Clam Lake Tower Road, but they did not flush into eternity in vain.

They provided the main course next day at a shore lunch on the banks of the Chippewa Flowage. With wild rice, mushrooms, bacon and fried potatoes prepared by Milt Dieckman of Hayward, they left this old world with style and grace. The wind was sweet and the sun was warm and you had to be happy because there were three birds in the pan.

You had to be happier still that the others survived. Maybe they will still be there when you hunt the Tower Road again.

Wounded Buck Slipped
Through Enemy Lines

There is a medium-size buck that lives today, as far as I know, in the federal swamplands between the Burlington Northern railroad tracks and the Mississippi River near Durand, Wisconsin.

He's been winged, the buck has, but I think not seriously. What he has, more than likely, is a graze mark across the top of his back from a shotgun slug.

I don't know a lot about that deer first hand. I saw him for only a moment or two when he was shot at by another hunter some distance away. I know he has, as the saying goes, horns, but I never could tell the size of his rack. I don't think it's a big deer. I didn't see it that close.

What I do know about that deer is that it stands as a living, breathing symbol of all the wonderful things I know wild animals to be. Especially deer.

> **"In the fresh snow you could read the entire story of what happened..."**

I know that a buck is smarter than a roomful of journalists. He's rougher than a cob. He knows when to run and when to walk. He knows how to survive in a world that is mostly against him.

Our paths crossed in the middle of a cold, gray morning in the swamps off what is called, locally, the Pepin Road. The buck stepped into the edge of a clearing and was shot by a hunter who stood a couple of hundred yards from my stand.

The buck took about three jumps and disappeared into a stand of hardwoods.

I stood around for about half an hour after that. The hunter who had done the shooting walked back in the direction of the road.

With nothing particular in mind, I headed over to the spot where the deer had first appeared in the clearing. In the fresh snow you could read the entire story of what happened. First there was the measured stride as the deer approached the clearing. Then there was the moment of hesitation before it stepped out of the cover. And then there were the great, bounding strides that came after the shot.

But there was something else as well…a couple of drops of blood.

I followed the tracks for a hundred feet, finding blood spots all the way. The deer, obviously, had been hit. And the hunter who did the shooting wasn't aware of it.

It was about 10 a.m. when I decided to take the track to see what would happen. Hunting hadn't been all that great anyway. I had seen three deer that morning, but all out of shooting range.

So what the heck?

The trail was easy to follow in the snow. So I did it right out of the book on tracking. I moved slowly, keeping a close watch ahead. If it had been hit hard enough, it would stop in some brushy cover. There it would stiffen up, I would jump it and kill it. Right? Wrong.

I followed the track for the next 3-1/2 hours. Toward the end, there was no more blood on the snow, but I'd find small smears of it on the trees or brush where the deer passed.

The trail took me across beaver dams, around little flowages, through thickets of heavy cover. Within an hour it was obvious to me that the deer was heading for the railroad tracks, the other side of which was federal refuge where deer hunting was not allowed at the time.

Along the way, the deer worked around three other individual hunters and two groups of three men each. None had seen the deer.

Beyond that, it managed to cross the railroad tracks unseen between two other hunters who had taken stands there several hundred yards apart.

I walked up on the tracks and followed, with my eyes, the trail the deer left in the snow. The bleeding had all but stopped and the deer's strides seemed stronger, even, than they had been in the beginning.

Now I'm no different than any other hunter. I like to shoot deer. That's the name of the game. But I was glad I didn't get this one. And I was even happier nobody else did either.

If ever a buck deserved to live, this one did. He had taken all that men and guns could dish out. He outsmarted every other living thing in those woods that day, including a bunch of guys in red suits who are supposed to know it all.

I know that deer beat the hell out of me. I was wet with sweat, dead tired and two hours of walking away from my truck. The day was shot and so was I.

But the deer lived. I hope it still does.

A Song of Death for the Bear

It was a motel room like all motel rooms. There was a bed, a basin, a stool, a shower and a TV. Its decor was vintage lonely.

The man from Milwaukee was a prisoner in this one the same way he had been a prisoner in so many others so many times before.

The hunt, for the time being, was over. Two bears had died that day in the woods near Grantsburg. It was good for the hunters, bad for the bears. Outside, rain came down in windblown sheets and lightning streaked through the black sky, stabbing at trees like an orange and yellow knife. Thunder was so close it rattled the windows.

There was no place to go. Nothing to do except think, smoke and sip at a drink.

What is there, really, about the bear hunt that turns you on; that starts the juice flowing? So many detest it. Yet you love it. Why?

It's not the kill, certainly. You've shot a couple in your lifetime; drilled them neat, dead center and skinned them out. You don't need that part anymore.

Maybe it's the company of a band of rough, tough, hell-for-leather men who know how to hunt, who know how to kill better than

BEAR DOWN. Two fallen bruins raised a number of thoughts in Jay Reed on the evening after the hunt. This contemplative essay appeared September 20, 1978.

any you've known since Vietnam and the Marine Corps killer patrols.

You look at the portable tape deck sitting silently on a ledge below the window. It could be spouting golden horns and mellow strings and the throbbing beat of jungle drums that could carry you back to the place where it all began.

But it has no voice this afternoon. Its transistors are cold as a dead man's lips. Its horizontal, numbered face looks back at you, unsmiling, voiceless, devoid of warmth and comfort and care. Sometimes, even, it looks like it laughs at you.

Then there's your head and your heart and, when you peek inside, you suddenly know what the bear hunt is all about. Really. Truly.

You light another cigarette and you pour another drink and you look out into the rain and you can smile because, at last, it is all there before you.

It's the sound. It's the song. It's the music of the hunt. It's got nothing to do with men or machines or blood or death or smells of the deepest wilderness.

That's what it is. Sound.

The hounds pick up the track and then the music starts. They sing as they go, telling a story of a wild animal, of what it does and what it thinks and what it plans in a time of the greatest stress it will ever know.

> **"The hounds pick up the track and then the music starts..."**

The hounds know only of the track they must follow. They sing by instinct.

The bear, king of the wilderness, knows only that death is on its trail. It must run like the wind. It must use all of its wit and strength.

And so the music of the hounds fills the chamber that is the woods. The bear hears it. So do the hunters. It is a magic melody that prods them both.

So the man from Milwaukee knows the truth of it now. It is the song. It is the music. It catches and captivates. It enthralls. It will make him a prisoner to as many hunts as the future will provide for him.

He smiles to himself, then, in the loneliness of the room. What, after all, are the sweetest sounds? A woman's voice whispering softly in the night? Water lapping at a sand beach?

The man from Milwaukee snubbed out his cigarette. He finished his drink. He turned out the light.

Do the hounds really sing a song of death? Or is it the music of eternity that echoes through the woods when the chase is on?

It was still raining when he fell asleep.

130

Deer Season Ends,
The Woods Fall Silent

This must be the time to say goodbye. This must be the time to break camp, to put out the fire, to let the stove grow cold. Deer hunting ends today. It ends, as everyone knew it must, on a wintry note. Only the forests are really ready. Such peace and quiet as astounds men not accustomed to them have already begun to settle over the state's Northwoods.

Sedans and station wagons are loaded. Some carry the carcasses of deer on top. Others carry Christmas trees. Most have nothing more than the ill-stacked stuff, tarpaulin covered, which was brought into the northland 10 days ago.

It was ever thus on the last day of deer hunting season. Men who looked forward to that magic time now stand in dismay beside their cars knowing that it all must end.

> **"Winter has claimed this land and a deer hunter has no more part of it..."**

The taste of seared beans hangs rich and sweet in their mouths. They smell the smoke of a campfire. They feel a little gnawing deep inside because they know they must wait another year for it all to come into being once again.

That is the way it is here in Lac du Flambeau, Wisconsin, today, November 29, 1964. No car tracks cut the paper whiteness of the back roads. As far as a man can see, there is nothing except shadows of ice and snow and ridges.

Winter has claimed this land and a deer hunter has no more part of it. Chickadees have staked new claims around human habitation. Snowbirds have traveled to the shoulders of highways where traffic and plows have exposed weed seeds and specks of sand for their crops.

Walk a ridge tomorrow and there will not be a red coat in sight. For they will be gone—back to the cocktail parties and the bowling events and the little social activities which make a man's life complete. The unwashed, unshaven days of deer hunting are done.

There are those of us who love this northland and we like to think that the best is yet to come. The woods will be quiet. A deer need fear no movement. From here on until spring there will be such silence that no man not on friendly terms with himself can long endure.

If it hasn't already done so, snow will cover every evidence of man. The deer hunter's brass shell casings will be buried deep beneath the white. Stumps and brush in the cutover will be hidden. Old campsites will blend and become lost among the trees and it will seem, after a while, that no man ever came this way before.

Those days, then, those to come, will be good ones for a man to be in the woods. His mission will not be to kill, but to live.

And he will have nothing to face up to except himself.

Woodcock Drive Sane Men To Distraction

It is a well-know fact that in the outdoor community, a select group of hunters burn out early.

Their nerves go first, as a general rule. Their eyeballs get to spinning like the wheels of a slot machine. Their legs go trembly and their arms go jerky.

As the season progresses, their complexion tends to pale from blood seepage through a thousand gashes in hands and arms and necks.

They are called woodcock hunters.

I know all of the above to be true, for I have just completed a woodcock hunt here in northwestern Wisconsin, near the town of Webster.

I know it was successful because I now resemble a raw hamburger that walks, I figure I lost at least two pints of blood, and I don't know if I ever will be able to stride normally again.

My boots may never dry, and my pants look like

© ISTOCKPHOTO.COM

TIMBERDOODLES, more commonly known as woodcock, are famous for their aerobatic maneuvering through thick cover.

they've been clawed by a cougar. I do not have nearly as many shotgun shells as when the hunt began, and the barrel of my 12-gauge is still smoking hot.

What I do have, though, stowed carefully away in the back of my truck, are the gutted carcasses of three woodcock, the net result of the day-long efforts of three hunters, two dogs and a photographer.

It ain't much, considering the size of a woodcock breast. Put them all together and you wouldn't have enough to feed a midget. If you were going to serve them as an entrée, you'd need a lot of gravy to go around.

133

So, it is reasonable to ask, why bother? Why go hunting for woodcock, anyway?

The answer is locked in the hearts of those who hunt them, and there is a considerable number of people who do in Wisconsin. It has something to do with both pain and pleasure.

Perhaps more than any other game bird legally available to state hunters, the woodcock is the most challenging to someone with a gun.

They can fly, seemingly, in three directions at the same time. Unlike the flush of the ruffed grouse, their take-off is not loud. They hold close, as a general rule, climbing into the sky from a point almost always at or near the feet of the approaching hunter or dog.

The trick to successful woodcock shooting is to have a fast gun. Their initial flight is usually straight. That's the time to get them.

Then there's one other thing. When woodcock are in Wisconsin (they are migrators, you know), they hang out in places that drive a man crazy.

> **"They can fly, seemingly, in three directions at the same time..."**

They like thick, wet, swampy cover, where there are windfalls of trees higher than a giant's head, where brambles and prickly ash grow in equal profusion.

Maybe you know about prickly ash. Unless you've ever walked through a stand of the stuff, you can't really appreciate it. It's got corners of razor blades growing out of each branch and stem.

Woodcock, like grouse, tend to flush at the least-opportune time for the gunner. Most often, it happens when you are on your hands and knees, crawling under or over a windfall.

Or when you have three feet of vine wrapped around one arm. Or when you are holding your head, trying to stem the flow of tears that started when you asked yourself why you got into this mess in the first place.

I got into it because the Canada geese at Crex Meadows had not yet started their feeding flights off the refuge there. So blame the geese.

Or blame Max Harter of Grantsburg, who said we should do it because the Canadas were not flying and because I had never written a woodcock story out of that part of the state.

So with Max's American water spaniel, Finney, and my yellow Labrador, Thor, plus writer Don Bluhm and photographer Sam Kosholek of the Journal, we headed into a patch of cover near this Burnett County community.

Bluhm killed the first woodcock. And I got the second. Max hit the third one.

In between, we flushed, shot at, missed and cursed perhaps 30 to 35 other birds.

Back in town, there were people who said we had done quite well. And maybe we did. I guess it depends on how you measure such things.

But we shot up enough shells to make the ammunition manufacturers smile and editors who sign expense reports cry. And we cut corners off our lives.

But that's what woodcock hunting is all about.

A Time to Live…
A Time to Die

For every man, there is a time to live and a time to die. At best, life will be sweet and full and death, when it comes, will be swift and sure and without deep pain. But it does not always work out that way and maybe there is good reason for it.

I'd like to think that for wild birds and animals there, also, is a proper time to live and time to die. But the proposition doesn't always work."

Trouble is that humans so often these days roam the woods in the guise of hunters — pseudo sportsmen who have never learned when to stop killing. You see evidence of it all over the north these days, from Hayward to Eagle River; from Crandon to Cameron — a doe carcass with the back quarters cut away. Bits of bones from an illegal summer kill.

You see it in the duck marshes of western Wisconsin — a couple of wood ducks or a mallard rotting in the dead grass, birds that would not fit into a man's bag limit. Maybe there were mistakes. Or maybe they were sent into eternity by men who couldn't resist the opportunity to kill.

You see it in the fields of the Fox River Valley — a pheasant gone to waste because a man shot too far for a clean kill. And along the Wolf River, a dead mink, a bullet hole in its head.

You hear it in little crossroads taverns where men gather to sip beer and talk about the big kill, the easy kill, the illegal kill. You hear it, too, in big cities, for the men who can't stop killing are never definable by the size of the community where they live, by their professions or by the cut of their clothes.

And you can't set the activity apart by species.

Anywhere there is something wild living, you can bet next week's paycheck that someone, somewhere is figuring out a way to kill it without being caught.

It happens with squirrels and rabbits as well as deer and the occasional moose which has strayed into Wisconsin in recent years.

I have no argument with killing wild animals, as such. My personal bloodletting has been monumental over the years since hunting has always been the largest part of living for me. It was more than a hobby. It was the axis around which life revolved, and work was something to do only in the off season.

My argument is with indiscriminate killing—killing for the sake of seeing something die.

The man who kills within the framework and limits of hunting regulations is one thing. He tempers his killing with respect for the animals he pursues. He sees a wild thing not only as a target but as a living, breathing creature of more freedom than he, himself, will ever be. He takes that life and that freedom, if he can, only if the law permits it. And he may even do it with some regret.

This man stands with the majority of men who hunt. But the others?

Well, the sad truth of the matter is that there are people in this world who can't stand to see any bird or animal alive in the woods. They will blast an otter into eternity while hunting ducks. They will riddle a heron with birdshot if there is nothing else in the air to shoot.

They will kill simply because, while carrying a gun, they have found something with life which can be rendered dead.

They are predators, senseless slayers, more harmful than the bloodiest four-footed killer that exists. They don't even have the good sense of the wild predator. They don't eat what they kill. They just kill. They have no feeling for the woods or the forests or the animals living there.

> **"My argument is with indiscriminate killing... for the sake of seeing something die..."**

They are the ones with black-and-white values: a gun is to shoot, a bird or animal is to be shot. They are children with men's bodies, wearing men's boots. No more.

Maybe they feel good when they kill a deer they know they can never eat. Maybe it makes them stand 10 feet tall in the duck blind when they continue to kill mallards knowing they can only take one home legally.

Maybe joy seeps into their hearts when they take an otter from a world that already has too few. Maybe they feel a sense of accomplishment at blasting an eagle simple because the eagle lives.

I don't know the answer. I wish I did.

But one thing is certain: Those who kill for no reason; those who let the blood continue to flow long after it should have stopped; those who do such things...are already dead themselves, inside.

For them there is no time to live; only a time to die.

What Possible Gain
In Shooting a Dog?

Wonder what pleasure a man derives from killing a dog? Does it make him feel good? Is he filled with the throbbing joy of accomplishment? Will his future be brighter, his world more secure now that the golden voice of a beagle hound has been choked off forever?

There must be something to it because an assassin with a shotgun killed a lady friend of mine here the other night. And today the world is a little more tarnished because Sally is dead and because we live with such people as would gun down a little beagle dog.

> **"Today the world is a little more tarnished..."**

Sally had no claims on me nor I on her. We were just good friends. She belonged to Ted Eberly, of Land O' Lakes, and was running mate of another beagle named Silkie.

I met her first on a cold, windy day in January. With Eberly's father, Abe, we hunted snowshoe hares in the spruce swamps along the Michigan border. Sally liked me, I think, if for no other reason than I was willing to prowl the swamps with her.

She had naturally friendly tendencies and bore ill to no man or animal except snowshoe hares. And that is why I can't understand why anyone would want to kill her.

But someone did. A blast from a shotgun rolled her over a hill and into eternity one recent night behind the Congregational Church here. The same assassin wounded Silkie. She survived although she will now live out her life with a bobbed tail.

This winter we will run the snowshoes again through the swamps along the Michigan border. Silkie will drive them over the snow-covered logs and down the swales. And the frost will tip her black muzzle with beads of white. But it won't be quite the same as before because Sally won't be there.

Wonder what pleasure a man derives from killing a dog?

138

Ducks Lurk in Land
Of Vines and Razors

Come hunt with me. This is the Tiffany Public Hunting Grounds, more than 16 square miles of swamps and marsh, of sloughs and highland, stretched out along the Chippewa River where it joins forces with the Mississippi. Highway 35 forms the hunting grounds' general southern boundary, Highway 25 its eastern edge.

We drive out Highway 35 from Nelson. Those swamps mark the Tiffany. There are six bridges here. Just past the fifth, we'll turn onto a logging road to the right.

Park the car; load your shotgun. We'll walk the logging road; there's a running slough alongside that might hold ducks. End of the road. We go across the slough to the left; along a ridge running out into the swamp. If you are inclined to squirrel hunting, this is a good place.

© ISTOCKPHOTO.COM

Twenty minutes gone. Cross another slough. Now, a narrow cut that leads to two potholes. Quietly. Quietly. Beware the prickly ash trees; they have razors on their branches. Slowly now. Step. Halt. Wait. Step again. Wait.

JUMP SHOOTING mallards on the backwater sloughs of the Chippewa River was something Jay Reed did as a youngster...and was paid to do many years later as an outdoor writer.

A rush of wings. Seven mallards break into the open, on the elevator going up, too distant to shoot. Kneel. Keep still. They may circle. They do. But they are cupping their wings. They are going to sit in the next pothole on the far end of the meadow.

Now we must stalk. It takes half an hour to cover 40 yards. A strip of willows is between us and the ducks. We have a good chance here.

139

Move carefully. Don't cough. Don't breathe hard. Don't let your feet so stick in the mud that they make a sucking sound when you lift them.

We are in range. Quiet. You can hear the ducks feeding, hear the little splashing sounds they make? Another step. Be ready.

The birds flush—mallards everywhere. Pick out a greenhead. Shoot. It goes down. Pick another. It, too, falls.

Pick up the ducks. Go back to the strip of willows. You have two mallards. That's the limit on them for the day. Now you must try for a couple of wood ducks, or black ducks or teal.

You hear the steady "beep, beep, beep" of feeding wood ducks in a little slough 500 yards or so away.

You know where they are. It is brushy—thick with willows, prickly ash and fallen logs. Again move slowly. But it is impossible to be quiet. The willows scrape your canvas hunting coat. Vines cling to your arms.

> **"The air suddenly erupts with thrashing wings and quacking ducks..."**

You feel hot blood where a prickly ash has slashed. You see the little puddle of green water where the wood ducks are. You hear a whirr of wings. You can't get a clear shot. The ducks are gone.

You break through the final barrier of willows, stand knee-deep in water with a sinking feeling in your stomach.

You take three steps forward. The air suddenly erupts with thrashing wings and quacking ducks. A half dozen black ducks have remained, out of sight, in a little bay directly ahead. They are airborne now.

Pick out one. Fire. Down. Another. Fire. Down. The flock is out of sight. One bird is dead. The other is crippled, making for the bank. You fire once more. The duck becomes still in the little puddle.

You retrieve your ducks, stuff them into the hunting coat with the other two.

Your shotgun is empty. Turn around, now, and walk out the way you came in. The hunt is over. And you have ducks to clean. 🐕

140

Buck Meets Slug
With His Number on It

There was no snow on the ground the day the buck went down. When the eight-pointer leaped over a windfall on his way to eternity, it didn't even seem like deer hunting season.

Except for the men with red coats and back tags, it didn't look like a time to hunt deer. It was warm and you could smell the rain in the air. The ground was soft and muddy and the lakes were free of ice.

But the buck came moving through the brown marsh grass like a ghost from out of the misty past. He hesitated for a moment at the base of a tree knocked to the ground long years before by the wind. And then he bounded over it and out into an open space.

The hunter was ready for he had seen the deer while it was still in the marsh. And when the buck stopped, the silence was broken by the metallic click made by the gun's safety.

The buck leaped up and away from the man sound and smell.

The hunter got off a quick shot as the buck broke out of the willows. He saw the animal hunch its shoulders. Now he was sure the deer would be his.

Without waiting, he picked up the trail. Spots of blood were well up on the grass and trees, indicating the deer was hit high and hard.

When he came over a ridge, he saw the buck moving slowly toward a stand of brush. He aimed carefully, the weapon spoke and the buck went down.

If you measure a man by his style, his class, his depth of character, you can measure a deer the same way.

Old Buck went into eternity with style and grace. He did not go out kicking or crying or whimpering like a child. There was no hint of hate in his eyes, or regret or remorse. He had taken the best a man had to offer. He had fought against uneven odds and had almost won. He had run a good race and he knew it. So weep no tears for Old Buck. Let there be no sadness at his passing. He died with dignity and he pulled it off better than most men ever could.

There is no way of knowing how long the animal might have lived if he had not come across the marsh that day.

But however long it might have been, he will survive for years as yet uncounted in the memory of one man who remembers how it was the day the buck died.

Pain Before Pleasure
In the Duck Blind

You wonder, sometimes, why you are there, shotgun cradled like a baby in your arms. Why sit where the wind curls under your coat collar sending cold caresses across your back?

Why project yourself into a black, hostile world where darkness presses all around and even the promise of a lightening sky is a sour reward for the ache in your legs and the gnawing in your belly?

This, you tell yourself, is the way of it with duck hunters: Pain before pleasure, gloom before glory.

So you sit and you wait and you watch the decoys bobbing silently in the choppy water. What is hidden behind those unchanging expressions? Do their wooden hearts pound with anticipation? Do they know joy at the killing they make possible? Or do they weep wooden tears because they might lure to certain death living things in their own likeness?

Across the lake, the shoreline stretches dark and forbidding, a pencil line on the foolscap of sky. Shadows tell no stories, sing no songs. But they dominate now in this never-never time when it is too dark to be day and too light to be night.

In the blind, booted feet scuffle, mud squooshes, hot breath turns into little clouds of temporary fog.

SWING and then follow through. Wingshooting wild waterfowl is not easy, but Jay Reed often made it look that way.

Willows whisper. A face, half shadowed, all whiskered, shows briefly in the glow of a cigarette, then disappears. There is a smell of smoke. Canvas coats, crisp with cold, rustle like leaves long dead.

A question slowly scales the peaks in the mountains of your mind. If duck hunting is such a wondrous balm for the soul, why are the surrounding blinds empty? Why did not others forsake the warmth of a bed, the comfort of a home? Why did you and a companion, to the exclusion of all others, select the cold, dark, painful path?

You reach for the Thermos. The stopper sticks, then releases. Steam spirals out, up. Black liquid splashes into the red, plastic cup. You palm it, letting the heat sear the numbness from your hands. You burn your lips, tongue on the first sip. You feel better. More coffee. Then a cigarette. It tastes bitter, good.

The whistle of wings overhead ends the coffee break. It is shooting time. A brace of bluebills swings over the blocks. You pull on one, take a lead and squeeze. The weapon bucks into your shoulder, the bird crumples. Now the blind holds a faint smell of cordite.

Later there is more action. More feathered forms bob among the decoys.

A mallard drake, riding the wind, swings over the blind. You pull and fire once, twice. Clean miss. The mallard turns again, this time out of gun range, and makes another circle, You can almost hear him laughing.

> **"The whistle of wings overhead ends the coffee break. It is shooting time..."**

There's no need to wonder any more. You know why you are there. Let the others sleep in their warm beds. Let them grow fat and soft amid the comfort of four walls. Let them live the easy way.

You have met the wild duck in his own land. You have given much, taken a little. You absorbed the cold, accepted the wind, battled the darkness. You lost some sleep and maybe there is less of you left than before you started — because anyone who hunts for love leaves something of himself out where the willows whisper and the water sings. You tried and triumphed.

That's a rose in any man's garden.

A Grand Stand Seat
Is Deer to a Hunter's Heart

There is a place where dreams are made. Hunting dreams. Dreams that throb with excitement, that smell of gun smoke, that crack with action.

It's called "the stand," and everybody's got one. Everybody, that is, who hunts for deer.

It is the exact, specific spot where a hunter will be on opening day of deer season, there to play those cards The Great Dealer provides in the most fascinating of all Wisconsin hunting games.

It is the place where it all begins, where the hunter spends those first magic moments, where the shadows of hope become the images of reality.

A hunter selects a particular deer stand because either his instinct, his experience or his ability to "read sign" tell him that a deer is likely to pass within shooting distance of that spot.

JAY'S STAND. A buck like this would raise the pulse of any deer hunter watching from a stand on opening morning. This ode to deer stands appeared on November 12, 1980.

Some hunters use the same stand for years. There are places in the state known as "Einer's Stand" or "Frank's Stump" or "Randy's Rock" simply because the same guy hunted from that spot for a lifetime.

Hunters develop something like squatter's rights after a while, and you'd no more take over one of those stands than you would another man's house.

A few hunters do it the easy way. They wander into the woods an hour before shooting time and stop at some particular spot for no particular reason. This becomes their stand.

They might luck out and get a deer, but mostly they won't, and, beyond that, they will have missed some of the best parts of the hunt.

I point out all this now because in less than two weeks, Wisconsin's deer hunting season will open. And I can report to you that there already has

144

taken place a fairly substantial pilgrimage to the deer woods of the state.

The reason is that while many hunters have a sort of tenure agreement on deer stands, and others really don't give a rip one way or the other, the majority of serious deer hunters go into the woods a week or two ahead of time to check things out.

They take a peek at paradise, in other words. They sip from the cup. They look for that place where dreams are made.

I know I did. And I found it, too, north and west of the little lumber town of Seeley, Wisconsin. The country here rolls violently. There are drops deep enough so you'd need a parachute if you were going to jump. But the ridges have oaks and where you've got oaks you've got acorns, and where you've got acorns you almost always have deer.

I found their trails and the rubs the bucks made to get the velvet off their racks. I found the places where they pawed through the carpet of leaves to get at the acorns.

And I found where a timber cut had been made; where the new popple shoots are head high; where the deer go to sleep when daylight comes.

> ## "I found my stand, my place where dreams are made..."

It was on a ridge top near the timber cut where I found my stand, my place where dreams are made. There is a stump to sit where I can watch in three directions. If I get a shot, it won't be more than 75 or 100 yards. It is sheltered from the wind.

I sat on that stump for a while and dreamed the dreams of how it is going to be. I saw the shadows of the big bucks and the images of the slender, bright-eyed does.

I don't know how opening day is going to be for me. Mostly it never turns out exactly the way you think it will. But right now, I really don't care. I'm thinking positive.

My little brush gun, the .30-30 lever action carbine is ready. At 100 yards it shoots a tight group an inch low and to the left and that's plenty good enough for me.

My gear is ready and I have a Hunter's Choice permit No. 010950 for Management Unit 13, so I really won't have to look for antlers if I don't want to.

And the stand is ready. Right now it's a place where dreams are made. Maybe memories will be made there, too.

This Cagey Bird
Leaves 'Em Grousing

It has been said that nothing in the world can make a fool of a man quicker than a belly full of whisky and an armful of woman. Given the Reed track record, I would endorse that, except for one thing:

You've gotta put grouse in there somewhere. Grouse as in ruffed. Grouse as in partridge. Grouse as in clown-maker.

I have hunted grouse all my life, which means a long time. There have been the easy shots, the ground swats. Hell, I admit it, which is more than most people do.

There have been the explosively quick snap shots, the flush, the swing, the squeeze, the kill.

And there have been those graceful shots, the ones where the bird bombs into the air and hangs suspended for a split second, magnificently silhouetted against the gray fall sky.

You bet. All of those. But, mostly, this innocent-appearing bird, this fluff of feathers, this creation of speed, grace and style, has faked me out of my boots, tied me in knots and left me for dead while it flew off, laughing, to some other place of refuge.

I'm not kidding. Grouse do that to me. And I'd bet a month's pay they've done it to you, too, if you've spent any time at all hunting for them.

That's why the thought persists that these little brown birds are really instruments of the devil. They are here to humble us, to bring us down a notch or two when we start to thinking we are pretty hot stuff.

They are like country boys at the county fair. They look dumb. And they act dumb. But they manage to beat the guy in the silk vest who runs the shell game. And they win free tickets to the hoochie-koochie show.

I got to thinking about all that after a recent grouse hunt near Clam Lake, Wisconsin. Journal photographer Sherm Gessert and my old friend, Milt Dieckman of Hayward, were part of it. That made all of us witnesses.

Three grown men, right? Arguably of sound mind. And possessed of reasonable hunting skill. We hunted grouse for half a day and we killed two. When you fill in the blank spaces in between is when you get to the part about being outfoxed, outsmarted and out-maneuvered.

In one way or another, we saw, heard, flushed, shot at, walked after, ran after and otherwise pursued about two dozen grouse. And, as noted, we killed two. That's two for 24. That kind of average wouldn't keep you in the neighborhood softball league. As percentages go, it would be labeled insignificant.

If you did two things right out of 24 on the job, you'd get canned, right?

And one of those birds performed magic on us. It did the old disappearing act. It fell, dead, almost literally at our feet. But when we went over to pick it up, it was gone. Like all gone. Not there. Vanished. To this very day, I have no idea what happened to that grouse.

Unfortunately, we had no dog. Thor was at home because this started out to be a fishing trip and my yellow Lab, truthfully, is a pain in the butt when it comes to angling. A great hunter, but no fisherman.

We flushed six birds out of one small patch of cover. One at a time. Two at a time. Three guns. Six birds. No shots. Maybe now you get the idea. Grouse are like that.

The good thing about it all was that what we found that day tended to confirm the stories that Wisconsin's ruffed grouse population is coming back.

"This fluff of feathers has faked me out of my boots..."

Last year, Dieckman and I hunted some of this same cover and we never saw a bird. This year it has been different.

Nearly every serious grouse hunter with whom I've talked says the same thing. In this year of 1984, the birds are back. Hunting has been significantly better in virtually every part of the state.

In fact, grouse hunting, generally, has been better around Wisconsin than most anyone was willing to hope for back in September.

Given that as a truth, it is predictable that this would be one of those years when I did not hunt for them very much. I opted mostly for ducks. The truth is that the grouse hunt here was only the second for me this year.

Don Bluhm of Whitefish Bay and I had spent a day grouse hunting in Buffalo County in mid-October.

It was one of those hot, sunny, misplaced summer days when the ducks were not flying, so we turned to grouse. It didn't work.

We found a rattlesnake sunning itself at the base of a turned-over white pine and that was about it.

But, in the end, there were these two grouse that died in the sprawling wilderness country here, and they found their way back to Milwaukee.

147

And that is how it came to pass that Nancy and Sherm Gessert and Chris and Jay Reed dined, one November night, on breast of grouse and fillet of mallard duck.

Shadows of candlelight danced in the wine and there was wild rice and soft music and the memory of the birds that drove us crazy and lived in the process.

The two that came back, you can be sure, did not die in vain.

Ringneck Pheasant is One Bad Bird

Show me a long-tailed razor-spurred ringneck pheasant that never has seen the inside of a pen and I'll show you one of the world's original bad guys.

Just because he's dressed to kill only hides the mean streak in him. If he were human and rode into town you'd have to hide the women and children and pour the whisky into the gulch. He'd rob the bank and take over the saloon. He'd buffalo the men and sweet-talk the schoolmarm into riding off with him.

If he traveled on a Mississippi riverboat, he'd wear a velvet vest and a black string tie and he'd have a waxed mustache. He'd turn a jack into a king quicker than the eye could see. He'd send the country boys home with empty pockets and tears in their eyes. He'd take everything but the hayseeds behind their ears.

If that ringneck were human, he'd be the town tough. He'd be wide at the shoulders and narrow at the

A COCKY CHARACTER is the wild ring-necked pheasant. He'll run, fight and fly to survive.

hips and he'd have eyes so cold they'd freeze you solid with one glance. He'd have every woman babbling after him and he'd have every man crossing the street to stay out of his way.

You think that overstates the case? I don't. Every year I hunt for ringnecks and every year something happens that reaffirms my belief that these are birds of the devil, put on Earth only to make hunters humble.

Here's my case for this year...

Journal photographer Sherm Gessert and I were hunting with Pete

Macaluso of Milwaukee, Wayne Rajchel of Hartland, and Denny Kinatender of Slinger.

We had Rajchel's German shorthair pointer, Lady, and Gessert's English setter, Beast. And we had my yellow Lab, Thor.

We were hunting north of Berlin on land familiar to everybody except Gessert and me. There were pheasants, too. Rajchel had seen them. So had Macaluso and Kinatender. The thing is, they were not the pen-reared stock available on public hunting grounds.

These birds were what state game managers call natives. They were survivors, and kin of survivors—of long hunting seasons and even longer winters. They had lived while most everything else had either died or migrated south. They were tough and smart.

You have to understand that we had hunted hard. Because pointers and flushing dogs do not normally work that well together, I tried to stay somewhat distant from Rajchel and Gessert and their pointers. But we did

> **"These are birds of the devil, put on Earth to make hunters humble..."**

hunt as a group, more or less, covering a variety of terrain from grassy fields to swamps to fence rows.

After three hours of tough, hard, persistent hunting, our party had put not one bird in the air. All the dogs worked well and hard. And we had combed cover both tight and thin.

And then there was this field of standing corn. If the birds were nowhere else they had to be there, right? Now standing corn is tough work for pointing dogs. It's better for flushing dogs.

So Thor and I went down the middle of the field with the others flanking on either side. But nothing. Absolutely nothing.

We met at the end of the field in a little clearing that was ringed with heavy grass at the edges and some stunted tree growth.

We were tired. We were disappointed. We were baffled. We had to regroup. We had to figure out new tactics. So we gathered in the clearing in a sort of informal semi-circle to smoke cigarettes and talk it over.

The two pointing dogs had already cast through the clearing. I confess I wasn't really paying attention to what my dog was doing, although I know that the first rule in the Book of Hunting is that you should always watch your dog. Especially if it's a flushing dog.

We were standing there, all of us. And we were off guard. Really off guard.

That's when Thor burrowed into a knot of tight, heavy grass and sent this long-tailed, razor-spurred ringneck rooster cackling into the sky with two hens following.

Not one of us was able to get a gun up in time to shoot while the rooster was in range. And that was that.

Five grown men stood there looking sheepishly at each other. And one yellow Labrador stood there boiling mad because nobody had finished what he had started.

That ringneck had picked us clean. It had faked us right out of our hunting boots. And that's why I'll tell you again that ringneck roosters are bad guys.

Modesty does not permit me to tell you how proud I was that my dog had put that rooster in the air after the pointing dogs had already gone through.

Ego does not permit me to tell you how embarrassed I was to be caught scratching my butt while my dog was doing what he was born to do.

But there were other red faces, too. In fact, together we looked like the finest sunset you've ever seen.

An Old Friend Has Returned

Allow me, please to introduce myself.

I'm the Wisconsin duck hunting season. That's a name, not a paragraph, by the way.

I arrived here at noon Thursday to the joy of many and the consternation of a few. But isn't that always the way?

In any case, though, some of you know me and some of you don't. So let me tell you something of myself because it's important.

I'm both good and bad, you know. Wise and dumb, cold and hot, wet and dry, kind and evil, sweet and sour, soft and hard.

I am the carrier of such joy, such inner pleasure, such supreme well being as to turn pale other recreational endeavors. Unlike my close kin, the Wisconsin deer hunting season in which most everyone takes part, I am for a select few.

I am also honest, which is why I must tell you right here up front that I am a killer. That's right. Not only of ducks but of people, hunters.

I have frozen hunters to death right here in good old Wisconsin. I have tipped them out of their boats and drowned them. I have caused them to have fatal heart attacks. I have gotten them hopelessly lost in the swamps where the muck and mud finally swallowed them and reduced them to turtle bait.

But that is the dark side. We should not dwell on it for it is the exception rather than rule.

I am the stuff, you see, of which nervous stomachs are made. But I am also that which sends the soul soaring toward those highest places it can reach.

Some of you have waited for me an entire year. You have thought of little else over the months of winter, spring and summer.

First you counted months and then weeks and then days. Finally, you counted hours and minutes until I arrived. You planned for me. You talked about me. You went to your boss for time off so you could embrace me.

You know me, those of you who have gone down the road before. I'm the dream you have cherished, the hope you have clung to, the time you thought would never come.

You know me for certain, every one of you who holds the sound of beating wings in the darkness of dawn as music eternal. I'm your Lorelei and you've heard my song and you've risked the rocks to come to me.

152

I am the muskrat house upon which you sit to catch your breath or eat a sandwich. I am the little cut of water too deep for you to wade. I am the beaver dam that serves as a bridge to that place that looks better than where you are right now.

I am the decoys you so carefully set out according to the wind and the points of grass and the strips of trees and the bend of the bays. I am the mud that sucks your legs up to mid-thigh and holds you like a vice until your face turns purple in the effort to take one more step.

I am the wind you hoped would come and the rain you hoped would fall. I am the formation of ducks in the sky that tells you "V" is for very and valiant and velvet, as in the feel of the feathers of that most beautiful bird you have just killed.

And I am the dog that does your dirty work, who picks up for you after you spray the sky with shot and the luckless duck falls to some hidden place that you could never find or reach yourself.

> **"You hold the sound of beating wings in the darkness as music eternal..."**

I am the sweet smell of gun oil and swamp water, the perfume that drives you wild with a lust that has nothing to do with sex. And I am the warm red blood that stains the brown and brittle marsh grass, marking one more place where one more bird has gone down.

I am yesterday and today and tomorrow. I'm a memory of other times. And I'm the laughter of a friend who shares with you those quiet moments in camp when the day is done.

If, indeed, I am but a dream, then I have come true for you this day. I have fed your soul with that which is good and pure and you should count yourself among the lucky, the endowed.

And if I am the dream come true, then, this very night, I am also the sweet soft sleep that cleanses you of weariness and prepares you for another walk through those places where angels dwell.

Have a good hunt.

Hunting Ripples Fishing's Water

Hello, Doc?

You see, I've got this problem.

No, it's not physical. I mean I don't hurt or anything. There's no pain. What it is, really, is mental. It's like I've lost a couple bricks somewhere along the line.

You know this is fishing time. Sure it's hot and sure it's slow but what the heck? Hunting seasons are still quite a way off yet.

The thing is, my head tells me to think fishing but my heart won't let me. Neither will circumstance.

Right now I'm lining up a duck hunting trip into Canada for this fall. Me and Ken Coyle and Charley Morgan are working like crazy on it.

It's tough to think of fishing when you've got this vision of greenheads bombing in over a grain field in Saskatchewan.

At the same time, I'm laying some final plans for the opening of next November's deer hunt. I'm setting up a place for me and Gregg Kales and Joe Shoquist to hang our hats.

Now how are you going to think about fishing when you have those big, Bayfield County bucks running through your mind?

Then there's the matter of a pheasant hunt in Iowa or Kansas. I have to work on that, too, and fish just can't compare.

FISHING IS FUN but nothing can beat hunting. That's the way it was for Jay Reed, despite this stringer full of fish taken from the Chippewa River.

Heck, every time I look at my dog I think about duck hunting or grouse, or pheasants. I pull on my hip boots to go trout fishing and I find myself dreaming about the swamps.

Every meeting I've attended recently had to do with hunting. Most everybody who calls has a question or comment about hunting.

In the meantime, spiders spin webs on my fishing rods. My boss hounds me for fishing stories, but my typewriter only forms words about hunting.

It's a crazy time of year, Doc. I'm telling you. The other night it was so hot I thought I was back in the jungle, but when I went to sleep I dreamed I was in a duck blind in the middle of a snowstorm. When I woke up I was just about frozen.

I got a postcard from my buddy, Don Bluhm, who was in California on assignment for The Journal. He said the pelicans were starting to look like mallards.

I know what he was talking about. The other day a robin flushed out of the bird bath. My heart skipped a beat and for a minute there I thought it was a teal.

I thought I had a sure cure for all this, Doc. I made plans to go fishing this week with the Spooner Musky Club. If anything can rekindle the old fishing spirit, that will, right?

We are going to launch a full-scale attack on the Chippewa Flowage with bucktails and plugs and suckers. We are going to do the dawn-to-dusk routine with a shore lunch in the middle.

> **"My head tells me to think fishing but my heart won't let me..."**

It's going to be fish, fish, fish and I'm going to get off this hunting kick. That's how it's going to be.

Well, not exactly. I've already figured out how to slip in some time to scout for grouse. And I want to check some of the back bays off the flowage to see what kind of local duck hatch there has been.

I figure, too, that it won't hurt to take a short walk through some of the deer hunting country up there. Nothing major, you understand, because it's awfully early for that. But I just want to get a sort of feel for the land.

So, you see what I mean, Doc. This ain't serious like a heart attack or something, but it's a problem. What can I do about it?

What's that, Doc? How do I think hunting will be this fall?

Geez, I don't know. It depends. Now, what about my problem?

I see. Take two aspirin and call you when I know something about hunting.

Gotcha, Doc. You're all heart. Goodbye.

See? Even a quack reminds me of duck hunting.

A Day of Anguish in the Northwoods

Four hunters were killed by gunshots during November's deer hunting season. This is the story of one…

It's Thanksgiving Day, 1977. There's a heavy overcast and it is cold and gray in Sawyer County. It's threatening to snow.

Your name is Milton Dieckman. You are a Wisconsin conservation warden. You are on patrol. It has already been a hectic deer season.

Lost hunters. More than the normal number. You have been moving about your county, coordinating, directing, helping in whatever way you can.

The weather hasn't helped. It went from bitter cold to warm to rain to snow and back to cold again. You know the woods. You know they can kill. And so you worry.

But it's Thanksgiving Day, and the hunt is more than half over, and if it stays quiet this day, you'll join your family and other relatives for a holiday dinner, and maybe, a good night's sleep. Something you haven't had since the hunt began.

So you stop at the ranger station in Hayward. The time is about 1:00 p.m. You are just inside the door when the phone rings.

It's the sheriff's department. There has been a report of a fatality about 25 miles from town. No other information. Just a report. A death.

© ISTOCKPHOTO.COM

HUNTING BLIND. Deadly trouble can happen in an instant with firearms, whose reach often exceed our ability to clearly see a target— or what is beyond. Hunter's safety rules aren't only for beginners.

The sheriff's office has dispatched a deputy. You hurry to your squad car. You call DNR district headquarters at Spooner by radio. You ask for help.

Bill Hoyt, DNR safety specialist for the Northwest District, has been sent to the scene.

A township road. That's the place. There will be a car and a hunter waiting. You find the spot. You stop.

A deputy sheriff is there. And a hunter is waiting to take you to the scene.

You get as much general information from him as you can. Then you tell the deputy to stay with the squad to keep in radio contact.

The hunter guides you into the woods. You don't talk. It's about a quarter of a mile through the hardwoods to the place where the shooting took place.

You walk in silence, thinking.

You approach the area and you can see a small fire. A deputy sheriff is there. And another member of the hunting party.

The shooter is there, too.

They stand in silence around the fire trying to keep warm. Introductions are made. Credentials are shown.

You look at the victim. His body is crumpled in the snow. Nothing has been touched.

You attempt, then, to piece the story together.

The shooter is in his middle years. The victim is an old man, a veteran of many hunts.

> **"You look at the victim...his body is crumpled in the snow..."**

There are no tears, no overt emotion. But there is deep anguish, deep sorrow, shattered spirit, a collapse of all that once was good and clean and bright and exciting.

How did it happen?

Both the shooter and the victim had been standers on what was to be a routine drive through some hardwoods. There have been a thousand hunts on a thousand different days run off exactly the same way.

The man who was to become a victim was put on his stand. The middle-aged man was put on his. Others took stands. And others participated in the drive.

The middle-aged man watched the area for which he was responsible. He could see no signs of life, no other person within his range of vision.

About 10 minutes into the drive, he saw two deer moving through the hardwoods. When the animals stopped on a logging road he leaned against a tree and took aim at one. He could see it clearly through his scope.

He fired once. And the deer ran.

The animal at which he had shot showed no sign of being hit.

It has been the rule of the hunt since time began that you stay on your stand until you see the drivers approaching. And that's what the shooter did.

157

In about 20 minutes from the time he fired the shot, the first of the drivers came into view. The shooter walked over to where the deer had stood when he fired.

Nothing. No spots of blood. No tufts of hair. Just the tracks of two deer.

He walked in little circles looking, seeking. But there was no sign of a wounded deer.

And then he saw it.

A body in the snow looks like nothing more than a lot of dull red in the distance. But he knew it was a man.

My God. He's had a heart attack. He's down.

He rushes to the spot. He sees the wound. Then he knows.

That is how it was, you see, that death came to the hardwoods on Thanksgiving Day.

You walk with the shooter to the place where he had stood. You pace off the distance to where the victim is down.

It is 225 yards.

You pace off the distance to where the deer were when the hunter shot at them.

It is 160 yards.

There is little brush in the stand of hardwoods. It is open country, except for the trees. You can see farther than you can shoot, as the saying goes.

But the shooter did not see the victim. He saw nothing but trees and the deer and the expanse of open area.

The victim was wearing dark red, the traditional garb of the old-time hunter. The shooter was wearing blaze orange.

So you run off some sight tests on the spot. Standing at the point where the shooter stood, you find you can't see another hunter in dark red at the 225 yard distance. The dark red blends perfectly with the shadows of the trees.

Safety specialist Hoyt and Earl Gingles, staff specialist for law enforcement at the Spooner DNR headquarters, ran tests the next day at the spot of the fatality.

Had the victim been wearing blaze orange, he might have been seen. The dark red, however, had the effect of making the wearer disappear.

The coroner has arrived. He hears the story of the shooter. He speaks with others in the hunting party. He discusses the results of the DNR investigation.

He will rule later that the shooting was accidental, that the shooter was in no way at fault.

With the shooter and the coroner you leave the scene. You walk slowly back to the squad car, where you radio for a mortician and crew.

You stand and you wait. You have confiscated, temporarily, the shooter's rifle.

You have all the details, all the facts.

The mortician arrives. Somebody drives the shooter back home.

Then you walk back to the scene of the shooting. You help load the victim onto a stretcher. You help carry him out of the woods, back to the waiting cars.

And then, suddenly, you are alone. It's late, approaching 5:00 p.m. The woods are nearly dark. The sky sags low over the line of trees.

Thanksgiving dinner will have to wait because you are a state conservation warden and you have just assisted in an investigation of the first fatal deer hunting accident in Sawyer County in about a dozen years.

You drive away, then, thinking about how it was that death came to a patch of hardwoods on this cold, gray Thanksgiving Day.

159

Gunning Down an Accusation

Sometimes, as the saying goes, you have to fight fire with fire, right?

This, then, is the way it was on a warm, sun-kissed day in the grouse woods near Danbury, Wisconsin, where men hunt for bears in September, partridge in October, deer in November and bobcats and coyotes when the snow lies thick across the land.

Max Harter of Grantsburg and I were driving down this logging road that was barely more than a pair of ruts slicing though some of the thickest country you've ever seen.

At one point, the trail curled out to the left and made a gentle, curving swing to the right. Down beyond the curve, we saw this grouse on the road, standing a couple of feet into the opening.

Harter, who was driving, stopped the truck.

"Get that bird," he said.

I got out of the truck, took my shotgun from its case and put in two rounds of No. 7-1/2 lead.

The idea was I'd walk within shooting distance of the grouse and either kill it on the ground or shoot it if it flushed.

Now, Lord let the truth be known, I have ground-swatted grouse in my lifetime. Once I told Journal writer Bill Stokes, a purist if there ever was one, that I was of drinking and voting age before I knew grouse could fly. And, in truth, I would have blasted this one on the ground if I could.

PRETTY POSE. This ruffed grouse made an inviting target for a photographer. Would Jay Reed ever shoot one out of a tree? Read on and find out...

In any case, I rounded the bend and there was no bird to be seen. Because it had not crossed the road, I reasoned it had gone back into the brush. You don't have to be smart to figure out things like that.

So I walked about 50 feet into the brush, flushed the bird, shot and killed it in full flight.

In the meantime, Harter had driven the truck down the road and, as I was coming out, he asked:

"Did you get it?"

"Of course," I answered. "That's what you told me to do, isn't it?"

Inspecting the bird, Harter noted there was considerable blood up toward its head.

"Shot it out of a tree, it looks like," was his reaction.

Right then I knew the line had been drawn. Fire with fire, right?

"No, Max," I said, keeping my voice calm. "I didn't shoot it out of a tree. I didn't ground swat it.

"What happened was that I was walking into the brush and fell into this deep, vine-covered swale. I landed on my back under a log. There was barbed wire wrapped around both my arms and blood was burning into my eyes from savage cuts on my forehead.

> **"Shot it out of a tree, it looks like..."**

"But at that moment, the grouse flushed. And so, using all of the wisdom and experience of a lifetime, I whipped a hand mirror out of my pocket, put my gun over my nearly broken shoulder, drew a reflected bead on the grouse that was flying away at rocket speed and killed it with one well-placed shot.

"That, darn it, is what happened."

Max dropped the bird into our game bag. He started the truck and we drove on. He didn't bring the subject up again.

CHAPTER 3

Fish Tales

INTRODUCTION

Jay Reed began his angling life as a subsistence fisherman, using trotlines, seines and any other efficient means to harvest a living from the Mississippi River. It was tough, dirty, smelly work.

In comparison, the fishing he enjoyed as an outdoor writer was a picnic...brook trout on a cool western stream...voracious muskies from the pine-fringed lakes of northern Wisconsin... walleyes in abundance at a remote camp in Canada.

Further south, he enjoyed even more varieties of fishing with opportunity beyond compare....bucket-mouthed bass in Kentucky, tarpon off the coast of Florida, and all types of finfish and billfish to be had with guides who know the waters of the Caribbean and South America.

Jay enjoyed the finest fishing in the world, but to him, it never got any better than this:

A lazy day on the bank of the Mississippi with a cane pole, a big gob of worms, and a bobber. Prop the pole on a forked stick, lean back against a tree, and wait for a golden-bellied bullhead to bite.

You can't take the river out of a river rat.

On the First Cast
You Snag a Dream

Hey, you know me, I'm big in this state. My name is fishing. I'm rods and reels and cobweb lines. And angleworms. I'm tears and laughter and pain and pleasure. I'm water. I'm ice. And I'm little islands where the wind goes to hide once the storm is over.

If you are like most people, we met when you were a kid. Your father introduced us. Or maybe your uncle. Or your granddad.

But we met on a sun-kissed summer day beside a pond where lily pads floated like green pancakes on the water. You tried me then for the very first time. And when the bobber disappeared and you lifted your pole and hoisted that little sunfish out of the water, you shrieked with joy and did a little dance in the grass.

At that instant you were as happy as you would ever be again in your life, for it was all clean and exciting and trouble-free and triumphant. You were a child giant and there would never again be a moment quite like it.

That's why I knew I had you hooked for life. That memory would stay in your heart forever, and I knew you would spend all of your remaining years trying to duplicate it or surpass it. I also knew you would grow very old before realizing that you never could, never would.

But my name is fishing...

I am one of Wisconsin's single most valuable assets. Measure my worth in the millions if you are dealing with dollars. Count it incalculable if you are measuring with the heart.

There are people who plan their lives around me. Babies have been conceived so as not to interfere with one of my opening days. Weddings have been so planned, too, and christenings and house closings and conventions and job interviews and meetings of people in high places.

So powerful is my hold on many that national holidays have been considered before establishing those times and dates when I would come upon the land.

In the beginning, I was a gift of the Creator, but through the centuries, the decades, you have done me wrong. You thought I was endless so you killed me indiscriminately.

Of all the mistakes you made against me, though, the worst was your inclination to dispose in my water those things you no longer needed. You soured that which was once clean and pure. And you are still doing it.

But to this day, this very moment, I survive, because my name is fishing.

Look for me first inside your heart, because that is where I live.

I will be the yearning, the tightening, the eagerness that develops when there is that first warm turn of the wind in spring.

You'll recognize me, for I'll be the dream in your soul, the warmth of the sun, the memory of a cottage on a lake. I'll be a day of sunshine and a day of cold, an ice storm and a dozen inches of wet snow. I'll be the earth turned soft and sweet.

I'll be a dock that needs painting, a lawn that needs raking, flowers that need planting. I'll be a trip to the sporting goods store. I'll be things you want but can't afford. I'll be money spent.

You will know me by the plans you make for Opening Day. I'll be those sleepless hours of night, those workless hours of day when your mind takes flight

"When the bobber disappeared, you hoisted that little sunfish, and shrieked with joy..."

and lifts your body to a boat on a lake or a river where, certainly this year, you will catch a fish bigger and better and more beautiful than any that man has ever caught before.

I will be the vacant space on the wall where you will put the mount.

For I am your dream, you see; your hope, your wish. I am a reflection of yourself.

So listen for me.

You'll hear me in the rush of water curling beneath the ice. My sounds will be the soft splash of melting snow, the grinding crunch of shifting ice floes, the beat of migrating wings.

You'll see me in streets wet with slush. I'll be dead leaves awash in the rain. My song will throb in the throat of a bird, sob in the sigh of a breeze, echo in the emptiness of the night.

You'll know me by all of this, and more, because we met a long time ago, and you got hooked on me then. And I've still got you. Solid.

My name, you know, is fishing.

The Mother Flowage Is Feeling Change

The day is right and so is the time, so I don't think it unreasonable to ask this favor of you and you and you.

Come fish with me today. Please. Ride my boat and share my lunch and sip my beer. There are things I want to show you here on the Chippewa Flowage and there are questions I want to ask.

There are things I need to know and you have the answers. There are thoughts I want to bounce off of you. There are ideas I want to share.

It's important because, increasingly, it comes to me that time is running out.

This is my boat, right here. I'll get in and run the outboard. You shove us off, OK?

Yes. That's right. This is my favorite lake. I call it the Mother Flowage because she has given up so much to me. She's taken care of me like a mother would. And you'd better believe she's whacked me on the knuckles a lot more than once. She's never been known to spare the rod. But I've mostly felt her love, and that's what makes me love her.

Dead ahead, there, is Popple Island. It's one of the most famous landmarks on the flowage. You'd have trouble counting the number of muskies that have been caught there.

And that's Eagle's Nest and Hell's

FISHING THE FLOWAGE. Jay Reed tends the boat while a companion fights a fish on the Chippewa Flowage. This column appeared in the *Milwaukee Journal* **on May 18, 1980.**

Half Acre. I once caught a big musky there. Down that way is the Hay Creek Narrows. Over the other way is Moss Creek and the mouth of the Chief River. Right beside it is Clutcher's Bar. That's dangerous musky water, too.

Across those trees is Pete's Bar, where, they say, the biggest musky ever caught in Wisconsin was taken. And back the other way is Flemming's Bar. The red cabin you see on the point belongs to Nate DeLong. I spent a night there once a hundred years ago.

The resort you see up the shoreline is called Herman's Landing and the Golden Fawn is down that narrow cut on a little bay. The blacktop road is Double C.

And this is just one little corner of the flowage. There's a lot more of it out there that I know very little about. There's some, in fact, that I haven't even seen. But then there are not many people who can say they've seen it all. And there are fewer still who can say they know it all.

My plan for today is to work around the narrows at Hay Creek for a while. Then we'll spend some time at Eagle's Nest and after that we'll drift the shoreline around the bend from Moss Creek.

About an hour before dark, we'll slip over to the mouth of the Chief and finish off the day there.

What kind of lure should you use? Well, if you've got some special method or technique for fishing walleyes then give it a try. It can't hurt.

I'm going to use two lines, one with a jig and a minnow and the other with a live minnow on a common hook weighted with split shot about a foot or so up the line.

I'll cast 'em both out, let 'em settle and then pick up one and retrieve it slow. Then I'll cast it out and pick up the other one. Sort of alternate, you see.

No. I've never been able to figure out walleyes. Have you? The books tell you lots of things. But not everything.

Like for two days we caught 'em pretty good. It was hot and cloudy. But then the weather turned cold and clear. The sun like to burn you blind. And the wind was so strong the anchor couldn't hold.

The walleyes turned off, just like that. I mean you couldn't buy a fish. It affected the big-name guys the same as us punks.

We at least have a chance today with the wind down and the clouds.

When you do get a fish working your minnow, you'll find those walleyes are feeding so slow as to make you sick to your stomach with the waiting.

The thing you've got to remember is not to take 'em too soon. If you forget that, you'll miss most everything.

Let's pop a top now, and talk to pass the time. Why thank you, friend, and here's to you and to the hunt.

What's the size limit on walleyes? There isn't any. Keep whatever you want so long as it's not more than five. The state took the size limit off last year, and they say a lot of wonderful things are going to happen because of it. We'll have to wait and see, but I have my doubts.

They say we are going to have a real quality fishing experience out here on the flowage now. I guess that wasn't quality when we were taking walleyes no smaller than 13 inches.

I've never been able to figure how a mess of 10- or 11-inch walleyes could represent quality. But then I never said I was smart.

One thing it did do, though. It allowed a lot more people to catch limits of walleyes. Most everything I've seen in the fish house back at camp would have been too small to keep when the size limit was on.

Yes, sir. The season does open on the first Saturday of May now. Sure it's early. A lot of folks say it's too early. It used to open on the second Saturday of May, but that conflicted with Mother's Day.

The DNR can take a lot of pounding, but it couldn't take the heat applied by wives and mothers, so they changed it. Now we can catch walleyes that haven't even spawned yet. That happens some years.

The fish managers say that makes no difference; that it does not matter when you catch the fish. That's a tough one to figure out, too, especially if you've got a simple mind like mine.

What's that, you ask? Why, sure. They'll be looking at year-round fishing here on this flowage someday. They close the season in November now, but there's some talk about setting up an ice fishing season.

It will probably come some day. I sure wouldn't bet against it.

You see how most of this shoreline is wild. Looks a lot like Canada, right? In time to come that could change, too.

They could build big launching ramps and pavilions and campgrounds here. They could open it up to the public, is the way the saying goes.

Well, you certainly are right. Time does go fast when you are fishing. Since we don't have running lights, we'd best get to shore while there's still some daylight.

The fish? You're welcome to them. I hope you don't mind that we put back the stuff that was less than a foot long. I'm just not ready for this no-size-limit thing yet.

And I'm glad you liked the lunch. Fresh liver sausage and onions and crackers go pretty good together.

Listen, I hope we can fish together again. And I hope you get to the flowage a lot.

Yes, sir. You are right. This is a beautiful place. I hope it stays this way. But you never know. Times are changing. But at least you've had a chance to see it and enjoy it. Not everybody has been that lucky.

So thanks again for your company. Have a safe trip home, and always, remember…

Jackpine Dispenses Some Fishy Advice

Upnorth, Wisconsin—When I walked into Jackpine Joe's Saloon this recent day, the proprietor himself was elbow deep in conversation with a lone customer at the bar.

"Lucky for me I called ahead for reservations," I said, by way of greeting.

"Well, if it ain't the scribbler," Jackpine said. "I can only surmise that you dangled a participle and they ran you out of Milwaukee in disgrace."

"Nothing like that," I said. "Actually, I am on my way to a big job in Ashland. Given the heavy trade you are doing, I can only conclude that you must be having a sale on beer. I'll snap for the house."

"Considering there ain't but three of us, your generosity is overwhelming, although

> **"See yourself standing at the tee, resplendent in matching socks, shoes, shirt, slacks and jockstrap..."**

typical," Jackpine said. "This boy here is Harlan. Shake and howdy while I draw three."

"Glad to meet you, Harlan," I said, as Jackpine put the beer down. "What's happening?"

"Likewise, I'm sure," Harlan said politely. "You see, I got this big problem so I stopped to ask Jackpine for a little advice."

"Good thinking," I replied, "except that Jackpine has never been known to dispense a little advice. Usually, he offers a pile of it, most of which is best dispersed with a pitchfork, if you get my meaning."

"Button your lip, scribe," Jackpine snarled. "This is serious business. Old Harlan here was just about to lay his troubles on me when you walked in. So why don't you be seen and not heard?"

"You got it," I said. "Who am I to disturb The Ann Landers of Upnorth?"

Jackpine growled like a coyote on raw meat and turned his attention to Harlan.

"Well, you see, Jackpine," the young man said with his face shading toward pink. "You know my girlfriend? Well, I popped the question last night and she said she would...under one condition."

169

"Now hold on right there, Harlan!" Jackpine interrupted. "I ain't talking sex with you. What you do down at the boat landing in the dead of night is your own business."

"No! No!" Harlan protested. "I asked her to marry me and she said she would if I quit fishing. I mean give it up entirely. She says that is the only way if we are to have a life together with a mortgage and other fun things like raising kids."

Jackpine gasped and Harlan continued:

"Fishing has been my life. You know how much I love it. But I love this girl, too. Heck, I love her almost as much as I do my split bamboo fly rod that my grandfather gave to me along with his deathbed wish that I use it for the rest of my natural life—to which I agreed, by the way.

"That much?" Jackpine asked.

"That much," Harlan replied, taking a box of trout flies from his pocket and placing them on the bar where he looked at them with adoring eyes.

"She says fishing is a waste of an honest man's time and those who indulge in it are not to be trusted. So what should I do?"

Jackpine didn't say anything right away. He picked up our empty glasses and filled them without asking for cash money, so I knew he was in deep, inner deliberation.

"You know, son" Jackpine said, his voice taking on a fatherly tone. "Your girl makes a fine point. When you think about it, fishing really is an activity for the shiftless and shameless. It is a waste of time to say nothing of money and effort. It is a killer of pride, a destroyer of ambition, a crusher of dreams."

Jackpine paused to sip his beer and take a deep breath. His eyes grew misty and his fingers trembled.

"Let me tell you a story, son, that few people know about. You remember Mattress Mike, the old guy who sweeps out this joint at closing time for a free beer? Well, as a young man, he stood on the brink of a brilliant career as a brain surgeon.

"But he frittered it all away on trout streams and bass lakes and walleye holes. He fell into ill repute, shunned by his friends, disowned by relatives. He's a broken man today and you can blame fishing for it."

"Gosh, I didn't know that," Harlan said. "I always thought fishing was fun. You mean we should spend the rest of our lives just doing married things?"

"Not at all," Jackpine said. "You and your girl should take up golf."

"Golf!" Harlan exclaimed.

"Golf!" Jackpine repeated. "Unlike fishing, golf is a game of meaning and value. It will build your character and enhance your standing in life. You will win the respect of your contemporaries. You will stand tall with a driver in your hands.

"See yourself, Harlan, standing at the tee, resplendent in matching socks, shoes, shirt, slacks and jockstrap. With one mighty swing, you drive that ball high into the sky where eagles fly. It splits the fairway and lands perfectly at the dogleg right for an easy chip to the green. The entire world will applaud and you will see yourself as you really are.

"Picture yourself, Harlan, you and your bride, spending weekends together at the country club, hand in hand, sharing life's pars and birdies. You will forget all about fishing."

"God bless you," Harlan said, shaking Jackpine's hand. "You've convinced me. I'm going to give my fishing tackle to Goodwill, take up golf, marry my true love and live happily ever after."

With that, he ran out the door shouting, "Fore!"

"What kind of a con are you running here?" I asked. "If the kid believes all that, his shelves need restocking. Mattress Mike dropped out of school because he couldn't master the alphabet, to say nothing of the scalpel. And you hate golf. What gives?"

"You don't learn everything in journalism school," Jackpine said. "Harlan is maybe the best fisherman I know. And except for me, he is the only person in the world who knows about a hole on Plum Creek where lives a brown trout as long as your arm. I had to get him out of the fishing business so he wouldn't catch it before I do."

"Now it makes sense," I said, getting up to leave. "You get the trout and old Harlan gets a fishless marriage."

"You got it, " Jackpine said. "Now I'm going to lock up this joint and head out for Plum Creek, where I will catch that trout.

"I'll get it mounted and have it photographed and give the picture, framed, of course, to Harlan for a wedding present.

"It's the least I can do."

Good Walleye Anglers
Enjoy a Magic Touch

There is something peculiar about walleye fishermen.

I don't mean the ordinary ones. I mean the ones who are really good at it, those who are almost always successful, those who put fish in the boat.

It isn't something you can see because it has nothing to do with their dapper clothes or their generally handsome profiles.

It isn't the way they carry themselves or the way they talk or the cars they drive or the women they are seen with.

Really good walleye fishermen do not sign contracts. They don't have agents. They don't call press conferences. They are never greeted at the dock by giggling groupies.

No, sir. There is none of that.

What sets the really good walleye fisherman apart from ordinary mortals is his touch, his ability to feel, his talent to sense movement as transmitted through water from fish to bait to hook to line to rod to reel to hand.

Show me a really good walleye fisherman and I'll show you somebody who would make an outstanding pick-pocket. Show me a really good walleye fisherman, and I'll show you someone who could defuse bombs, pick locks, fix watches or build ships inside bottles.

It is a delicate business, this matter of catching walleyes here in northern Wisconsin these days. The fish are hitting short, as the saying goes, which means they are biting lightly.

LIGHT BITE. Walleyes are notorious for striking lightly, requiring sensitivity in any fisherman's hands. Newspaper photographer Sherman Gessert, and not Jay Reed, likely caught these fish.

The "smashing strike" we read about so often in the big outdoor magazines is not to be found in the real world of cold wind and high water. What walleye fishermen are finding, instead, is a good population of generally small fish that approach the bait about the same way you'd try to pick up a live rattlesnake—carefully.

That's why, at least so far this young fishing season, the premium has been on a fisherman's ability to feel light-biting fish and sense when the time is right to set the hook.

That is the way it is most every walleye fishing season in early spring. But to those of us who have been involved in it for a long time, it seems it is even more so this season. The guys with radar in their fingers and steel in their wrists are the ones who have been making out.

It is appropriate now, in light of all of this, to talk about my friend from Menomonee Falls, Sherman Gessert, with whom I shared a boat for several days in Hayward, Wisconsin.

> **"It took awhile to discover I'd been hustled..."**

Gessert is a professional photographer employed by the *Milwaukee Journal* and was here on a working assignment. He has built a fine reputation over the years by being quick on the shutter, so there was no question about the sensitivity of his hands.

But, by his own admission, Gessert has never really been into walleye fishing. Bass are his bag. Or tarpon if he is in Costa Rica. And trout, too, if the time is right.

Walleyes, though?

"I don't think I've ever fished walleyes," he said, as we were loading our boat at the Golden Fawn Resort on the Chippewa Flowage this recent day. "How the heck do you fish for them?"

You should know that it was just minutes after 5:00 a.m. It was cold and the wind was coming straight down the pipe from the northeast. The night had been long and sleep time short.

I was not exactly in the mood to give lessons.

"Just tie on a plain jig," I told him. "Bait it with a minnow when we get to the spot."

We motored to the mouth of the Chief River, which is not exactly a secret place when it comes to walleye fishing. It is a good spot, but popular, and so there were a number of other boats in place when we got there. I found the area I wanted and we anchored.

"How do I hook the minnow?" Gessert asked.

"Lightly through its lips and try not to kill it," I told him.

"OK. Now what?" he asked.

"Well start fishing, dammit," I said.

And that right there, let me tell you, was the last instruction I gave to Sherman Gessert on the fine art of walleye fishing.

Country boys are slow, I'll admit. So it took awhile to discover that I'd been hustled.

Gessert put a fish in the boat. And then another and another.

That much I could lay to beginner's luck and, of course, my expert instruction.

When he landed two more while I was still thinking about it, I knew I had been had.

Gessert did it the way experts do. He could feel the bite and he'd lay off, keeping the line just tight enough to follow the fish. He'd feed it, then, like a mother swallow with a baby.

And when he sensed that the time was right to set the hook, he did, with a short, sharp flex of his wrist.

These fish were small, at least too small for us to keep, even though there is no size limit where we were fishing. But what the heck. If nothing else, I can count. And Gessert had brought in what could have been a limit while I was still getting untracked.

I tried to laugh it off, suggesting that when you are guiding, you don't have time to fish well. But the truth was in me and I knew that Gessert was one of those rare ones with the magic walleye touch.

So we worked the water seriously after that and we collected a stringer of respectable walleyes plus a northern pike of about 30 inches.

Gessert took some pictures later in the day when the light was right and we were home free. That was that.

Except for one thing. I'm glad we didn't make any bets.

A Sad End for Prince of the Sea

I've learned some things down here in Isla de Coiba, Panama, a place where the winds are warm and sweet as perfume in the night.

Having been a freshwater fisherman all my life and a virgin in this particular atmosphere, that is to be expected, I suppose.

Among the things I have discovered is that there isn't really very much you can do with a sailfish once you've caught one.

You can't eat it. You can't sell it. You can't even give it away.

It has no real value except, perhaps, to the person who caught it.

So far as I know now, there are only two things to do with a sailfish once you've killed it.

You can have it mounted. Some people do that. But you've got to have some extra wall space available because they run 10 feet in length or more. And unless you like the plastic look, you probably wouldn't go to the time and expense.

The other thing you can do is have your picture taken with it.

Deep sea camps have the facilities for that. They consist of a white scaffold with yellow rope and a pulley plus hook so that your fish can be hoisted up to camera level.

To that scenario, they'll add a blackboard on which will be written your name, the species of fish you've caught, its weight, its length, its girth, the line weight, etc.

Now all you have to do is stand up there beside your fish and the blackboard. You've got to hold your fishing rod in your hand because that's obligatory.

If you are a man you should smile triumphantly and look macho. If you are a woman you should smile triumphantly and look however it is a woman who has just killed a great fish should look.

Now somebody will take your picture.

With any kind of luck at all, they'll send it back to your hometown newspaper and they'll publish it someday when the news is thin and a portion of the world will then know what a great fisherman you are.

It's hero work, for certain.

Bull!

I hooked and battled a sailfish. Maybe it was 80 pounds. Or maybe 100.

175

Nobody will ever know because we released it.

It gave three of us — me, the captain and a photographer — all we could handle. Except for some tarpon I caught last year in Costa Rica, it was the toughest, hardest, meanest, fightingest fish I've ever dealt with.

But when we came to camp tonight, they had a sailfish hanging from the scaffold. The guy who caught it had his picture taken with it.

We shook his hand and congratulated him and he was modest, but proud. He said it was the toughest fight he'd ever had with a fish.

He bought a round of drinks for all hands and we bought back and it was a wonderful cocktail hour.

After that we went to our respective cottages and showered and changed for dinner, and then we all went to the dining room, where, again, we toasted the sailfish and the man who did it in.

And when the softest light of late evening in the tropics descended over all, we sipped after-dinner drinks and strong black coffee in the open-air lounge and laughed with Ortega, the bartender who said we were the greatest fishermen to have visited the camp.

But there was this shadow, don't you see. It came from the sailfish still hanging from the scaffold.

Once it was the most beautiful fluorescent green, blue, lavender, crimson, and sweet orange you ever saw. Once it was muscle and blood and steel and bone and unbridled anger and hatred toward those who would kill it.

Once it was the prince of the sea.

But it was dead now. Its color was gone. Its skin had dried and crinkled like old parchment. Its eyes were vacant with the stare of death.

Sometime later tonight or early in the morning they'll come for the big sailfish and cut it down. They'll drag it across the sandy beach beyond the line of rocks and, there, they'll push it and pull it out to the water where it will slowly sink to become feed for sharks.

Because I don't know any better, I think that is sad.

Because I don't know any better, I think that's a hell of an inappropriate ending for a magnificent fish that has three times the strength and courage and guts of the people who killed it.

Because I don't know any better, I think there should be another way.

But what else can you do with a sailfish once it is dead? Take its picture. Have it mounted.

Or feed it to the sharks…

Fables for Fishers:
The Trout Angler

Sometimes when howling wind sends slants of rain across the ocean of forests, fishermen hunch cheek by jowl in a place of shelter. And they tell stories.

This is one.

A successful man, highly regarded in his community and a trout fisherman his entire life, died. Upon arrival in the next world, he was greeted by a man.

"Welcome, sir," the man said. "We want to make your stay here as enjoyable as possible. If there is some recreation you especially enjoy, tell me about it and we'll try to arrange it. Anything at all."

The fisherman was pleased.

"I've worked hard all my life," he said. "I've never had enough time to fish trout as much as I wanted so, if it's possible, I'd like to fish trout just as often as I can."

OUT FOR TROUT. This clever short story was written early in Jay Reed's tenure with the *Milwaukee Journal*. It appeared June 19, 1966.

"No problem at all," the man said. "In fact, it will be your duty here to fish trout every day. Nothing else. Just fish trout."

"Wonderful," the fisherman said. "But what about equipment? As you can see, I've none with me."

The man showed the way to a building which contained more angling equipment than the fisherman had ever seen before.

"Take your choice of whatever you want," the man said. "But, if you'll take advice, it really does not matter what kind of equipment you select. Fishing is so good here you'll have no problem, no matter what you choose."

The fisherman had heard such advice before. So, he carefully selected the gear he wanted, paying particular attention to rod weight, leader strength and reel action. "Since fishing is to be your only activity here, we might as well get started," the man said.

Together they walked along a road, over a hill and down into a wooded valley. Presently they came upon a beautiful trout stream.

"What fly would you suggest for this stretch of water?" the angler asked.

"Everything works well here," the guide replied. "Just pick out any fly at all and give it a try."

The fisherman selected a nymph. He cast. The fly had hardly settled on the water when he heard the familiar "slurp" and saw the water boil. He was fast to a trout. It fought briskly, bulling into the current, across it, toward a log and back. At last it came to net.

It was a brook trout.

"That's a beautiful fish," the angler said. "One of the nicest I've ever taken. Let's see how much it weighs."

"Don't bother," the guide said. "It weighs exactly three and a half pounds."

"I think it might go four or better," the fisherman said, getting out his pocket scale. He weighed the fish.

"You're right," he told the guide. "You really know your fish. It weighs exactly three and a half pounds."

The fisherman cast again. Another trout hit and fought just the way the first one did. Four more casts, four more brook trout, all the same size and weight.

"This is the most fantastic fishing I've ever had," the fisherman said. "I never dreamed I'd find anything like this. Let's go down the stream a bit."

Around the bend they found another pool, another log, another trough of fast water. It looked exactly the same as the first place he'd fished.

"What's this?" the fisherman asked. "Everything looks the same."

"That's the way it is here," the guide said. "Around the next bend and the next and the next there are other pools exactly like this. It will be no different no matter where you go.

"Every stream looks the same. The fish are all the same size, same color. They all fight the same. You will never lose a fish here. You will never miss a strike. There is no bag limit. You will catch a trout on every cast every time. And by your own request you are obliged to fish here under these conditions through all eternity."

And then the trout fisherman wept.

He had not, he realized, attained heaven after all. 🐦

Another Case of Musky Heartbreak

I f it's true that men tend to covet most that which they can never really have, then I know why I get excited over musky fishing.

Ever since I first tried to catch one, the musky has been my all-time, hands-down, bar-none favorite fish. And that's strange because I don't like punishment any more than the next guy. I don't like to be made the fool. I like to be let down easy. Hanging by the thumbs has never been for me.

But muskies have done all that to me, and more, down through the years. They are born heartbreakers. And now, here's the latest:

Less than a week ago I was fishing near Couderay, Wisconsin, with August Otto Gruenwaldt of Chippewa Falls, an old compadre with whom I have hunted, fished and caroused since the beginning of time.

We were on the Chippewa Flowage, which should be

FISH OF 10,000 CASTS. This husky musky was taken by Jay Reed on the Chippewa Flowage during a more successful outing than the one described here.

no great surprise to anyone. More than that, though, we were fishing the water around Popple Island, which has produced as many big muskies as any place, anywhere in the state.

And even more than that, we were working the precise corner off the island where at least three reputable fishermen have, this very year, raised the same musky that all three believe to weigh well over 35 pounds.

Gruenwaldt was working a surface bait because the day was dark, with as heavy an overcast as you've ever seen. I was throwing a black bucktail with a silver blade and had dressed it with a strip of pork rind. My scientific professional reason for using the rig was simply that I like it.

We were also trailing a sucker, which is the style of most of the best musky fishermen I know. And while we both worked our artificial baits with what passes for skill and determination, it was the sucker that produced the action.

We had a small musky on early in the day. It had hit the sucker, mouthed it for a time, and then broke water and spit it out, evidently figuring it was just too big.

Shortly before noon in the spot described above, we got a good hit on the sucker. We both saw it happen. The cork suddenly jerked about two feet across the top of the water and there was this big boil and swirl.

It just had to be a good fish to do that. Every sense we had told us that. It could only be the big one those other guys had seen. I mean this was it. For sure. For positive.

So we cleared the decks for appropriate action. We took in the other lines. We closed the tackle boxes. We lifted the outboard. We got everything out of the way. Gruenwaldt got both the landing net and the gaff hook ready. He'd use either one or both to get that baby in the boat.

I took the rod and Gruenwaldt took the oars. And together we watched the movement of the fish. Depending upon what the fish would do, we decided to give it 20 minutes to take the sucker. Then we'd take the fish.

The musky didn't really move all that much. We took this to mean it was big. At the 10-minute mark, I tightened the line to "feel" the fish. It had moved straight to the bottom and, through the line, I could feel the side-to-side movement of its head.

Now that could only mean it was a good musky, right? So maybe, just maybe, we were tied to a fish that might make the boys in the back room look up and take notice.

The last 10 minutes dragged. My palms were sweaty, as they always are at times like that. My nerves were grinding and I could feel a tight pain building deep in my gut.

"Let's take him," Gruenwaldt said.

As soon as I made the set I knew I had been had by the muskies again.

The fish rolled with the set, turned, made a short run, dived for the bottom and came back to the net with little line pressure.

We never took that musky out of the net. It was an imposter, an actor playing the part of a big fish.

The ruler said it was 29 inches long. We cut the cable on the hook and watched the fish swim away.

The musky had taken us to the top of the mountain and dropped us over the side. That's the way it is with muskies.

Musky of a Lifetime
Nearly Ends a Lifetime

You could smell the storm coming. It was heavy in the air like something sick and evil.

But, at first, you couldn't really see it.

The sky had that dead gray look about it. It was heavy, hanging down toward the top of the tree line around the Chippewa Flowage. But the thunderheads had not yet started to build and there was no wind save a little ruffle of the leaves once in a while.

Now if you are a musky fisherman there are times when you know you must fish. You just know it. You feel it down to the bottom of your gut clawing away at your insides like some kind of cancer. And that's the way it was that day for the man from Milwaukee.

Such little wisdom as he had told him to leave the lake, head for shore, get the hell out of there and beat the storm. But that, of course, is practical knowledge created for people who live in cells.

BOAT HANDLING ABILITY has saved more than one fisherman in rough water. Jay Reed lived to tell about it in this story that appeared on July 17, 1977.

It is designed for those who live their lives on the ends of short leashes.

It has nothing to do with a pounding heart, an instinct that tells you to hang in for another half hour because maybe, just maybe, you'll get a shot at that fish you've been seeking for a lifetime.

It has nothing to do with the freedom that boils within, the voice that whispers in your heart, urging you to push that extra inch, to take that one more step, to toss the dice just one more time.

It is not smart. It is just natural for some of us.

But it is why, nevertheless, he was fishing the shoreline opposite the

181

Hay Creek Narrows campground in Couderay, Wisconsin, at a time when others had retreated to the comfort of camp, the safety of shelter.

He didn't know it at the time but, for years to come, men will remember it as the day of the big northland holiday storm, the day the gods went crazy and sent wind and rain slashing across a strip of Wisconsin's north, smashing cabins and houses in its path, splintering stands of huge trees that had withstood the ravages of time for a hundred years or more.

But all of that which was to become history was of no concern to the man from Milwaukee. He'd come north to fish in this place that had given so much to him over the years.

They had seen him slink away from the resort-campground like a tired coyote seeking refuge where the sound of Independence Day's exploding firecrackers and whistling rockets and flaming fireworks couldn't reach him.

"The musky was gone. But the storm was not..."

And he found that solitude, that refuge deep in the chambered depths of the lake that men call Chippewa.

And so, at first, he had smelled the storm. He had felt it, sensed its coming. It would've been wise of him to leave because, clearly, nature was mad about something and she was soon to let the world know about it.

He fished the shoreline near Hay Creek Narrows the lazy man's way. He soaked suckers. In the ominous calm he watched the bobbers floating listlessly on the glass-flat surface of the water.

He pulled easily at the oars every minute or so to give a little movement to the boat. He wasn't even aware when the first drops of rain began to fall because, at the same time, a musky hit one of his suckers.

It was a good hit, the kind that pops the cork free the first time. He made sure the spool on the reel was free. Then he brought in the other line and tilted the outboard. He checked his watch and lit a cigarette. That's when he first realized it was really raining. The cigarette was wet. But the musky was moving again, stripping line from the reel.

He worked the oars to follow it, to keep the line entirely free. Milt Dieckman, a fine musky fisherman, had told him years ago that the trick is to keep the line free while the musky works. The fish should feel no resistance.

It was raining harder now and the wind was kicking up. Across the line of trees, he could see the black thunderheads building, rolling, moving

182

almost as if they were alive.

The minutes dragged.

There are men who say, who believed, that those minutes from the time a musky hits a sucker until they set the hook are the most exciting in all of fresh water fishing. He believed it. He smoked another damp cigarette.

When is the time right to hit a fish working a sucker? Who knows? Theory abounds. In this case he never got a chance to find out for, unaccountably, the musky dropped the sucker.

The line stopped moving. It was still for a long time. He reeled up the slack carefully. He took the line between two fingers and pulled gently. Nothing. No feel. No movement. The musky was gone. But the storm was not.

By the time he had retrieved the battered sucker, the water was boiling in the now high wind. The sky had become alive with black, rolling clouds. In the distance he could see the surface of the water lathered white with caps of foam.

Do you head for camp or do you retreat to the nearest island shelter? He decided to make a run for camp. It was about a 20-minute run. It turned out to be a nightmare.

The boat was all but uncontrollable in the wind. The waves sucked at it one second and battered it the next. He tried to quarter into the waves, but, mostly, it didn't work. He was taking on water over the bow and over the sides.

But he made it.

Once in the cabin, he heard a portable radio tell of the severity of the storm then in progress. A tree crunched down on the cabin next to his to underline the point.

You already know the story of the storm, the damage it did, the destruction it caused. And now you know what it was like out there on the water in the moments when it all began.

Smart, sure minds would have never been there. But the thought persists that every man should be able to see it, to feel it once.

Then he will know, as the man from Milwaukee has learned again, that he still is the tenant and not the master.

Ghosts Return
For Fishing Trip

It does not happen much anymore, and that is good.

Because when you fish with ghosts too often, people tend to believe your elevator does not go all the way to the top, and you might even get to thinking that yourself.

But it still happens to me every once in a while. In fact, it did right here in Reserve, Wisconsin, on an early June day. Conditions were right for it, don't you see, and that's a primary requisite if you are going to fish with ghosts.

I shook myself out of the sack in the neighborhood of 5:00 a.m. and when I looked out the cabin door to take a reading on the day, I thought my eyes were going bad.

Fog had rolled in overnight and I could barely see my boat down on the beach less than 50 yards away. I made some fake coffee and listened to a guy on the radio telling about how there had been a collision of air masses during the night, probably right over my cabin.

I put on rain gear, then, and picked up my musky rod, a box of baits and a landing net and headed for the boat, where I eased my butt down on the wet cushion I'd forgotten to bring in the night before.

© ISTOCKPHOTO.COM

MISTY MEMORIES. Jay Reed often wrote with reverence about the wise and experienced sportsmen who'd gone before him...and lived on vividly in his mind.

The outboard started on the third pull and in moments I was floating through another world. The fog was thicker on the water, but by hugging the shoreline I was able to find the cut that leads to the big water beyond the islands.

Then it was dead reckoning across a wide bay to a point of land where I knew at least one musky lived.

As long as I could see the shoreline, the world had some sense of place to it. But once away from the shore, I was surrounded by four walls of fog. Windless as it was, there were no sounds save for my feet scuffing on the boat's bottom.

I cast a bucktail and the bait would disappear just off the rod tip. I'd hear it splash when it hit the water. But I couldn't see it.

In that place and at that time, the stark pleasures of solitude were all around me. There was just me and the fog and the boat. God, how I loved it. I fished like an automaton, acting mechanically to the routine of cast, retrieve; cast, retrieve.

The flat fog, the loneliness, the silence, were spellbinding.

And that's when the ghosts came to fish with me.

Charley Inglass was first. In my presence, he was blown into three separate, but more or less distinct, pieces when he stepped on a land mine one soft, sweet November evening in Vietnam, thus becoming another sacrificial token of political stupidity.

> ### "Just me and the fog and the boat. God, how I loved it..."

But he was a friend of mine, and since I shipped his body bag home we have been together at more than one gathering of ghosts.

Ralph Raiche came along, then. He bought the farm more than 20 years ago because of a disease they didn't even have a name for at the time. Hell, he was 26 years old.

And Garnie Johnson was there. He was as close to me as anybody ever was. Mel Ellis, Tom Guyant, Wally Neimuth, and Johnny Helsing were there. Some of those names you'll recognize. Some you won't. Dion Henderson showed up, too. This was his first ghost gathering.

My uncle Anton came by, wearing his World War I uniform. So did Nels Fuhr and some of the others from Nelson.

There were many others, too. But I didn't have their names.

You see, I have always believed that I rode with the Seventh Cavalry when Custer went down at Little Big Horn. I took an arrow in the butt in that one, and when they found my bones they kicked them aside and kept the arrowhead, which is now on display in South Dakota, maybe at the Corn Palace in Mitchell or that famous drugstore in Rapid City.

Anyway, the troopers were there, and so were some people I used to know from the First Marine Division.

Faces swirled about in the fog like crazy circles and humps and bumps and so did other times and other places.

There were empty bottles and gutters and hotel rooms with carpets that smelled of wine and vomit and urine and body sweat.

There was an alley where the wind piled street garbage high in the corners, but it was a place to sleep, home for a little while. There were freight trains to ride and long roads to walk and there were doors that closed never to reopen again.

I smelled the sweet scent of perfume in the night and I felt the sticky warmth of blood on my hands. I was locked in the cold and left out in the rain.

My ghosts were riding high there in the fog, let me tell you.

But I kept on casting, kept on fishing harder and harder, faster and faster.

And then, suddenly, they were gone, all of them. The names, the faces, the places, the times and I was sitting alone in a boat and the sun was chasing the fog like a beagle after a rabbit.

There was no feeling, then, or at least none I could distinguish. I was wet with sweat and I could see steam rising off my rain parka where the sun hit it.

I put the musky rod down and watched the lake lick itself clean of fog. There was a breeze now so I drifted, but it didn't really matter.

The ghosts were gone and I wondered where they went. I would catch no muskies this morning. Maybe later in the day, but not now.

And I knew the ghosts would come back to visit me again. Maybe some morning in the fall when I'm in a duck blind, or it could happen in deer season when I'm standing on a runway somewhere in the north.

Or maybe they'll come again in the middle of the night and I'll wake up screaming.

Somewhere, sometime, someplace, though, there will be another gathering of ghosts. Like memories, they never really go away.

I wonder why.

Float Trip on Two Rivers Is a Taste of Yesterday

Trevino-on-the-Chippewa...
    You won't find this place on the map of Wisconsin because nobody lives here anymore. And nobody comes here much except hunters, fishermen and trappers.

But it's a place, all right. It's a parking lot and a boat landing and a long time ago there was a tavern and dance hall, but all that's left of it is the foundation, now hidden under 30 years of undergrowth.

It's eight miles or so north and west of Nelson, near the Mississippi River in northwest Wisconsin. The approach road is just before you cross the Highway 35 bridge spanning the Chippewa River, but you'll have to look close because the weed growth is high and the dirt road is narrow. It's easy to miss.

"We came to sip from the cup of yesterday..."

This is a place out of my boyhood past. It's a spot where I used to come to worship the gods that gave me the catfish and the bass and the beaver and the deer and the rattlesnakes.

I came back here again the other day with my yellow Labrador retriever, Thor, and Dave Van Wormer of Wisconsin Rapids, who is one of only a handful of people in this world who I count as the closest and truest of friends.

The three of us came to sip from the cup of yesterday.

We left one car at the Highway 35 bridge spanning the Mississippi River toward Wabasha, Minnesota, and trailered the boat and motor with the other car to this spot on the Chippewa.

The idea was to float and fish the Chippewa down to where it meets the Mississippi at the foot of Lake Pepin and then go down the Mississippi to the bridge at Wabasha where we had left the other car.

And that, of course, is what we did.

It was a page from the book of yesterday, wrinkled and yellowed with age and pockmarked with notations of things that had happened down through the years.

It was overcast and hazy and heavy with heat, and thunder rumbled over the distant Minnesota hills. You could smell rain every time the soft breeze turned, but mostly there was the scent of the swamps; of fish and frogs and mud and sand and rotted trees and fresh, green marsh grass.

There were no minnows to be had in town so we baited with nightcrawlers and spinners and jigs and little wobbling plugs.

We drifted with the Chippewa's current, casting to the bank, working the pools and scraping the sandbars.

We stopped at an open stretch of shoreline to let the dog run and swim. We sucked at cans of cold beer and ate bologna and rotten cheese and raw onions. We smoked cigarettes and slapped at mosquitoes.

When we hit the Mississippi, we trolled along the edge of a reef that runs far out into the river where the big towboats go.

Then we floated downstream with the current. We bobbed like a cork in the wake of passing pleasure boats and we worked our way around a big dredge operated by the Corps of Engineers.

We cut back into a slough off the Mississippi and went back into the woods as far as we could go. There was only silence except for the buzzing of mosquitoes and the jungle sounds of birds.

We dragged the boat in those places where there was not enough water to run the motor, and, finally, when the water ran out, we turned and went back to the big river.

It was nearly dusk when we got back to the landing off the Mississippi. Then it was a matter of driving back to get the boat trailer, returning and loading up.

We got back to the motel before dark to shower and change and go out for dinner.

At the Durand House in Durand, Wisconsin, we sat again beside the Chippewa. And, over wine and blood-rare steaks, we talked about the rivers, the Chippewa and the Mississippi; of the magic of yesterday and the reality of today and the hope of tomorrow.

If you measure the day as a fishing trip you'd say it was a bummer because we caught one smallmouth bass and one sheepshead. Another day, another time, it would be different.

But nobody who knows rivers, who loves them, ever measures them that way. Especially the Chippewa. Especially, times two, the Mississippi.

What we did that day, me and Thor and Van Wormer, was worship.

What I did was remember...

Outdoorsman Skips
The Indoor Stream

Royale Coachman, the noted trouter, connoisseur of good brandy and famed bon vivant who lives in the cabin behind Jackpine Joe's Saloon in Upnorth, Wisconsin, was a recent visitor to Milwaukee.

He came down to take in the 1984 Sports, Travel and Boat Show, and was understandably pooped when we met at Turner Hall, having been in Duluth the day before.

"You bet your best fly rod I'm tired," he said. "We call it Chevy lag back home. Get that? Chevy lag," he chuckled, digging my ribs with his elbow.

"Got it," I said, ordering a round.

"You big city guys ain't much for humor. That's a funny line Upnorth. Gets a laugh every time. Jackpine thought it up, you know. He's a card. Calls a spade a spade, get that? Card? Spade?"

"I got it, I got it," I said, lighting another cigarette.

He sipped at his drink

THE TROUT POND at the *Milwaukee Journal Sentinel* **Sports Show is always a big hit with the little kids.**

thoughtfully and then asked, "How are the bucks doing?"

"Pretty good," I said. "They beat the Detroits the other night."

"I don't mean them Bucks. I mean the real bucks. The deer. You got them down here, ain't you?"

"Well, they are doing all right, I guess. Somebody said they saw a couple out at the Nature Center."

"You are lucky, then. Back home they are starving to death. Hell, all of the wild game is gone, you know? Jackpine Joe said he saw a snowshoe rabbit the other day and it was the talk of the town for a week. It's the DNR's fault."

"You mean the Department of Natural Resources?"

"No. I mean Do Nothing Right. I mean Damn Near Retarded. I mean what God giveth, DNR taketh away. That's what I mean."

"Be serious," I said. "You can't blame the DNR for everything."

"The hell I can't," he said. "You remember Maribou Muddler, the town assessor, don't you? Well, he had to raise Jackpine Joe's taxes on account of the new rinse tank he installed. Said it was the DNR's fault. That's proof enough, ain't it? Would Muddler lie?"

"You may be right at that," I said.

"Hey, Sonny. Let's have one more round and then get over to the Sports Show. I want to fish some trout in that wilderness stream they got over there. All my gear is outside in the car."

"You mean you'd actually want to try for those factory fish in that tank?"

"Of course I do. Maybe I'll win a vacation in Cleveland. I've always wanted to go to Cleveland, you know? Or Buff-

"Don't blame the DNR. Instead, blame the *Milwaukee Sentinel...*"

alo. What do you think? I got a box of my best flies. Even got some worms if it is really tough going. Will I need waders or hip boots?"

I ordered another round.

"They won't let you use your own stuff," I told him. "They've got rules, you know. Exactly two dozen of them, in fact."

"Boy, I hope I don't win a trip to Duluth," he said, paying no attention. "I've been to Duluth, you know. Just yesterday. Hope I never have to go there again. Cleveland yes. Buffalo, maybe. But Duluth, no."

"Are you crazy?" I said. "You can't use your own fishing tackle. Rule Seven says only equipment supplied by trout stream attendants may be used. No special flies, artificial lures, live bait or scent will be permitted. You can't even put your rod tip in the water. That's rule 14."

"Say, that sounds pretty tough," he said. "That ain't a sting operation for the DNR is it? I mean, it's not like I'm going to set up a vending machine company. I just want to go to Cleveland."

"I don't think so," I said. "But you have to be pretty careful. Rule 15 says all fish must be hooked in the mouth. Snagged fish will be returned to the water."

"Well, I'll be danged," he said. "That does it. I suppose you can't put a little crab trap in there, either. What do you think about that hand net of mine?"

"I think they are all disallowed under the rules," I said.

190

"Didn't I tell you?" he asked. "That's the DNR for you. Always taking the fun out of fishing. If they let me use my net, I'd sure get to Cleveland."

"I'm afraid that's out of the question," I said. "But don't blame the DNR. Blame the *Milwaukee Sentinel*. It's their show."

"Hey, Sonny. Those are magic words. Tell you what. Let's have another round or three and forget about the show. I'll tell you a true story that happened a long time ago up at Jackpine Joe's Saloon. Deal?"

I said it was.

"You never knew Gordon MacQuarrie, did you?

I said I hadn't.

"Well, he worked for your outfit. The Journal, is it? Anyway, they called him the Old Eskimo. Finest writer ever in the world, bar none and damned well including you.

"Me and Jackpine Joe and Muddler and some others had been down to the Sports Show and we talked about it for days.

"Later that spring Old Mac dropped by when we was all enjoying a drop with Jackpine at his saloon and we told Mac how great the Sports Show had been.

"He said it should have been good because it is the only Sports Show in the whole country that owns a newspaper.

"Now what do you think of that, Sonny? Got you a good story, right? If you got guts enough to print it, that is. The Old Eskimo had guts."

I gave him my gratitude and put more jingle on the bar.

And then I ordered another round.

191

World's Oldest Profession Is Moving to Ice

What is desperately needed here this day is a barn burner, a tub thumper.

But they are in short supply.

So let's mix leeches and lust and see what happens. Let's examine parka passion and all its scarlet implications

But be warned up front that if it is something significant, something meaningful you seek from this space this day, we are all in trouble.

It does, however, have to do with fishing, which is why you turned to this page in the first place.

First, you need to know this: There was a report aired nationally the other day that said authorities in Minnesota were investigating allegations that a prostitution ring was flourishing among ice fishermen at Mille Lacs, which is about a hundred miles north of Minneapolis as the walleye swims.

Mille Lacs, as most any angler knows, was once regarded as the best place in the universe, or beyond, to go sport fishing.

Although fishing success there is said to have declined somewhat, it still draws a crowd, a large crowd, of anglers, especially in winter, when community-size clusters of shacks spring up as soon as the ice is safe.

And the fishermen have fun, as ice anglers almost always do. As it turns out, some have more fun than others.

Now please understand that I have no problem with prostitution. If it shakes your tree, go for it. If it does not, don't. It's your choice. Of course, it is against the law, you know.

It does bother me a little that hookers would ply their trade out among the fishing shacks on Mille Lacs or any other lake for that matter.

The thing is, fishing and fishermen have a bad enough reputation as it is.

They say the truth is not in us, first of all. They say we lie like wet rugs. They say we cheat in tournaments. They say we wouldn't tell our own mothers about a secret fishing hole.

And, it is said, we run heavy to strong drink. They say we buy more beer than bait. They say we are terrors at the local bars when we get off the water. They say we have not yet consumed all the beer in town, but that we have kept the delivery people working overtime.

Although there is no substance to those allegations, they are believed by many, nevertheless, and now with this hooker business at Mille Lacs, there are some guys who may never get out of the house again.

Just personally, I have my doubts about the Mille Lacs story. I mean the logistics of paid love in an ice fishing shack are enough to boggle the mind. Those little structures can hardly be looked upon as passion palaces.

You get a fisherman dressed for a day on the ice and you've got a guy with more zippers and buttons and buckles than scales on a walleye's back.

Then there is the matter of attractiveness. Those parts of the human body normally considered attractive just do not show through from under a parka. Insulated boots do nothing for a well-turned ankle. And long underwear, while functional, may be the ugliest garment ever designed.

And ice fishermen themselves rate right at the top of the ugly chart, although that may have nothing to do with it if money is involved. Ice fishermen have red noses that are constantly moist. Their hands are curled from cold and they smell of fish bait and stove smoke.

> **"The logistics of paid love in an ice fishing shack boggle the mind..."**

The breath of an ice fisherman is so bad, usually, that a dog would roll in it. It is strong enough to crumble concrete given his intake of rotten cheese and raw onions and garlic sausage.

Put a man in an ice fishing shack and he will never, ever be confused with Prince Charming.

For these reasons I have my doubts about the report from Mille Lacs. It is possible, though. Minnesota has always been a peculiar state.

In any case, there have been no such rumors of hookermania on Wisconsin's major ice fishing lakes like Winnebago or Big Green or Pewaukee. Perhaps that's just as well.

193

High-Tech Gizmo
Doesn't Catch On

A new fishing reel came on the market awhile back. It is high-tech stuff.

Manufactured by Daiwa, the instruments are called the Microcomputer Procaster Tournament Baitcasting Reels.

They sell for about 140 bucks a clatter. They may or may not revolutionize the grand old game of sport fishing. But they'd have old Izaak Walton looking twice, I guarantee.

The reels are said to be able to do about everything except mix drinks, grill steaks and row your boat. They are not much into computerized dating either so scratch that idea.

But if you attach one to a fishing rod, what you have is a computer on a stick. It was bound to come sooner or later.

By programming simple inputs such as the line test and length of line you are using, the reel will employ time signal processing to give you instantaneous information, according to the manufacturers.

It will tell you, for example, the length of your cast; the speed of your retrieve and how much line is still out at any given time. The computer beeps once each second as the lure sinks and once for each 10 feet of line retrieved. There is more, too, but you get the idea.

When the news about this amazing instrument first came out, it spread like wildfire through the valley where the Wolf River runs from Northport to New London to Gills Landing to Fremont to Winneconne.

It had a lot of us on the edge of our chairs, let me tell you.

But, alas, we expected too much, too soon. This is what happened...

A few of us had this plan, you see. We were going to put some money in a pot and buy one of those computerized reels. Then we figured we would feed it some essential information like water temperature, air temperature, rate of river flow and the number of hours of available sunlight.

We were going to tell that reel what kind of bait we intended to use, the color of our boat, the weight of our river rigs, the size of our hooks, the names of our dogs and the cut of our clothes.

We were, in fact, prepared to 'fess up to the reel anything it wanted to know up to and including what happened on Saturday night in Fremont after the poker game ended.

In return, of course, we thought the reel would digest all that input, cough, groan, grunt, wheeze, roll its ball bearings and, eventually, spit out information that would tell us exactly when, where and how to catch walleyes on the Wolf River in spring.

It would be even more accurate than a telephone call from a fisheries biologist at the Department of Natural Resources. It would be more reliable than last year's records. Certainly it would be better than checking oak leaves to see when they are the size of a squirrel's ear.

That's what we figured, anyway. The list of benefits that would accrue would be nearly endless.

There would be no more wasted hours on the river waiting for the walleyes to run. We'd know exactly when it would happen. The reel would tell us.

Never again would we have to sit for long periods of time in rain and snow and wind. The reel would tell us when to fish and we'd go out and bang a limit before the first pair of hands grew numb.

> **"What you have is a computer on a stick..."**

With the information the reel would give us, we could plan our trips to the Wolf right down to the precise minute.

It was a dream, of course, and like all dreams, it was made to be broken.

While the Microcomputerized Procaster Tournament Baitcasting Reel may very well be an astonishing marvel of high technology as that relates to recreational fishing now, it is not yet ready for the plans we had for it. Maybe it needs a bigger chip.

In any case, that is why we were back working our old stand on the Wolf River last weekend, our dreams of bringing technology to its knees through technology drowned in stinging slants of rain and snow.

We thought about it all as we waited for walleyes that never did arrive.

Right now the river is bank high or better and its water is cold. There'll be no big walleye run for a while yet until warm days are combined with warm nights. You don't need a computer to figure that out.

I'm just glad we never told that reel what happened on Saturday night in Fremont after the poker game broke up.

I mean, reely.

Fishing for Solution
To a Maddening Dilemma

When you are sick, you see a doctor. Right? When you've got a toothache, you go to a dentist. When you are thirsty and need whisky, you head for a bar.

Makes sense.

So when I had trouble catching fish, particularly walleyes, this spring, I requested an audience with that Great Guru of the North, Jackpine Joe, who moonlights as a saloon keeper and sports authority supreme.

"What can I do for you, my son? Except this, I mean," he said, calculating the depth of the head that stood atop the golden shoulders of the beer he placed in front of me.

"Jackpine," I blurted, "You gotta help me. I'm in trouble. Real trouble. I'm up to my butt in crocodiles."

"If it's a jealous husband you are worried about, I suggest you consider leaving the country, since you are too old to fight. As a matter of fact, I figured you to be too old for that sort of thing in the first place."

ANOTHER FISH STORY. The "Jackpine Joe" series of humor articles was created by the legendary outdoor writer Gordon MacQuarrie who started with the *Milwaukee Journal* in 1936. Jay Reed continued the tradition by writing the stories regularly and with flair.

"No! No! It is nothing like that," I said. "My problem is fishing. I've been catching walleyes at about the same rate the Milwaukee Brewers have been hitting home runs. I want you to tell me what I'm doing wrong.

"Why don't you ask me something simple?" Jackpine said. "Like the real meaning of truth or the state tax program or the Packers' draft."

"Be serious, Jackpine. This could be my professional life we are dealing with here. Have you ever heard of an outdoor writer who couldn't catch

196

walleyes? That's like a surgeon who can't remove tonsils or a mechanic who can't fix an engine or an editor who can't punctuate."

He turned deadly serious then, Jackpine did. He peered at me intently with his sickly, green eyes. And then he spoke:

"Too bad," he said.

"Too bad!" I screamed. "Too bad! I lie my way out of work for three days and drive all the way up here so you can save my life and all you can say is too bad? Geez, Jackpine!"

"Well, OK. Tell me more about your problems. I can see you have several, one of which is that your glass is empty. You got any money?"

"How can you think about money at a time like this? You are looking at a desperate man. I haven't been able to catch walleyes this spring. I'm snake-bit. I've lost my confidence. My timing is gone. I've got a hitch in my stroke. I write one more no-fish story and Terry Galvin, my boss, will personally escort me to the rescue mission.

"Of course I've got money. I'll buy for the house if you'll help me."

"What a deal, considering we are the only ones here," Jackpine said.

"Well, I ain't on an expense account," I argued. "Anyway, it's the thought that counts."

> **"Just because you write about fishing doesn't mean you have to be good at it..."**

"OK," he said. "Let's examine your situation. Have you tried fishing in shallow water?"

"You bet," I said. "And I came up zilch."

"How about deep water?"

"I tried that, too, and it didn't work. I tried minnows and I tried junk. I fished early. I fished late. I fished in the rain and I fished in the sun. I fished hot. I fished cold. I even tried fishing in the moonlight, which is what they said to do in the Expert's Field Guide to Successful Fishing. It was zip all the way."

Jackpine's lip curled into a snarl. "You dummy!" he hissed. "There are a couple of things to be done in the moonlight, but fishing ain't one of them. If you buy that, you also believe that Salmonella is an Italian singer."

"You mean he ain't?" I asked.

Jackpine smiled. "You are in deeper fertilizer than I thought. Maybe you better consider another line of work.

"Why is it so important for you to catch walleyes anyway? Just because you write about fishing does not mean you have to be good at it. Your baseball writer never played shortstop for the Chicago Cubs, although God knows he could do a better job than that rookie they just shipped out.

"Your football writer never played linebacker for the Packers. Your golf writer never won the Masters. Your racing writer never got the checkered flag at Indy. So what if the outdoor writer can't catch fish? No big deal."

"All of that is different," I said. "Since the beginning of time, Journal outdoor writers have been expected to eat raw meat, drink a vat of whisky, chase women, kill game and catch fish. It is a sort of job requirement. Up until now I've done it all except the fish part. What the hell is going on?"

"As I see it, your problem is simple," Jackpine said. "You have been unable to catch walleyes. You are snake-bit. You've lost your confidence. Your timing is gone. You've got a hitch in your stroke. And if you write one more no-fish story Terry Galvin will personally escort you to the rescue mission."

"Hey, Jackpine," I said. "Ain't that exactly what I told you a little while ago?"

"Sure it is," he said. "You had it all along. It just took me to bring it out."

"Well, I really appreciate your help," I said. "You have saved my life. If there is anything I can do in return..."

"As a matter of fact, there is," Jackpine said. "I'm taking donations for Salmonella's spring concert next month and if you'd care to contribute..."

One More Summer Song

The sands of time pile mountain high these hot, sweet, heavy days of summer.

And the fisherman is tired.

He has sucked his own blood from a thousand cuts and bites and now his stomach is sour from the salty taste.

His head aches and echoes with the whine and scream of a hundred outboard motors; the creaking, squeaking of oar locks; the rush of water curling around the bows of a dozen boats that have carried him to those places where the song begins.

The skin on his ears is tissue thin after having peeled and peeled and peeled from the burn of the sun and the slice of the wind.

He feels, generally, like an old horse that has been run hard and put up wet.

But it has been a good summer for the fisherman.

The bag has been full more than it has been empty. Kentucky crappies, Wolf River walleyes, Wisconsin trout, Michigan

> **"There'll be a turn in the wind that only old dogs like the fisherman will recognize..."**

bass...they've all fallen, in order, at one time or another. Because of it, the fisherman has been the chief fish fry sponsor more times than he can count.

And that's good. But now he's tired.

The fishing rod that has been an extension of his arm ever since the dogwoods bloomed in western Kentucky has turned dead weight. It's no longer a magic wand. It's a shovel to dig a trench, a maul to break a rock. It's work.

So what the fisherman wants to do now is follow the muskrats to their runs under the banks where it's cool and damp and dark and quiet. He wants to follow the summer-red deer deep into the tamarack swamps where they curl in the shadows and wait for night to come.

He wants to go with the osprey to the perch atop the gnarled basswood tree, there to squeeze the last drop of coolness from every riffle of wind that blows. He wants to hide in the deepest forest glade where the coyotes go, there to snap at flies and scratch at ticks and roll in the dew-damp grass.

The fisherman wants to do all this because he's tired of tourists and traffic. He has had it to the top of his waders with waiting lines in northwoods restaurants and no-vacancy motels and crowded boat ramps.

But he knows his problem, the fisherman does. It's the reverse of cabin fever.

Like the wolf grown sick from eating too much of a fresh kill, the fisherman simply has had too much of a good thing. He has fished too much, too hard, too often.

That's why the stink is forever in his nostrils. That's why soap can't wash away the constant feel of slime from his hands. That's why a gallon of whisky can't chase the corroding pain in his gut.

And that's why the magic is gone from the lakes and streams, why there's music without a melody.

But one day soon that all will change.

There will be a turn in the wind and only old dogs like the fisherman will recognize it. But it will come and the air won't be as sticky-sweet and heavy. It will be sharper, cleaner, and it will carry the edge of hope.

And somewhere down the road the lady will be waiting. Her name is autumn, and she will take the fisherman by the hand and lead him to those secret, secluded places where only the heart can go.

She'll restore the magic with her kiss. She'll paint the sumac and curl the leaves and cool the world with a touch of her fingertips. She'll put the glitter back in the stars and make them worth counting again, or worth wishing upon. She'll silver the moon and turn its beams to the forest paths where the wild ones walk.

The fisherman knows all this to be true.

That's why he closes, now, the cabin door behind him.

That's why he heads for the boat where his fishing rods and tackle box and minnow bucket wait.

That's why he is ready, once more time, to fish again.

He knows about tomorrow, the fisherman does. And maybe the music never really goes away.

In Search of the Mid-Summer Fishing Spirit

The cattails are pencil slender now…and the deer are summer red… and shadows are plastered, like wallpaper, to the lakes at night, crinkling at the edges where the water ripples.

This is when the fisherman within me dies a little.

Muskrats move only when there's need to bring more green grass for a new litter…ravens desert the sky…mother grouse draws her brood around and huddles tightly in the growth of quack grass beneath a gnarled apple tree…and the sky is lifeless blue…

This is when the fisherman within me dies a little more.

Surface water turns teacup warm…lakes thicken with weed growth…trout streams tinkle against the rocks but they are clear as your mother's crystal and the fish brood under the overhangs.

> **"There's camping on the sandbars and swimming at the beaches…"**

And so the fisherman within me dies yet another death and another after that.

This, then, is how it is.

Door County, beautiful as only Door County can be in summer: A sign along Highway 42 in Sister Bay says 384 bass have been caught since July 1. But you don't see people rushing down to the boats, fishing rods in hands.

It's more informal, this business of sport fishing in a land created for, and geared to serve, those who do not live there. The fishing opportunity is there, but somehow, I'll never think of Door County in summer as a fish camp.

And so the fisherman within me dies a little…

Lake Michigan, from Algoma to Racine: It's exotic fish country now and the boats go out every day. They catch and they kill. But it's an up-and-down thing.

You can see them from the lakefront between Two Rivers and Manitowoc. And on that beach the bones of countless alewives lie rotting in the sun. It's not a massive die-off. It's not even an altogether unpleasant thing unless you are in the company of a dog who eats the dead fish until he gets bloating sick.

But the excitement of fishing isn't there the way you'd expect it to be and that's because it's summer and the heat has burned the spirit and the breezes are cooler away from shore.

It's the same, and different, in Milwaukee where there are more people at Bradford Beach than there are out on the water trying to catch salmon or trout.

They lie along the lakeshore turning either fish-flesh red or statue bronze and watch the boats moving slowly back and forth partway to the horizon.

The fisherman within me sees nothing and senses nothing and so dies a little…

The search turns west now, first to the Wisconsin River and then to the Mississippi.

There's some camping on the sandbars and swimming at the beaches. Smoke from grills curls slowly, but inevitably, toward the sky. There's a fish fry going on here and there, but mostly it's bratwurst and hotdogs that will fill the bellies of the outdoor public.

Boat traffic is heavy and you'd like to think it's made by fishermen hurrying from one good hole to another. But, not true. The boats, mostly, are pulling people on water skis or else they contain groups trying to beat the heat and bugs by moving on the water.

And that's why the fisherman within me dies again.

The search for the midsummer fishing spirit now turns toward the north. This is the weekend and it's hot and the searcher soon discovers that every body of water, big or small, has already been discovered by a sea of people.

They lounge on blankets in the shade. Or they wade in the water. Or they swim. They suck cold drinks from cans or plastic glasses.

There's not a fishing pole in sight. And so the fisherman inside dies a little more.

But they are fishing in the north, at least the musky fishermen are. Some of the others are working at it, too; the ones who have waited a year for this two-week shot at something on the end of the rod.

But it's not like May, when you didn't know whether to wear a short-sleeved shirt or a snowmobile suit because the weather was that uncertain. It's not like those days when the rain came down in cold slants or when the wind dug holes in you.

And that's why the fisherman within me dies a little.

Depth of Fishing is Measured in Quality

I feel a sermon coming on.

What the heck, It's Sunday, isn't it? And there are those who say I'm a preacher. I know I'm a sinner. So I've got a right—it takes one to know one is how the saying goes.

So gather 'round, if you want. Listen, if you will. Or leave. Makes no difference because I'm going to sound off anyway.

We start with a parable about a man who spent his entire adult life seeking to catch a musky bigger than anyone had ever caught before.

He did not succeed.

On his deathbed, he was asked about this lifelong obsession. Was he sorry? Would he have lived life differently had he known, in the beginning, he would fail?

> **"The one question most often asked is, 'How many did you catch?'"**

Then the old man's eyes brightened. And with his final breath he said:

"Fail? What are you talking about? I didn't fail. The fishing was wonderful. I enjoyed every minute of it."

He died, then, with a smile on his lips and contentment in his heart leaving his mourners to wonder at his final words because they did not understand.

That's the first part. And now there is this...

Two men recently returned from a fishing trip to a faraway place. It was renowned because the fish there were as numerous as the hairs on a dog's back. When the men reached home the multitude gathered and asked this question:

"How many fish did you catch?"

"Six," the fishermen replied.

And the multitude mourned.

"It was a bummer, eh?" one said.

"Only six!" another said. "Did you spend all your time in saloons?"

"If you'd have caught one more you could have fed the multitudes," another said, laughing. "With a little bread, of course."

And that is the way it has been for the two men since their return from this faraway place. What it does, of course, is serve to remind that people are numbers oriented. Fishermen are good at talking conservation, but the success they recognize is the big kill, the bag limit. Anything less is failure.

Most can't understand why anyone would forego catching a bagful of small fish in favor of the opportunity to take one big one. Most are inclined to label as a waste of time any fishing effort that does not result in a big kill.

Think about it. The one question most often asked of returning fishermen is this:

"How MANY did you catch?"

How many? How many?

That's it, don't you see? That's the criterion for fishing success in this day and age. Maybe it always has been.

That's why some can slobber all over the place at getting into a bunch of emaciated northern pike. That's why some can beat their chests at having hoisted half a dozen tainted salmon out of a holding tank called Lake Michigan.

I know all about that because I've done it. I'm already guilty of the thing I'm complaining about. And, most likely, I'll be guilty of it again somewhere down the line.

But that does not make it right.

One of the most serious mistakes a man can make, not only about himself but about the environment in which he lives, is to measure the quality of recreational fishing by the weight of his stringer once he is finished.

It is wrong to do it, plainly and simply, because if you do, you are doomed to disappointment. Unless you are very good or very lucky you will never catch fish in the amount and size you hope to.

With that in your head and your heart as a measure of fishing success, you will go to those faraway places where fishing is said to be good, excellent, superb and you will be disappointed because, even in those places, fish do not jump into your boat and die.

You will find that, in those places, you may have to work hard to find the fish. You may discover there is no such thing as the easy catch, the easy kill.

In that process, you may forsake the joy that is fishing.

That would be sad.

The old guy on his deathbed had the right idea.

End of sermon. 🐾

Reed's Retreat Is Underway

W hat you see waving here today is a white flag. That means surrender; like uncircle the wagons or give me the 10 count.

Winter has won, you see. It's won big, as a matter of fact.

I'm tired of cutting holes through ice that is thicker than my spud handle is long. I'm tired of wind that likes to cut a man in two.

You can have these days when a zero temperature reading is like a heat wave. I don't want to have to coax my car to start anymore.

I no longer like the feel of my parka. It's more prison than coat.

I want to forget for a while the problems of deer hunting. I don't want to hear more of the "rights" of anti-hunters. The steel shot, lead shot argument lies simmering somewhere in the background of my memory, holding far less significance right now than the cut of the winter wind.

FAR FROM WISCONSIN. As an outdoor writer, Jay Reed enjoyed fishing in Cuba, Costa Rica and other exotic locations. This story ran on Feburary 6, 1977.

It's been a long fall and a longer winter, and open water fishing is Wisconsin is still an eternity away.

So, as you read these words, I'll be in full retreat, heading south. There's a bunch of highway ahead, and I don't figure to stop until I reach the Florida Keys.

Maybe it will be Key Largo first or maybe Islamorada, where I'll pause long enough to wet my throat with rum and fill my belly with stone crabs and soothe my soul by catching a string of ladyfish.

Maybe I'll take a run out to Alabama Jack's fishing camp on Key Largo, where the crab meat is sweet and the beer is cool and there is protection from the wind that sometimes howls in off Card Sound.

Maybe I can find an inn where the bartender wears a patch over one eye and where the spirit of Humphrey Bogart haunts the halls at night when the wind blows in fresh off the Gulf.

And, when that wears thin, I'll keep on moving until I run out of highway at Key West. There, for sure, the sun will soak the cold from my bones and chase winter from my heart. I'm going to find a place where I can watch my back trail. I'm going to let the sun do its thing and, at last, when I've turned the color of medium rare steak, I'm going to turn to some serious fishing.

It abounds in the Keys, you know. There are tarpon and bonefish and permit, spotted sea trout, barracuda, snappers, groupers and red drum.

Maybe I'll grab a charter and work for sailfish, dorado, kingfish, wahoo and amberjack. I know for sure I'm going to spend lots of time in small boats poking about the islands and mangrove outcroppings.

> **"I'm going to be in small boats, poking about the islands and mangrove outcroppings..."**

When all of that is out of my system, I'm going to head back north—SLOWLY. I'm going to fish every bridge that's fishable between Key West and Miami. There's more than 100 miles of that sort of thing just waiting for any man willing to stop his car and cast a line.

And it's not just a labor of love, either. They catch pompano, bluefish, snook, kingfish, crevalle, Spanish mackerel and more.

There's no way I'm going to leave Florida without trying for bass. Maybe that will come at Lake Seminole near Clearwater or Okeechobee or one of the rivers like St. Johns or Chipola or Oklawaha.

And you can bet I'm going to scrounge around in the Everglades for whatever the purpose.

Before it's over, I'm going to eat steamed clams on a beach while the moon hangs bright in the sky and I'm going to fry some fish out where the wind blows soft and warm and free. And when Wisconsin is in my sights again, spring will be a lot closer.

So that's the story, friends.

Reed's retreat is underway.

Come along, if you like. There's plenty of room.

When Bullheads Bite
In the Summer Sun

Talk, if you will, of trout—gleaming, gallant, glittering creatures leaping toward the sky.

Talk, if you will, of muskies—brutish, melancholy killers whose world runs red with blood; trophies hunted by many, captured by few, cherished by all who hear the song of eternity in the whine of a casting reel.

But save today for a sermon that deals with something of the heart. Save it for the slippery feeling of fish slime, the sting of a mosquito bite. Save it for mud and murky water and memories of days so long ago when there was such a wonderful thing as youth.

Save it, if you will, for a fond look backward at the bullhead.

It starts with a town—Nelson, Wisconsin—a bend in the road. The sun is hot, flies drone and the leaves of elms yet unblighted, hang thick and heavy and green. The fisherman remembers how it was when he grew up in that town. It is only a little different now.

YOU CAN'T BEAT BULLHEADS! Some may turn up their noses at these whiskered, golden-bellied fish, but Jay Reed knew better. A self-described "child of the river," he grew up catching and eating them during the Depression years of the 1930s.

Pete Armstrong's store on the corner is gone and a small, sleek, brown brick bank building stands in its place. Tourists who drive along the Mississippi on the Great River Road (Highway 35) see it when they pass.

Many of the familiar faces are gone, too, so there is some sadness. But the locals who remain in this community about 60 miles southwest of Eau Claire gather at Shorty's café in the morning. They talk about fishing or rattlesnake hunting or trapping, depending on the time of year. Bertha, or

Maymie, Alberta, or Bob dispense beer, booze and good conversation in the adjoining tavern.

And there is a railroad track within a short cast of the café.

So the fisherman from Milwaukee rolls back the years. He digs a bucket of garden worms, rigs a cane pole and walks up the track toward the first bridge to a stream called Shively Slough.

Walk a railroad track some time. The ties are too far apart to easily step on every other one. They are too close together to step on each. After a while your legs begin to tingle if you are not used to it.

And the fisherman remembers while he walks. He remembers the deer he once killed just off the right of way. He remembers the pheasants he used to shoot where the old track bed runs. He remembers the countless times he walked the railroad to look at traps or hunt ducks or just to go where he could be alone.

"Bullhead fishing is an affair of the heart…"

Then he reaches the bridge. The slough looks the same as it did so long ago when he used to swim in it. It looks the same as it did the time he smoked his first cigarette while sitting on its banks. His memory is clouded but he remembers the slough as the place where he caught the first fish of his life — a bullhead.

So he walks down to its banks again. He rigs the cane pole with a single hook and a sinker and baits up with a gob of worms. He pitches the line out into the coffee-colored water. There is no current he can see. Bits of moss float motionless on the surface. He jams the butt of the pole into the mud bank. Then he rigs a fly rod the same way and props its tip up on a forked stick left there by some earlier fisherman.

That, friends, is the way to fish.

You sit on the grass and put your back against a tree. You soak up the sun and look at the sky and, for a little while, at least, the years roll away and you go back to the time when there were more tomorrows than yesterdays, more miles ahead than behind.

Then the line on the cane pole begins to twitch, jerk. The fisherman from Milwaukee takes the pole, heaves upward and a bullhead, its yellow gut gleaming in the sunlight, flops upon the grass. The fisherman removes the hook, being careful to avoid the spikes that can send pain shooting up a man's arm, that can bring blood streaming down his fingertips.

After that it is all fishing. The bullheads bite fast, just as it used to be.

The dirt from the bait can mingles with slime from the bullheads and the fisherman's hands become caked with the smelly mixture. The fisherman is soon drawing more flies than the fish he has caught.

When the count reaches 16, he stops fishing. He cuts a forked stick and slides the bullheads down each side. It is the kind of homemade stringer he used to use when such money he had was better spent for shotgun shells than metal contraptions to hang fish upon.

And that is all there is to it except that the fish were cleaned and eaten.

Well, it really wasn't all.

Bullhead fishing now, as it always has been, is an affair of the heart. And for those who care enough, the feeling grows that a man will be remembered not for the bridges he built, or the buildings he designed, but for the bullheads he caught while sitting on the bank of some muddy stream where time cannot reach.

CHAPTER 4

A Mixed Bag

INTRODUCTION

Jay Reed likely covered a million miles chasing stories across three continents over 40 years, leading him to some surprises along the way. A lot of unexpected things came round the bend in the form of tales not ordinarily told by the average hook-and-bullet writer. Jay Reed dug into such stories enthusiastically.

The stories Jay selected for this chapter reveal a lot about the man, especially his river-town past and the characters who taught him how to work hard and play hard. As you'll see, the pupil learned well from his teachers.

Some stories showcase a sly sense of humor, oftentimes more than a little ribald. And the topics he covered sometimes ranged far from whitetails and walleyes.

So, turn the page and enjoy a tasty blend of stories just a little bit different from the rest.

Imagination Soars
On Magic Mountain

There is a twin-knobbed hill at rural Nelson from which, if you believe in good and happy magic, it is possible to touch the stars.

Its flanks are slashed with scarlet now where sumac has spilled its blood-red stain. And it wears a crown of rust and lemon and burnished brown. Approaching dusk turns it all softly purple.

You have seen it standing stately on your right if you have ever driven north from LaCrosse on Highway 35 through this little bend-in-the-road town on what is called the Great River Road.

What the hill shows, to those who care enough to look, is its craggy, wrinkled, limestone face.

On its right cheek there is a pockmark. You see it clearly from your car window as a black dot. It is a cave—time's penetration of the rock formations, enlarged by the probing fingers of the wind.

The hill and the cave once made a magic mountain for a young man. As he approached manhood, all the roads to all the exciting places of the world began there.

From his hill, the youth prowled the back alleys of Hong Kong, where he smelled the smells of the sea and rotting fish flesh and unwashed bodies. He saw

SCENIC OVERLOOK. Jay Reed returned to this sweet scene from his youth to write a piece for his column entitled, "Jay Reed's Wisconsin."

the women with almond eyes. He rode a junk on the China Sea and he breathed deeply of the heady, acrid stuff called opium.

From his hill, he worked the deck of a sailing ship. He went to Madrid, where he drank wine straight from the bottle, spilling some on the glistening hair of a willing companion for the night.

He ate himself bloating sick on roast suckling pig and steamed clams. And then he drank the thick, black coffee and sipped sweet brandy. And afterwards, soft Spanish moonlight splashed upon a balcony.

From his hill he went to war. He marched with the bravest of the brave. The sound of shot and shell rang gloriously in his head and the mountain became a battlefield where the enemy always died and he was always a hero.

Then the years mounted as ever, one upon the other, and he began to walk the magic roads leading from his hill. They became real roads that led him to the back alleys of Hong Kong. He drank wine in Madrid and beer in Australia. He ate rice in Korea and raw fish in Vietnam. He met some of the men and loved some of the women.

And he went to war. But it was different. There was no magic then, even in the exotic places. There was hunger and there was fear and there was loneliness.

Once on a black night he sat on another hill and the sky turned bright with shell fire and

"It is where my insight into the world begins..."

the air was filled with the crackling sounds of guns spitting death. His guts ached from tightness and his throat turned sandy dry.

No magic could help him then, for the possibility was very real that this was the place where he was going to die. So he pressed his face close to the ground, still hot from the day's sun.

He closed his eyes...

And he went back to his magic mountain.

But he was not a hero anymore.

That is the way of it, you see.

If you should one day drive up the Great River Road and if the spirit should so move, stop at the south edge of Nelson. Take a long, hard look at the magic mountain.

It is a place where the boy, now a man, still goes to look for a little bit of yesterday.

Perhaps, if you listen with your heart, you'll hear the wind sing of eternity. You may see a golden road paved with such dreams as never can be broken.

Maybe you'll taste wine from a bottle and feel the swell of a ship beneath your feet. Maybe you'll see Hong Kong and the women with almond eyes.

I go there, you see, because this is my magic mountain. It is where my Wisconsin and my insight into the world begins.

It is the place where, if you believe in magic, you can touch the stars.

The Trapper Touched Many, And Now He's Gone

There are no happy words here today. Just syllables damp with tears. The Trapper is dead, you see, and that's why. He took it on home last month, too tough to die but too sick to live.

We dressed him in wool pants and flannel shirt, open at the neck. We put a pair of trail moccasins on his feet. And then we put him in a gray box with a flag over it and we sent him down the Hanging Road to the place of the dead, a waxen replica of what he had been in life.

The Trapper was really dead and a lot of people couldn't believe that because he was of such stuff as stability and continuity are made.

So they came to the chapel in the little river town of Nelson, Wisconsin, on that Sunday of hearts, Valentine's Day, the other trappers did, and the hunters and the fishermen, for he was one of them, and the townsfolk who knew him because Nelson was the only place he had ever lived.

And there were others, too, because The Trapper's life was never a tunnel. So the artists came, the ones who put paint on canvas to make pictures, the ones from Chicago, the ones who had visited him in life because he was a painter, too, to be studied and to study with.

There were writers there because he had always been the one with words, the one with quotes to be published. And there were those from high places in the world of conservation because The Trapper had given of himself to them, as well, in the years gone before.

BROTHER AND MENTOR. Huck Siefert (left) was 10 years older than his little brother, Jay Reed. Huck helped raise Jay, was his father figure, and taught him how to hunt, fish and trap.

A man of God, who drives a school bus and digs graves on the side, said some words and read some verses and two women sang some songs of faith.

214

And that was that. Then they closed the gray box and that was the last we were to see of The Trapper as he was in life and death.

He touched the lives of many, The Trapper did, and rough, tough men talked about it, voices choking, after the funeral. Everybody had a story or three, most having to do with something they had learned from, or been given by, The Trapper.

But there was one who remembered more than the others. He was a boy grown old and through the tears of the moment the lessons, some of them, came back.

It was The Trapper who told him that he should never, ever kill a wild bird or animal just to watch it die.

It was The Trapper who showed him how it is that things wild are beautiful beyond all

> **"Live your life, The Trapper told him, so you will never have to lie..."**

other beauty and that they should be treasured and honored and saved within the context of solid conservation.

The Trapper had instructed him in gun safety long before that became an "in" thing. The Trapper had shown him how to take beaver and mink and muskrats; how and where to place setlines and how to set gill nets and mend them.

It was The Trapper who had told him how to read the story of animal movement by the tracks and trails they leave behind. The Trapper had shown him how to clean fish, how to skin an otter, how to stretch a fox pelt, how to sharpen a knife, how to walk through the woods silently as a soft breeze.

The Trapper had taught him about truth and honesty and ethics. Never molest another man's traps, never take the first shot when you can let a companion do it, never cut a fence or leave a gate open, never shoot the last duck or kill the last muskrat or catch the last fish. Live your life, The Trapper had told him, so that you will never have to lie.

The Trapper taught him how to paddle a canoe, watch for rattlesnakes, patch a pair of waders, how to read the wind, how to understand the stars and moon.

The Trapper had never married but he was able to tell the boy grown old about love and devotion and loyalty and respect. With all those things you have everything, he had said. Without them you have nothing.

It had been The Trapper who taught him about the joys of music, the beauty of color, the depth that feelings can run to, that softness and sensitivity, at the right time, are strengths to be cherished.

And The Trapper, by example, taught him about charity, sharing. The boy grown old spent a lifetime watching The Trapper share of himself, his knowledge and sometimes, what little money he had.

The Trapper was his own person with no pretenses. His priorities were in order. If the marshes and swamps of the Mississippi were his passion, and they were, then the paints and the brushes that could create images of beauty were the lights that guided him through the nights that would never end.

He could build a house but wasn't a carpenter. He could wire a room but he was no electrician. He could do plumbing but he was no plumber.

What he was, though, was special, very special, which is why so many people said things would never be the same now that The Trapper is gone.

The boy grown old knows all about that. For he, now, is diminished by that part of him which was The Trapper. And so is that considerable part of his life that was put together and molded and directed and nurtured by The Trapper.

That's why, when fall comes, the boy grown old will go back alone to the swamps. And maybe, when a pair of mallards sweep low over a point of trees or when a buck comes crashing out of a stand of willows or when a beaver slaps its tail on the water or when the wind moans sadly through dry marsh grass, he will see, through misty eyes, a shadow where there is no tree.

The Trapper's name, you see, was Glenn William (Huck) Siefert.

He Built
A Cathedral

To some men, life is a long, lonely tunnel with no beginning and no ending. The accident of birth puts them somewhere within it and they proceed down its course neither walking nor running, neither stumbling nor staggering, until the inevitability of death removes them from it.

Hanging, then, on a cobweb tie in between is a lifetime during which they have made no waves, rocked no man's boat, carved no etchings upon the rocks of time for which they might be remembered.

It's sad, really, for there is a better way. I know that to be true because I once knew a man—a simple man—who was never famous except to the few people around whom his life revolved. Yet, with the lumber of his life, he built a cathedral that will stand just as long as there are those living who remember him for what he was.

LIFE OF A RIVERMAN. A towboat pushes a barge down the Mississippi, near the local stretch of the river where Peter John Railes once lived.

His name isn't important anymore because the snows of seven winters have fallen upon his grave at the outskirts of the little river town in Wisconsin where he had lived. But, for the record, it was Peter John Railes.

He was a riverman, the likes of which you hardly ever see anymore. His house was a barge with a one-room shack built on it. He had it anchored in a sheltered bay off the Mississippi next to a high bank so that it would rise when the water went up and lower when it dropped. A 14-foot river scow was his automobile.

He wore hip boots and a hunting coat with more grace and style than most men wear a tuxedo. He handled a fishing rod the same way an

217

orchestra leader holds a baton. He was a magician with a boat. And he knew more about the birds, fish and other animals of Wisconsin than any man I've ever met.

I knew him for more years than I can remember. And to me he always seemed like an old man.

In those earlier days, if I ever wanted to catch some fish, all I had to do was go out to Railes' barge and ask the old man if I could fish with him. He'd almost always do it. We'd go out in his scow and he'd pole me through the back waters, saying "cast over there" or "try a minnow here".

If it was walleyes I wanted, he produced them. Or northerns or bass. And when it was over we'd go back to his barge and he'd brew coffee and we'd drink it black and hot.

A good way to measure any outdoorsman is by what he puts back in the woods and waters from which he takes each year. Well, in his lifetime the old man must have killed a mountain or more of meat. But whatever he took out, he put back a hundredfold.

> **"A good way to measure any outdoorsman is by what he puts back..."**

He was the man out in the woods each winter when the snow was deep, cutting brush piles for rabbits. He was the one who would snowshoe for miles with a sack of corn on his back to feed pheasants. He cut browse for deer. And his major expense in winter was buying seed for his bird feeder.

There must be generations of wildlife along the river right now only because long years ago the old man had stomach enough to fight the weather to see that their ancestors might live.

The old man was really something. He could talk to you intelligently about geology, biology, affairs of the world. He could show a boy how to make a whistle out of a slip of green willow. He could overhaul an outboard motor. He was a little bit of a plumber, a little bit of a carpenter.

He drank whisky neat—sometimes too much of it. And he wasn't a religious man. But he sometimes made it to the little white church in town on Sundays and if the weather was warm the flies had a way of buzzing about him because most often he smelled mighty like a fish.

Peter John Railes was not a recluse, in the normal sense of the word. He lived alone for most of his adult life. But it wasn't always that way. And you should know about that, too, if you are to understand.

The old man's river shack was furnished about the way you'd think an old riverman's house would be furnished. But there were two things inside that caught your eye right away. One was the sort of casual neatness with which he kept his house.

The other was a picture frame which held two faded photographs. One was of Railes as a much younger man. He wore the army uniform of World War I. In a corner of the frame there was a bit of frayed purple and white ribbon.

"I forgot to duck once," he'd say.

The other picture was of a young woman, dark haired, bright eyed and pretty.

"That was my wife," he'd mutter to a first-time visitor who'd ask.

And sometimes, if the mood was right and if he was pushed, he'd tell how it was long years before when, on a day late in May when the river was high, she was swept from a boat by an overhanging limb.

"I couldn't get to her," he would say.

And then, sometimes, he'd tell the rest: how it was he who pulled her body from a bank of rushes where it had been washed high. And he'd tell how he heard the bugles in the cemetery at town while he was poling the boat carrying his wife's body because it all happened, you see, on Memorial Day.

Anyway, a lot of years had passed in between and time had healed as best it could. But once the old man told me he was never more lonely than when he was feeding pheasants or cutting brush piles for the rabbits.

"She liked to go out in the snow," he recalled. She felt sorry for those animals so I've kept up the feeding all along and I suppose it was mostly because of her."

I had to live a long time before I realized how much it hurt the old man inside to do the things he did: that every time he went into the woods a ghost went with him.

So that is all there is to tell about Peter John Railes, a man whole life was never a tunnel.

I hope, one day, I'll meet the old man again. Maybe he'll take me fishing or maybe he'll make a whistle for me or maybe he'll help me build another tower in the sky.

But, for now, while winter is here and the snow lies thick and cold upon his grave and while there are pheasants to be fed and brush piles for rabbits to be cut, I'll remember the old man for what he was.

And God, I hope he isn't lonesome any more.

Beaver Tail Soup
Tastes Better than it Sounds

O ne of the fringe benefits involved in living with, and frequently in, the outdoors, is the opportunity to eat certain kinds of food not readily available to everyone else.

And if you live that way long enough, you get to the point where your stomach is hardly ever surprised at what you send along for its attention.

With that out of the way, we can move right along, then, to the story of the recent day when the outdoor writer cooked beaver tail soup.

You read it right: Beaver tail soup.

Now it may occur to someone that Providence intended the tail of a beaver to serve only those purposes to which a beaver might put it. But that's not true. If it were, the world would also have been forever deprived of such delicacies as fried fish jowls or baked heart of venison.

The most difficult part of making beaver tail soup is the acquisition of a beaver tail. You can't go to the market and buy one. You can't order one. And you can't substitute for it. You need the genuine article. Since we were trapping beaver recently with moderate success along the Mississippi River in Nelson, Wisconsin, there has been no shortage of beaver tails.

RODENT DELICACY? Some columnists will go to any length to get a great story idea….even facing down a steaming bowl of beaver tail soup.

What was needed was courage. Beaver tails in their natural form are not things of extreme beauty and are to be best admired only by other beaver. They are flat, rather oblong and covered with a thick, black coat of skin and scales.

The book on wild game cookery said removal of the tail covering was simple. Just put it in a hot pan, it said, then let the skin bubble up. Then peel it away, exposing a clean white section of bone, fat and gristle.

Let it be said now that the book on wild game cookery didn't really tell it like it is. You put a beaver tail in a hot pan and the first thing it does is smoke and smell a lot. But the skin did bubble and it did peel rather easily. Only what was left was still largely discolored and rough and not very good to look at.

But a fillet knife did the trick. I skinned the tail and what was left was a clean white section of bone, fat and gristle.

A beaver tail has bone running directly down its center. So I sliced the meat away from it, cubed the strips and, as they say in the food department, sautéed them in a little butter.

Then came water until the pot was half full. Into the water along with sautéed cubes of beaver tail went three diced onions, four sliced carrots, three sliced stalks of celery, a quarter cup of barley and a heck of a lot of salt and pepper.

> **"Put a beaver tail in a hot pan and the first thing it does is smoke and smell a lot..."**

Now I don't know if you should bring soup to a boil or not. But I did. Then I turned the flame down, put a cover on the pot and forgot the whole business for two hours.

Forgot? Not really.

If you ever cook beaver tail soup, you'll soon discover the best part about it, in the beginning, is the smell. It's good. Really good. So I didn't completely forget about it.

And the taste? Not bad. It's heavy soup. And rich. Very rich. It isn't something you could handle every day. But if you serve it with a light, dry wine between smoked carp and roast haunch of venison, you'll find it to be first-rate.

On the other hand, it has been said if you put enough onions, salt and pepper into a pot of water, you could boil your moccasins and they wouldn't taste bad.

That may be stretching it.

I'll take beaver tail every time.

One Man's Dreams Go
On the Block

They stood in the bland sunshine of an early Sunday afternoon here in Pepin, Wisconsin, and matched dollars for dreams and money for memories.

When they were finished, all that remained of the life and times of a man named R.L. (Pete) Armstrong were scattered to the winds of men, some who knew him and many who did not.

It was an auction, you see, and auctions are not normally the city fellow's bag. But he was on assignment here in this land of western Wisconsin to pick up a story or two related to the outdoors.

The city fellow had pulled into Dorothy's Café in Pepin for a sandwich break between fishing

> **"Pete had given him the first real job he ever had..."**

trips when he saw the orange auction bill with its black lettering.

"Household and antique auction, Russell and Pete Armstrong Estate," it said.

Pete had checked out last winter. The city fellow knew that. It wasn't really unexpected and there was even some reason to rejoice because winters were always tough on Pete. He was a little man, in body at least. He weighed barely 100 pounds and he used to say that if the winds of winter were any sharper they'd cut him in half. He never really knew what it was like to be physically warm from the last of August to the first of June of any year.

And so when Pete took that long, lonely walk last November, the city fellow thought to himself: "Well, at least Pete ain't going to be cold anymore."

So it was that an afternoon of fishing was canceled and the city fellow drove a mile east of Pepin on Highway 35 to the farm which once was the home of an old friend.

Friend — he was that all right. But he was something more and the city fellow tried to set it all straight in his mind as he walked up the pine-lined lane toward the house.

There was a time when the city fellow was a country boy and Pete had given him the first real job he ever had. The farm where the auction was held used to be a chicken ranch and Pete hired country boys to clean pens.

222

This was fine for it gave the boys pocket money at a time when there wasn't much money to be had.

But Pete knew that the country boy was hung up on hunting, trapping, and fishing. Even though he had no children of his own, he understood that the boy was more of a prisoner in those pens than the chickens they were designed to hold.

Pete also owned a grocery and feed store in a town called Nelson, six miles south of Pepin. So he agreed to let the boy trap mice and rats at the feed store, giving him a chance to make some money and still spend time in the swamps where the boy really wanted to be in the first place.

Once in a while, Pete would leave the boy in charge of the store and those were great moments because the cash drawer held more money than the youngster had ever seen before and protecting it was the first real responsibility he ever knew.

Then there were those once-a-month trips to a nearby town for steaks with Pete and Roy Ott. It was here the boy learned for the first time how to order from a menu, how to deal with a waitress. It is not big stuff unless you have ever been a country boy yourself. Then you know.

It is sad, really, that country boys grow into city fellows. Years sped by and a couple of wars happened that touched everybody and things were never really the same after that.

The country boy turned city fellow used to see Pete once in awhile. They would talk and laugh and remember the old days and Pete would always ask about hunting or fishing or trapping. He always wondered how the city fellow could make a living at outdoor writing when he did so poorly at such a simple thing as trapping mice in a feed store.

But the important thing is, you see, that Pete never forgot.

That is why the city fellow attended the auction that day. He didn't stay long. Just time enough to see the old bed where Pete slept out most of his last days. Just hours enough to see the old desk from his grocery store, some of the incubators from his chicken farm, a couple of saddles from his last days as a leather salesman.

The city fellow stood underneath a willow tree well away from the crowd and listened as somebody bought an old coal scuttle for $4.50, a trunk full of books and papers for $3. Everything went. But the city fellow didn't hang around to see it all.

He walked around the grounds and looked at the furniture and the jars and the harnesses and the shovels and the rolls of wire. And he knew that he was in the process of losing a grip on a little bit of yesterday.

Wisconsin Holds
Highways to Heaven

The steaks had been blood rare and thick as a plush carpet, but by the time the heady conversation began, they were no more than memories impaled upon toothpicks of time.

But there was coffee, black as a raven's wing, when the meal was done and there was cognac soft enough to bring just a gentle glow of warmth to the heart. And as the level inside of the bottle sank slowly downward, it became apparent that wisdom, too, had been captured in that fine French container.

Huddled inside the cottage near Bayfield, Wisconsin, that day were a pulp and paper industry technician, a biologist and this nomadic newspaperman. They hunched around a table laden now with the remnants of what had been a fine dinner just a short time before.

They were prisoners of the elements, for wind clawed at the cottage and made it creak. And the waves of Lake Superior danced to an ugly go-go beat and the sky drooped low enough to touch the tops of trees. Clearly, a storm was brewing and it was no day to test the intentions of the lake or the queen of fate that made it boil so ominously.

So the men talked, as men will when there is nothing else to do. They talked of fish they had landed and animals they had killed.

SUPERIOR VIEW. **The Lake Superior shoreline, from Ashland through Bayfield, was Jay Reed's favorite scenic drive. He enjoyed it often from Highway 13**

And they talked about roads, highways they had traveled at one time or another — which, significantly, happens to be the subject of this Sunday's sermon.

Somebody mentioned the slashed opening that glides across the near north of Wisconsin, the one that shows up on maps as Highway 70. Follow it from end to end and you see just about everything Wisconsin has to offer from dirt farms and smoke-stacked industrial communities to an ocean of greening timber.

And somebody mentioned Highway 32 which memorializes the famed Red Arrow Division from Wisconsin and Michigan, which fought on five fronts in World War I. If you are a fisherman and you follow 32 from beginning to end you will touch water that contains every kind of sport fish attainable in the state.

Somebody spoke of a little segment of Highway 11 from Benton west to Hazel Green and on to the Wisconsin-Iowa border, and of Highway 59 through the Kettle Moraine, and of Highway 35 north from LaCrosse to Maiden Rock and Bay City along the lip of the Mississippi River.

Sure enough, these are great roads. All of them. And there are so many more in Wisconsin. Broad strips of concrete that can carry all the cars in the state or little dirt-covered trails down which no more than one vehicle at a time can go.

> **"It is the prettiest and most comforting drive I know..."**

These roads can take a man to a corner of paradise; they can take him to exciting places or to places of great beauty, they can take a man, even, to eternity.

But let me tell you about a road up in the northwest corner of Wisconsin.

It is man tough and woman pretty. It sweeps and glides and dips over and around that bulge of land that marks Wisconsin's ceiling, the northernmost part of the state.

It is that segment of Highway 13 that curves off of Highway 2 just west of Ashland and then cuts north where Lake Superior crashes against the coastline. It is the prettiest, most comforting drive I know in this state.

It will take you to Washburn and to Bayfield and Cornucopia, Herbster and Port Wing.

Drive it in spring and you can smell the apple blossoms outside Washburn. You'll cross a bridge which spans the Big Sioux River, a stream as pretty as any you've ever seen. You'll see rocky cliffs where the surf rolls in and splashes high, leaving a spray of silvery diamonds in the air. And if the sun is shining you'll see a rainbow there.

If you've ever been to New England, you'll see it all again when you top a hill on Highway 13 and drop down into Bayfield. Its harbor is straight out of Moby Dick. Summer or winter, to these eyes, at least, it has to be among the prettiest of all pretty towns in Wisconsin. It is clean and bright. Its streets are uncluttered. The sand of its beaches shine as if they were paved with gold.

On a clear day you can see in the shadowy distance the shores of Madeline Island, largest of all the Apostles. And if you have an ounce of romance in your soul, you will have to remember the legend of the great Indian chief who pegged rocks at a fleeing enemy and how those rocks became the Apostles.

Drive northward then through the Red Cliff Indian Reservation and then into a sea of wilderness. You're going through the barrens now, one of this state's truly wild and remote forest areas.

Next you'll come to Cornucopia and, down on the beach, you'll see the remnants of the sailing ships that once worked the waters of Lake Superior. Then there will be Herbster where the Cranberry River flows and there will be Port Wing hard by the banks of the river called Flag.

You may, on your trip, see deer or bear. Ravens will circle in the sky. But, always, the landscape will change and around each bend there will be sights you may not have seen before.

There is no need to travel that segment of Highway 13 if you are in a hurry because the road was not built for speed. In fact, you do yourself an injustice if you even so much as hurry.

Travel it in winter and you will know it to be tough as leather, demanding of you and your vehicle.

I have driven the route many times. More than once, it was not because I had to be there, but simply because it brought me comfort to travel its length.

The thought persists now, as it did that windy day in the cottage on the shore of Lake Superior, that a man, in the end, will not be remembered for the whisky he drank or the women he loved or the novels he wrote.

Instead, he may be remembered for the roads he traveled.

So, one day soon, I'm going back to that portion of Highway 13... up where paradise begins.

In River's Bubble, Death Takes a Renegade

A dog, even a renegade, has a right to die with dignity. To go out with a bullet in its brain while chasing deer is one thing. For that, in the manner of any criminal, is playing the hand the way it is dealt. But to die screaming with fear in its eyes and terror in its heart, is something else.

In some places along the Chippewa River, there is a thin shelf of ice now, where the water is sheltered and the current slow. Beneath the ice, the water bubbles dark and deep.

The two men had left their car off highway 35 near Pepin, Wisconsin. They walked down the high bank toward the brushy corner where the Chippewa dumps into the Mississippi River. The December air, cold and clear, carried sounds of the woods, intermingled, faintly at first with the throaty yelps of dogs at trail.

© ISTOCKPHOTO.COM

The men walked and listened as the sounds of the running dogs grew louder. Ahead, through a clearing, a deer flashed into sight moving straight for the river.

HAUNTINGLY BEAUTIFUL, yet dangerous, is a bubbling stream with a shelf of winter ice. This story was published December 8, 1969.

It was a doe and it covered great chunks of ground in high, graceful leaps. The doe hesitated only for an instant at the bank of the river, cleared all but the outer edge of the ice shelf in one mighty jump and began the long swim across the Chippewa.

The dogs were only minutes behind. There were two of them and they bellowed into view with tails wagging and noses close to the ground. They came to the river edge, stopped and whirled in tight little circles, whining and barking as they watched the deer swim away.

227

One, brown and white with long ears and a lonesome baritone voice, scrambled down the bank and stood, front feet on the ice, for a moment, then took a half dozen steps forward to continue pursuit.

The ice gave way and the dog disappeared into the black water. It bobbed up and managed to get two front feet on the ice shelf. The ice broke. The dog tried again and again. Each time the ice gave way and the current pulled at the animal sucking it down.

The men hurried to the spot. They cut two poles and placed them on the ice. One man lay on his stomach and inched toward the struggling dog.

The animal's front legs were bleeding where the ice had slashed its skin. Its eyes were glazed with fright and its yelps turned to pleading screams of terror.

The man on the ice reached toward the animal, and the dog, in one final try for life, lurched toward the outstretched hand. Fingers closed on a bit of fur. Then they slipped and held nothing. Black water swirled over the dog's head.

> **"Its eyes were glazed with fright, its yelps turned to pleading screams of terror..."**

The air, filled moments before with the sounds of death, turned suddenly silent. The second dog disappeared into the woods. The man on the ice slid back to safety. The Chippewa rolled on. Its water lapped at the hole in the ice, washed away the stain of blood.

The hunters stared at the scene a moment, then walked away...haunted by the end of a renegade dog that was denied death with dignity.

Another Fine Mess
To Toss at the DNR

What God giveth, the DNR taketh away.
— Bumper sticker literature

The Wisconsin Department of Natural Resources, a sort of godfather to us all in one way or another, is a public punching bag to a greater degree than other state agencies.

You got a gripe? You got a complaint? Any kind. Any kind at all. Well, lay it on the DNR, then, because it has been a receptacle for public spittle since the beginning of time.

The DNR has been blamed for more wrong doing than tight underwear.

The public has left charges at the DNR's doorstep wrapped in everything but a blue blanket with a pinned-on note.

The agency has been accused of being too tough, or too easy, on water and air polluters; too conservative, or too liberal, with hunting and fishing regulations; too

DEVIL'S LAKE. An incident at Devil's Lake State Park near Baraboo, was a cause for concern and complaints to the DNR.

strong, or too weak, in promoting tourism; oversensitive, or insensitive, to the needs of people. It has been blamed for the weeds in Pewaukee Lake.

There's a lot more, too, but you get the idea.

Some of the charges, some of the complaints are deadly serious, significant and right on target. Some are funny. Some are sad. Some are ridiculous.

And here's the latest one that appeared in the statewide press last week. Damned if I know which category to put it in. Crazy, maybe.

It seems that a kindly grandmother from Chilton, Wisconsin, where morality runs rampant, recently visited Devil's Lake State Park, where it does not.

The grandmother complained that while she was at the park she observed a young woman take off her shirt, under which there was nothing but the young woman herself.

The woman, according to the complaint, while thus bare-breasted, not only sunned herself but walked freely around the park for an hour or two.

While admitting there was "no cavorting" involved, the Chilton grandmother was nonetheless disturbed by all of this and complained to her legislator, who has been harrumphing about it ever since. Legislators are good at harrumphing.

The grandmother and the legislator blamed the whole thing on the DNR. I mean what else would any good citizen and politician do?

DNR is in charge of parks, right? We can't have everybody at Devil's Lake going around taking their clothes off like they do at some of the beaches on the Wisconsin River, now can we?

"You got a complaint? Lay it on the DNR, a receptacle for public spittle since the beginning of time..."

That sort of thing can spread like sunburn or rash. God knows where it could end.

"If that happens today, what will happen next Saturday?" as the Chilton woman put it in her complaint.

It is that part about next Saturday that may trigger immediate action by the DNR.

While one could not expect the agency to drop its research projects, its work on water pollution, its fish and game management programs to get at this nudity thing, it is reasonable to believe that some little attention will be paid to it.

You can bet they won't send in a squad of game wardens equipped with binoculars to do the job. It would sniff of storm-trooper tactics.

Nor will they beef up park patrols significantly to prowl among patrons and pounce upon the first young lady to bare her breasts to the sun or whomever else might care to look, including grandmothers from Chilton and state legislators.

No. The DNR will be more subtle than that.

This looks like work for a district director, his assistant, perhaps, and maybe an underling or two.

They'll get the people in equipment to issue them spy glasses that look like pocket combs or something. They'll get out of their three-piece suits and neckties and into their grubbies. They'll infiltrate the throngs at Devil's Lake.

You can bet, then, that any young lady who bares her breasts will be observed. Boy, will she be observed.

And justice will be done.

OK. Enough is enough.

The point of this whole thing is to suggest, once again, that while the DNR is sometimes rapped with good cause, it is frequently hit with complaints over which the agency has little or no control.

And that is unfair.

Also unfair is the legislator's quoted outrage that the DNR would allow nudity on state property.

DNR does not "allow" it. Nor does it "allow" a lot of the other hanky-panky that sometimes goes on in state parks, some of which would curl the hair of the grandmother from Chilton if she ever saw it.

A bare-breasted maiden on the beach at Devil's Lake just does not seem to be an uplifting problem for DNR, given the context of the times.

Yesterday Rushes In, Then it Flees

Sometimes yesterday comes roaring at you like a freight train and you are stuck on the crossing. Can't move.

Then it smacks you broadside and bends you double, leaving you sulking in some dark corner and the only sounds are whimpers because you can't go back.

There was this recent day and the man felt as miserable inside as the weather was outside. There was no way he could face it so he retreated to the deepest, darkest recess of his cave, which is really a house in the suburbs.

He sat down on the stool in front of his work table, where he stared directly into the eye of chaos. The furnace hummed a dirge of dollars, so he turned on the radio to drown it out.

But the ghost of fuel bills yet to come had a voice like a bullhorn, so he turned his attention to the work table. Chaos gazed fixedly back at him, but the man vowed he would not blink first.

His eyes took casual inventory. My God! In just a glance he saw a can of Neatsfoot boot oil, six shotgun slugs, four .30-30 rifle shells, two boat lights, a coil of rope, a can of Browning extra fine gun oil

MESS O' TACKLE. Every serious fisherman is familiar with this sort of scene. Looks like time to tackle that mess!

and a pile of tailfeathers from ringneck pheasants that had died bloody but honorable deaths last fall.

There was an empty bottle from Outdoor Editor Ron Leys' Bayside Winery that once held velvet-smooth Zinfandel, vintage this very year. Beside it were two fishing reels, an old Pflueger Supreme and a new Zebco Omega 156.

And there was more.

Three boxes of nails, an unused deer tag No. 290-280 from last year, a gun cleaning kit, an empty coffee can, a container of WD-40, a cardboard box

232

holding potatoes and a bag of onions, an ash tray, a 300-yard spool of Nitro premium six-pound-test monofilament fishing line, a couple of fountain pens and a yellowed copy of the *Milwaukee Journal*.

There was something more, too: A tangled mound of spinners, plugs, spoons, plastic worms, jigs, sinkers, leaders and assorted other fishing tackle.

Anybody with an eye for order would have called it, politely, a mess. And that's what the man thought, too. That old line about a place for everything and everything in its place could in no way apply.

But he said he wouldn't be the first to blink and he wasn't. What he did, instead, was paw through the mound of assorted fishing tackle, and right there is where the part comes in about yesterday and freight trains.

From the tangle of metal, feathers, plastic, wood, lead, and line his eyes picked out a scarred and scraped spoon that once had been painted red and white. Its single set of treble hooks were corroded around the eye.

> **"He owned a grand total of three fishing lures..."**

He worked it free from the tangle and held it in the palm of his hand. Except for little patches here and there, the paint was gone. On the back side, the original silver side, was stamped: DAREDEVLE, Detroit, USA. It was a lure that clearly had been to the wars and back.

What the man knew, then, was that he was holding yesterday in his hand. He was holding a time from his own past, a time when he owned a grand total of three big-name fishing lures: a Bass-O-Reno, a red and white jointed River Runt and the Dardevele, Detroit, USA.

He was rich then. The richest, in fact.

He had carried them around on his bicycle in a tin can and when he took one out they all came out. He fished them from an old South Bend rod and a Pflueger Akron casting reel, a combination he never could have afforded at the time.

But he'd found the rod and reel beside a cottonwood tree off the old Wabasha Road up in Buffalo County, and his mother had made him wait three full days for someone to claim it before he could keep it.

Once he cleaned the reel and oiled it and filled it with black, nylon casting line, he had the greatest fishing outfit in the world. He could zing any one of those three baits for ungodly distances, with backlash only once every three or four casts.

Of the three baits, he remembered the Daredevle to be the absolute best most of the time. He caught northern pike on it and walleyes and bass. Once a channel catfish hit it and the fish weighed a couple of corn cobs and some chaff over eight pounds on the scale at Johnny Kennedy's feed store. He was a hero for several days after that.

The man looked at the bait in his hand. It was old and bent and scarred. He knew it hadn't seen water for years. In fact, the man couldn't remember the last time he had fished any red-and-white wobbling spoon, otherwise known as a Dardevele.

And he wondered why. It its day, it was the best.

He put it back, then, gently on the mound of tangled fishing gear. He knew he would never use the bait again. And he realized, too, that he could never, ever again fish with his South Bend rod and his Pflueger Akron reel. They were gone, he knew, just as those days were gone. Only the scarred fishing lure, and some lingering sorrow, remained.

I Am a Gun...
I Can Kill You

These are the days when many Wisconsin residents have already begun preparing for the hunting seasons. They are buying new weapons or caring for old ones. They are going to shooting ranges or to city dumps or old stone quarries or out-of-the- way forest lots to practice shooting. They are getting ready for a time of year which can bring ultimate joy—or deepest tragedy. It is time, then, to say this to them...

I am a gun.

Treat me right or I'll kill you.

You know me as a rifle or a shotgun or a handgun. I come in sizes and shapes to fit the tastes of everyone. But no matter what my model, size or cost, my mission is always the same—to kill.

What I kill depends upon the man who uses me. I'm used for hunting and this is where I'm at my best— or worst—depending, again, upon the man whose finger is at my trigger.

Is he a wise man or a fool? It makes no difference to me.

© ISTOCKPHOTO.COM

WATCH THAT MUZZLE! Firearm safety can never be overly stressed to sportsmen no matter how experienced they are. Jay Reed did his readers a service with this reminder.

The wise man will realize the power he commands each time he cradles me in his arms. He'll know that in less time than it takes to blink an eye. I can destroy what someone has taken a lifetime to build.

He will know, if he is wise, that in one blinding instant I can make children fatherless and turn wives into weeping widows. And it all depends on him.

But what of the fool who uses me to commit a crime or takes me into a forest crowded with humans? I'll do his bidding, too. My voice will roar and I'll spit leaden death when he points and squeezes. I'll help him rob. I'll help him murder. I'll help him take a life in the most senseless way of all — by accident.

If I have a failing, it is that I make no distinction between the wise man and the fool. I am a companion for both.

Race, creed, or color mean nothing to me. I am blindly faithful to whoever puts me in operation. I'll perform in the extremes of heat and cold, in wind and rain. I'll make my voice heard under conditions so varied and complex as to make my metal muscles seem strong beyond all comprehension.

I'll gleam brightly in a mahogany and glass case and I'll rust and corrode in mud and muck.

> **"My mission is always the same — to kill..."**

Men have paid thousands of dollars to own me. Others have paid less than a hundred. I have been the object of men's pride. I've been a conversation piece. I've been owned by some who never fired me at anything except a clay target.

But, for the most part, there is only one reason anyone would want me — not to frighten, not to wound, not to adore — but to kill. For that is my business.

I am a shotgun, a rifle, a handgun.

And you'd better treat me right. Or I'll kill you.

Or you...or you...or you...

How Do Bears Smell?
Something Like Bear Trappers

I've always had a particular envy for airline pilots, high-stakes gamblers, back country guides and fire-and-brimstone preachers.

That means, I guess, that I have a special liking for men who reach for the clouds, who laugh at high odds, who are sly as hungry coyotes, who believe, ultimately and forever, in what they say and do.

Given all that, add to the list today the wildlife researcher who, it turns out, is a combination of all of the above.

I wouldn't have believed that if I had not spent a couple of days with a genuine, in-the-flesh wildlife researcher whose name is Bruce E. Kohn. Now I am, indeed, a believer.

Kohn is involved in a five-year study of Wisconsin's black bear population. I liked everything I saw as I watched him work near Montreal, Wisconsin. I liked the dedication, the knowledge, the precision and the dawn-to-dusk, gut-busting work that Kohn and his associate, Ned Norton, deal with every day, for 10-day periods at a time.

WOODS PIG? Old timers in northern Wisconsin have referred to black bears with that moniker often in years gone by. Jay Reed and his partner likely would have answered to it, too, after the experience described here.

And I liked other things, too. Kohn, for instance, is a hunter. Because he is a hunter he kills wild animals. Yet he displays the inborn love for wild animals that good hunters have.

You can tell it by the way he affectionately slaps the rump of a tranquilized bear and murmurs softly: "Sleep it off, old girl. You'll feel better in the morning."

You can tell it by the way he handles animals, strongly, aggressively, but with a gentleness born of love and respect.

And that respect shows in other ways. Kohn will tell you, if asked, about how much and why he detests television programs that depict bears as pets; as kind, gentle, always-to-be-trusted animals with the disposition of the old family dog.

"It's a terrible and dangerous thing for children to grow up believing bears are really that way," he says. "There is nothing natural about it. Those television shows just do not portray bears the way they really are. It's tragic."

While the bear is not normally aggressively hostile, it can always be dangerous when approached at close range, even when caged.

"They must be respected for what they are, for what they can be," Kohn says.

Working alone as a solitary team deep in the northern wilderness, Kohn and Norton are faced with many problems, not the least of which is social.

"We've turned many a head in local restaurants..."

Bears, you see, smell unpleasant. And live-trapped bears tend to smell more than usual because of the dung and ripe bait meat that is in the barrel traps with them.

So, you handle bears on a daily basis. Sometimes as many as eight. Even with a shower every night and a clean change of clothes you tend to take on the natural odor of a bear.

"We've turned many a head in local restaurants," Kohn says with a laugh.

I know what he's talking about.

After a day of coming in contact with four live-trapped bears, Photographer Erv Gebhard and I checked into the Holiday Inn motel in Hurley. The day had been long and hot and filled with hard, sweaty work.

Before going to our rooms to clean up, we stopped at the downstairs bar for a beer to chase the dust of the day from our throats.

The nose on the young woman behind the bar began to wrinkle even before we sat down.

"You guys," she said, "smell like a couple of bears."

What could we say?

We took it as a compliment.

A Bar Can Be a Perfect Place To Spend an Evening

It has been sometimes suggested by colleagues and others that most, if not all, stories about hunting and fishing are produced from bars.

It is broadly hinted that the copy sniffs of brandy, that the pen has been dipped in beer, that the t's have been crossed with swizzle sticks and cherry stems.

They say the best of all sunsets are the ones that fall upon the top shelf, that the music of eternity really comes form a jukebox, that the only rings an outdoor writer knows about are the ones left by a wet glass.

Well this time, at least, they're right. Let the record show that this story was, indeed, written from a bar. Now that's official, like notary-signed official or wife-approved official or editor-initialed official.

It was written from a bar, all right...a sand bar... a sandbar on the Mississippi River...a sandbar where there were turtle tracks and heron feathers and willow leaves and a lot of other good things.

NOT THAT KIND OF BAR! An evening camp out on a Mississippi River sandbar shows that there always remained just a little bit of Huck Finn in Jay Reed.

What you are going to get today, should you decide to read along, is a perspective of the outdoors from a sandbar.

It won't be steeped in great knowledge. There will be nothing scientific about it. It will cause no great stir in the wonderful world of fish and game management. But it was fun for me, and so might it be for you.

Sandbars are nice places. Especially Mississippi River sandbars. I found that out a long time ago when I was young. Trouble is, you get older and start messing around with what you perceive to be serious stuff and you

239

tend to forget how clear and clean and simple things can be.

The sandbar from which I draw this perspective is located downriver from La Crosse. It is far enough away from the city so you can't see it or hear it or smell it. But it is close enough so you can get there in an old outboard without growing old.

I was alone, unless you count the blue-and-white houseboat beached down the shoreline a half mile away, or the ducks and herons that flew by. My camp was no great shakes if you measure it by the equipment ads you've seen.

My tent wasn't really a tent at all. It was what we used to call in the Marine Corps, "a shelter half." I never did put it up, because the weather was good. I also had a sleeping bag and a cardboard box that held a frying pan, some cooking oil, salt and pepper, a couple of onions and items like that. There was also a small cooler that held some ice, a six pack and two dozen night crawlers.

I had one fishing rod and a tackle box. It wasn't much, as camp gear goes, but it was all I needed because I was only going to stay the night.

> "I cut a forked stick, balanced the rod tip on it, and anchored the butt with a chunk of driftwood..."

I pulled my rented boat onto the sandbar at mid-afternoon. It was hot, as only the Mississippi River country can be hot in August. So the first thing I did was go swimming. After that I laid around in the sun, watching the boat traffic and sipping cold beer.

It must have been about 6 p.m. when I gathered some firewood. The sky was clear as a bell, so I spread the shelter half on the sand and put the sleeping bag on it.

I rigged a line with a common hook, a gob of nightcrawlers and some split shot. I cut a forked stick, balanced the rod tip on it and anchored the butt with a chunk of driftwood.

After that I started a campfire, a small one, just right to make smoke enough to smell and light enough to see.

Then I sat in the sand to wait and to watch and to look and remember.

From the count of ducks I made that evening, I'd say that waterfowl hunting along the Mississippi River this fall of 1980 will be good, assuming there is a season. But I'll tell you true, I didn't think about problems like that. There were mostly mallards and wood ducks. They flew low and often over and near my sandbar. They were alive and picture-pretty and they had prospered and that was good.

In the daylight, the Mississippi was mud-puddle dirty from rain. It looked like you could plow it and plant corn. But once the sky cleared of the sun, its water turned rainbow. It picked up the light from my little fire like a mirror.

An excursion boat went by. The *La Crosse Queen*, I think it was. I could hear the band playing the Basin Street Blues and people waved at me. I waved back and watched and listened until it was out of sight.

How was fishing? Well, it was pretty good, considering that I didn't try hard. I caught two white bass and a catfish about 15 inches long. I released the bass and kept the cat. I cut it around its head, stripped its skin with a pair of pliers, halved what was left and put the pieces on ice.

I didn't fish anymore after that. I had enough to eat, and if you can catch a couple without really working at it you can say that angling action on the river is midsummer good.

The night, as it turned out, wasn't long enough. I hiked the banks of the Mississippi with a shadow. I looked for turtle eggs and crow's nests and muskrat runs and I asked the shadow what had happened in those years in between, but he didn't know because he was very young. Only his eyes were old.

In the morning, I fried the catfish and ate it, washing it down with the last can of beer. Then I loaded my gear and went back to La Crosse.

After that there was a motel room with conditioned air and a shower and soft music from a leather box.

And there was truth.

My sandbar perspective was that duck hunting will be good and that fishing is good.

And you can believe it because the Mississippi never lies to those of us who love it.

Country Boys
Can't Survive

I paid seven sawmill dollars for a bracelet,
Just to satisfy her 14-carat mind...
— From an old country song

The Wisconsin Board of Natural Resources took a boat ride down a section of the Mississippi River near Wabasha, Minnesota recently. They boarded a flotilla of DNR craft at this river port, which is no more than a short cast or two from the Wisconsin border.

First they went upstream to a place near where the Chippewa River empties into the Mississippi. Then they went downstream to a place called the Weaver Bottoms to view some environmental work being done by the U.S. Army Corps of Engineers.

Along the way, they saw some of the most beautiful river and swampland scenery available anywhere in the universe and beyond, at least in the view of some.

Because that trip took the Board along the outer perimeter of what once was my world, it got me thinking about sawmill dollars. And swamp dollars. And rubber boots. And trot lines. And traps. And gill nets. And food on the table. And survival.

The Board didn't see any of that, of course, because it isn't there anymore. It's gone, just as the deep-running sloughs and guts and cuts are gone.

And the Board didn't see the farm boys either, the country boys and their families out cutting and bundling marsh hay, sidestepping over and around the rattlesnakes as they did their work.

The snakes are still there, but the hay meadows are gone and so are the county boys, at least in a sense.

The swamps were, and are, many things to many people but, back in earlier days, they were a ticket to survival for those who knew how to use them.

There was a sawmill then, for those who remember, and the pay for a day's work was one buck as in a dollar bill. It was the going rate and the people who could work there were glad to get it.

If you wanted some extra scratch then, and most everyone did, you had to turn to the swamps to get it.

There were families who made a portion of their living from the swamps. They ran setlines for catfish and gill nets for carp.

They trapped muskrats and mink and raccoon. They hunted wild bee trees for honey and they scrounged for berries when they were ripe. The Board had no way to see the clothes that the money bought, the rent it paid, the extras it provided.

Those swamps were no recreational playground to zip through with high-powered outboards. If fishing was fun, and it was, it had a more serious point to it.

The Board couldn't see any of that because you can't see what isn't there.

There is still a little cash fishing going on. But not much. Since the water soured, there is a limit on the size of fish that can be sold. That's sometimes hard to understand for those of us who remember because we used to drink the stuff like it came from a spring.

"Swamps were a ticket to survival for those who knew how to use them..."

There is still some trapping going on, in season, as well. And some duck hunting. But the seriousness of it is gone. It is called recreation now.

And if the sense of the hunting and fishing has changed, so has the face of the swamps. The deep-running sloughs have silted in over the years to the point where power boats have problems getting around.

The Board, on its trip downriver, passed within sight of sloughs that used to provide access to the swamps but don't any longer because they have filled in.

Some of those water passages were cut off by sand dunes, the residue of decades of dredging on the main river to maintain navigation channels for towboats. Pleasure boats stop at those dunes now and families picnic on them.

Maybe that's a plus. Or maybe it is not. It depends on how you look at it.

It is entirely fitting that the Board should have toured that part of the river for it is one of the great recreational assets of the state. But there was much they didn't see.

Memories of people and places and other times remain hidden in the hearts of only those yet alive who remember. And those memories never come out on warm, bright, sunny days when the world rings with laughter and the swamp smell seems like sweet perfume.

Fisherman Offers Respectful Ode To Mississippi River in All Her Fury

A dream denied…

She's been a mother to me over the years, the Mississippi has, and, God, I wanted her to embrace me once again. I needed to feel the comfort of her. I needed to test the texture of her currents. My heart yearned for her music and her magic.

It would be so easy. All I had to do was launch the 16-foot flatboat and its cargo of fish line, fry pans, coffee can and groceries.

Once I was on the water, the river would be mine again. I'd point downstream to where a slough cuts off the main channel and I'd find the little sandbar with its willow growth and beaver cuttings.

I'd work a pair of lines until I had two catfish on a stick or until dark, whichever came first. I'd clean the fish and start a fire. I'd hunch close to the smoke to discourage the bugs. And I'd suck on a cold beer.

And when the serenity of the moment finally chased the gnawing tension from my gut, I'd fry a couple of thick bacon chunks and eat the cracklings with another beer. When the fresh catfish slices turned desert brown in the bacon fat, I'd wolf them down with some ripe cheese and raw onion.

FLOOD OF 1993. Like the floodwaters above, a wall of water descended upon Cassville and other towns in western Wisconsin. Jay Reed reported it with this story from July 14 of that year.

After that, camp coffee, thick and rich and gritty, would bubble in the can and I'd sip it, carefully, after settling the grounds with a few droplets of pure Mississippi flood water. Then I could sit quietly, reflectively in the darkness with my mother, the river, and listen to her night sounds. And all the wounds of the heart would heal.

Once filled to overflowing with the richness of it all, I'd roll up in a blanket and count stars and fireflies until the sweet harmony of sleep descended.

Ah, but it was, indeed, a dream denied.

The Mississippi River near Cassville, Wisconsin, is in no mood for such frothy stuff right now. She's grouchy and cranky, suffering the painful, morning-after effects of her springtime high-water binge.

Nose a boat into the current of the big river now and the boils and undertow and freight-train current will grab its bow and twist it like a lion with a zebra's leg. You figure out quickly why, even in mid-July, state officials still do not recommend general river travel.

And the sandbar? You couldn't find it if you tried because water covers it like a deep, soggy blanket. Some willow tips, barely perceptible in the current, mark its location. You'd need a wetsuit to picnic there.

I remembered what Mark Alter, of New Berlin, told me the night before up in Alma: "The high water has screwed up my fishing, but I still wouldn't want to be anywhere else."

And he is right, of course.

> **"And the sandbar? You'd need a wetsuit to picnic there..."**

People who love the Mississippi with a passion do not begrudge the river its right to kick up its heels once in a while. A spokesman for the Army Corps of Engineers said relocations were rare among people who had homes in the Mississippi's floodplain.

"It requires something special," the spokesman said, "for someone to proclaim his love for the river at the same time it is pouring through his kitchen and living room."

Ron Benjamin, of the Wisconsin Department of Natural Resources at La Crosse, said he'd heard few complaints from people who had lived on the river for more than two decades. "The people who are complaining are the ones who've come to the river within the last five years," he said.

From Lake Pepin to this point on the Mississippi, where it puts Wisconsin in its rearview mirror, the river folks are not without complaints, however.

One is universal.

They blame newspaper people like me, plus television newscasters and radio broadcasters, for much of the financial loss business owners have experienced.

"The way newspapers and television report it, you'd think the entire

245

western edge of Wisconsin was under water," said Marianne Munro, of Alma.

"The media created the impression that we had to paddle canoes just to deliver food to the tables in my restaurant," she added.

Let the record be clear. I had a heck of a good steak in Marianne's place the other night. Marianne didn't paddle to my table with that steak. She walked.

I can't believe newspapers would mislead like that. I know mine wouldn't. Television? Maybe.

In any case, western Wisconsin is not under water. Except for those on the lowest ground nearest the river or its backwaters, roads are in good driving condition. One more exception: downtown Cassville, where the main drag is undergoing reconstruction having nothing to do with the floods.

The fact that most of us who have been here a long time have webbed feet and speak with a quack is of no consequence.

It's just that they say it will rain again tomorrow. The Mississippi does not need any more muscle. It's plenty tough right now, plenty strong.

And us river lovers wouldn't mind if she turned it around and got it on back to her kindly old self.

Ghosts Come Back
To Have Their Say

Between explosions of thunder that rattled the windows and bursts of lightning that brightened the darkest corners, the ghosts of yesterday came to visit.

They sat in a semi-circle around the main room of the hunting camp in Nelson, Wisconsin. They didn't wear sheets. No. they wore flannel shirts and bib overalls and they had hip boots on their feet.

Their hands were gnarled and their wrists displayed bloody scrapes and their facial skin was wind-burned brown.

There was G.W. "Huck" Siefert, the leader of the pack, a true Alpha. But he has been dead since 1988. And there was Ed Salwey, gone a few years after that. And there was Alex Reick, Anton Bush, and Elroy Reidt. Maybe there were others, no doubt were, but, sometimes, you can't see all the ghosts for years already spent.

They all share common ground on a little hill just out of town, but they were at the hunting camp this night.

They talked about the price of muskrat fur. Would it average $3? They talked about the little potholes up in the swamps, for duck hunting season was just around the bend. Was there enough water to draw the mallards?

Could you run an outboard up Dark Slough or would you have to use a canoe to get to paradise? They talked about that a lot.

Ghosts, like people, look ahead as much as they look back. So while there was talk of trapping seasons that had gone before, duck hunting seasons that had run their course, the ghosts, as they did in life, wondered about how things would be.

That's why the price of fur was important. That's why the availability of water was on their minds. Those are items of great significance.

Nobody talked, much, about the traps they would set or the ammunition they would shoot. They did, though, set a sort of agenda for how it would be on opening day.

And that's the way the talk went the night the ghosts came to the hunting camp.

But there was more than that. You should know about the smells of raw fur. Neat stacks of it were on the floor and the odor of it was sweet perfume to the nostrils so inclined.

A man whose name is now forgotten, but a ghost, nevertheless, had a ruler in his hand and he was measuring beaver pelts. A fur buyer. And when he wasn't measuring he was fingering, feeling, for the quality of the dried and semi-brittle muskrat skins.

He put them into stacks of his own, according to size and quality. He asked the ghosts if any of them had ever seen the pelt of a rare cross fox. Said he had one in his car and would bring it in later.

The thunder and lightning spawned rain, after awhile, as is right and correct. And wind. It whined around the camp while the ghosts talked about skinning knives and dirt hole sets and flights of mallards and mink tracks and whether raccoon pelts should be stretched square or cased.

And while they talked a parade of hunting dogs sniffed and snarled and whined happy whines. There was Mink, Star, Bugs, Towser, and the newest of the dog ghosts, Thor.

And then fog, clean and sweet and pure and heavy, filled the room of the hunting camp

> **"He remembered how the days of thunder ignited his spirit and fed his soul..."**

and the wind kicked in and the lightning flashed and when it was over the ghosts were gone.

The man from Milwaukee opened his eyes and realized that he had nodded off at the table covered by the red-and-white checked cloth. The country music station on the radio was playing an old song about memories.

He cleared the supper dishes from the table and put them in the sink. The washing could wait.

He took a walk then, and smoked and looked at the sky and remembered how it was when the days of thunder ignited his spirit and fed his soul.

Were those really the days? Or are these the days?

We are going to get at this serious business of hunting starting October 1. The camp is ready.

And the ghosts have visited. They will again when the time is right and conditions are perfect.

That's OK. It's proper. It's part of the game that we play and they played.

So the man from Milwaukee turns away from the grave of the old dog. And when he reaches the camp, there is this sound of thunder from somewhere deep in the sky. He looks up. There is nothing but darkness.

Ghosts of men and old dogs go on forever.

Old Friends Savor Reunion

The man from Milwaukee was standing at the nearly deserted bar at the Indian Shores Campground in Lake Tomahawk, Wisconsin, when the man from Madison walked in.

He was alone, the man from Madison was, which was unusual in itself, but then his purpose was to use the john, so they gave him some privacy for that.

When he came out, the man from Milwaukee asked him if he had time for a beer.

"I'd like to," he said. "But you can hear 'em out there. They want to get this fishing party started."

The man from Milwaukee said he understood.

The man from Madison turned then, toward the door. But he stopped. And turned again.

"What the hell," he said softly. "It can wait. You bet we'll have one. But I'm buying."

So they bellied to the bar, and the man from Madison put some folding green down that, in moments, turned into two cans of Old Style.

They raised them, then, as old friends do, in silent salute and there was this metallic clink as the two cans touched.

The man from Madison lit a fresh cigar as the man from Milwaukee picked a Camel from a crumpled pack and thumbed flame to it.

But even before the first pleasantries could be exchanged somebody appeared at the doorway to remind the man from Madison that he was needed outside. Like now.

The man from Madison took a long pull at the Old Style.

"Not now," he said. "Not yet. Give me just a few more minutes here."

And then they talked, the words rushing because there was so little time and so much ground to cover.

Mostly, it was light. It was about now. It was about yesterday. It was about fishing and good times past. In seconds they left this lush land of lakes and traveled to another where the West Fork of the Chippewa River flows.

They rode those currents again and they sat around a campfire, eons of time and space removed from the real world of pride and pressure, of power and puffery.

Then there was this voice from the doorway again reminding the man from Madison that there were schedules to be maintained, appointments to keep. There were people waiting.

"In a minute," he said. "In a minute."

He turned back and, for a fleeting instant, the man from Milwaukee thought he saw a shadow of sadness in his friend's eyes.

In the next couple of minutes, the man from Madison covered the full range of conservation problems for which he has concern.

Details, names, figures, times, places, events rolled form his tongue, an avalanche of data on complex issues and the man from Milwaukee was reminded again how this marvelous ability had first attracted him to the man from Madison so many years before.

The sounds of the crowd outside grew ever louder. The crowd was getting restless. So were the camp followers, the ones with big shoulder cameras and the ones who carried only pads and pencils. So were the hosts and others who yearned for their brief moment in the spotlight.

So the man from Madison and the man from Milwaukee stood back from the bar, their beer finished, their time together gone.

They shook hands, then, and wished each other luck. They promised their trails would cross again.

The man from Madison turned to the doorway. His shoulders stiffened and straightened. A wide smile played across his face. His eyes glistened.

He stepped outside and you could hear the response of the people gathered there and the television cameras made their whirring sounds and the still cameras clicked and the microphones bristled in the air like hairs on a deer's back.

The crowd surged around him, carrying him in human waves down toward the lakeshore where there would be ceremonies and a glorious getaway for some ceremonial fishing.

The man from Milwaukee watched this through a window. He turned back to the bar, then, and to a fresh beer and pondered it all.

The man from Madison had taken time to talk briefly with an old friend.

It was something only a good guy would do.

And that, all politics aside, is what Anthony (Tony) Earl is.

The man from Madison, you see, is also the governor of the State of Wisconsin.

With these thoughts in mind, the man from Milwaukee sat down and wrote the story you have just read. 🐾

Snow is Soft,
Spring is Near

Walk with me, this day, through the courtyard of kings and angels...

Walk with me to the cathedral of the woods, where priestly prayers whisper softly on the lips of the wind...

Walk with me to the house of love, where the kiss of snow is X-rated to all except those who can look beyond its sensuous being...

And walk with me—please, walk with me—to where the sounds of music go when the song has ended.

These are the woods, and winter is here. The crooked track of a fox shows how it staggered along its way, drunk with hunger and full of freedom, yet leashed to a prison cell bounded by fear and a growling gut.

But the snow is soft and spring is near...

The fox knows it because his coat is thinning and his guard hair, once December bright, is turning dull.

And then there is this place beside a tree at the edge of a flowage where the ice has been broken. Peeled twigs float in the black water and there is mud on the snow. A beaver has broken out here and the markings show where he crawled out on the ice to breathe deeply of the fresh air.

Maybe it was a female heavy with pups or maybe it was a male sick inside at its winter-long imprisonment.

In either case, they heard the song and followed the music and found that the snow was soft and that spring is near...

The buds of the cottonwood are brittle with cold but there is a softness inside that the partridge likes, so the bird sits high on the crown, filling its crop and looking down at a page out of February's book. Its feathers ruffle in the wind and it stretches its neck like a great, brown chicken pecking away at the seeds of eternity.

This night, for the partridge, will be easy because the snow is soft and spring is near...

And high in the sky where the angels live there are patches of blue 'midst patches of gray, and there are no shadows save one cast by the eagle. Its head glistens virginal white and its wings embrace the wind like a long-lost lover.

It sweeps and soars through the unseen drafts, and it spots the rabbit

251

where the brown grass pokes through folds of snow.

The eagle comes down to the land of February, and when it climbs back toward its place in the sky it leaves behind those stains of red — crimson tears on crystal eyelashes — and the screams of the rabbit are lost to the melody of death.

For the eagle — but not the rabbit — the snow is soft and spring is near...

And for the man who walks in this place of angels, this place of kings, this place of prayer and love and violence and death, there is solitude and comfort.

Fresh snow clinging thickly to the trees gives the woods an acoustical perfection of the concert hall. The sound of the wind is as vibrant as a violin ringing through the concert hall, and it comes back a hundredfold to the ear tuned to it.

And if the taste of moisture from the sky is like the finest of fine wines, then a snowflake on your lips is a sensation to be rolled over and across the

> **"These are the woods, and winter is here...**

tongue, measured not by degrees of goodness but by vibrations of the soul.

And if the softness of the time is an uncut gem to be stored in the velvet lining of the heart, then your moment in the woods with me should be a song to sing forever when the soul turns slack and the mind goes sour.

Roses do not grow in the garden of regret — when the snow is soft and spring is near...

Jackpine Pickets
To Make a Point

Upnorth, Wis. —On my way to a big job in Ashland the other day, I stopped for a beer at Jackpine Joe's Saloon here.

When I turned off the highway I could see right away that three guys were picketing the place. When I got to the parking lot I saw it was Jackpine Joe himself, sage of the north, plus Mattress Mike and Chilblain Charley. Carrying signs and chanting, they were.

"What are you doing?" I asked, getting out of my truck.

"You ARE sharp today," Jackpine said with a sarcastic growl. What does it look like we are doing?"

"Supporting the National Football League players, I see," I remarked. "But listen, you can't strike your own place."

"Who says I can't?" Jackpine asked. "Anyway, we are not exactly striking. We are making a public statement. We want to make everyone aware of the plight of the professional football player, downtrodden as he is."

"Is that right?" I said.

"You bet your typewriter that's right, " Jackpine said. "You know I've always been concerned about guys who make several hundred grand a year and more for about six months of work at what some call a child's game."

"That's for sure, Jackpine," I said. "You are all heart."

"My sympathy is with them," he said, holding his picket sign high in the air. "These guys got special problems. When a 280-pound tackle says he's got to put food on the table, you know he ain't blowing smoke.

Personally, I'd rather buy the Bradley Center than pay for steaks for a linebacker. They ain't tea-and-toast types, you know. *War and Peace* takes less reading time than some of their grocery lists. Putting food on the table of a football player ain't a responsibility, it's a project.

"I mean, these guys ain't got stomachs, they got sanitary landfills. When they talk about a quarter pounder, that's just the salt. When they order a barrel of chicken that's what they mean, a real barrel."

"You may be right about that," I said. "I hear there is mass picketing at some of the stadiums."

"What do you think this is?" Jackpine said. "You get three sign carriers together in Upnorth and what have you got? Mass picketing. There won't be any violence, though. Mattress Mike is the town constable. He won't allow it. Besides, the last fight he had was with his wife, and she pretty near wiped him out with a stiff arm and a body block. No wonder he calls her the Walter Payton of the north.

"By the way, the joint is open," Jackpine said, "if you care to indulge and don't mind crossing our picket line. Try to remember that I need your business even though I've got strike insurance. My accountant is tougher than a crackback block."

"Tell me something," I said. "If you are out here picketing your own place, who is in there tending bar?"

"I hired a B team to work during these troubled times," Jackpine said. "Young kid. I tried him out this summer but he couldn't cut it. Dumb. Didn't know beer from bourbon. I told him I enjoyed a Manhattan and he said he always liked New York, too.

"And when you put the kid in a uniform he looks just like a professional bartender. In fact, you can't tell the difference until he starts to work."

> **"Listen, you can't strike your own place..."**

"I see some similarities here with what is going on in the strike-torn world," I said.

"You bet your sweet free agency issue," Jackpine said. "You know none of us wanted this to happen. If they'd just let us work when we want, where we want, for who we want and for the amount of money we want with signing bonuses, no-cut contracts and incentive clauses thrown in for good measure, we could settle this thing in a minute. What is wrong, actually, with letting the animals run the zoo?"

"I guess that is what it comes down to," I said. "Listen, I've got to get on the road. I hope everything works out the way you want. The next time I come by, maybe there won't be a picket line and I'll be able to come inside."

"Not to worry," Jackpine said. "We're prepared to hold out as long as we have to, but the public loves us and they'll force the evil owners to bargain fairly with high purpose.

"Besides, the retail grocers can't afford to have us out very long. There are Big Macs going to waste even as we speak. There are steers that will die of old age unless we get back to playing."

"You and the players have a big stick there, that's for sure," I said. "See you sometime."

"A man's got to do what he's got to do, Pete Rozelle to the contrary," I heard Jackpine say, as I pointed my truck toward Ashland. 🐾

Onset of Winter
Mixes Feelings in the Soul

The sky was an old man, stooped at the shoulders and bent low at the waist. It sagged and sighed from the weight of the snow it carried. Its cloudy complexion was gray and it waited, as old men must, for death to come.

The wind moaned a slow and melancholy dirge through the brown, brittle leaves that carpeted the freeze-hardened ground.

The water of the lake had a mean look about it, almost as if it were ready to turn killer. But it brought a tinkling sound when the whitecaps cracked the skim of ice that had formed where sand and water met.

A shadow stalked the beach that day, puzzling whether loneliness was really nothing more than a state of mind.

He remembered how it used to be at the lake when the sky was blue and the sun was warm and the wind laughed a lovely melody. He remembered how it was when each tomorrow was an uncut diamond to be sliced and polished and brightened; when the next sunrise was a kiss to be anticipated, a steak to be eaten, a drink to be savored, a dream to be lived.

I don't know what the early days of Wisconsin winter do to you, but they turn me pulpy inside. The cold penetrates deeper than it ever did before and the days seem grayer and the nights seem endless and the wind always has a cut to it that rips me in two.

"Hell," you might say. "Winters are not so bad. There'll be snow and it will be clean and white and crisp and it will hide the scars of a summer of hard use. The air will be sharp and the morning bright and the evenings pretty.

"There'll be snowmobiles to ride and snowshoes to hike in. There will be trail picnics and ice fishing. And there will be nights to watch the flames dance from the fireplace and a drink to warm your insides and the glow of laughter even as the wind screams outside the house.

"There'll be cocktail parties and bowling. There'll be holidays. Friends will call and there will be comforting warmth from a heat register and the satisfaction that comes from good food and good conversation and good music. And there will be handshakes and cheek kisses and new clothes."

So the shadow stalked the beach once more, remembering winters that had gone before.

A hundred evening grosbeaks at the feeding table, their black-and-yellow feathering standing out against the white of the snow...a purple finch, unidentified until the bird book came out...a downy woodpecker chipping away at a block of suet.

Coffee black and steaming hot from a tin cup that stuck to the lips when you tried to drink...slabs of venison fried deep brown with chunks of bread spread thickly with butter...beans searing biting hot in a frying pan...a blood-red sunset...an aching heart...teardrops of rain splashing softly off the eyelashes of pine.

He remembered the time last year when the big snow came...how it piled high inch upon inch above the fence... and the man with the snowblower came and afterward there were steam-fogged glasses and dripping noses and wind-burned cheeks and warm, sweet brandy to chase it all away.

> **"The early days of Wisconsin winter turn me pulpy inside..."**

And when it was over, there was a little puddle of melted snow upon the floor...a puddle and a memory and nothing more.

So the shadow asked himself: What is eternity? Is it an uncommon place where there are no bag limits and no seasonal regulations? Is the sun always warm and the sky always bright? Can you cross over any man's fence without fear of retribution? Can a man, like a hound, scratch his back on any pole and sleep in the sun and dream of triumphs long past?

That is what the early days of winter do to me.

And so the shadow stalks the beach. The wind kicks up and the temperature drops in step with deepening darkness. A dog barks...and a light flickers, first on, then off...and the movement of the air sends the leaves to singing a stereophonic dirge.

The sky is truly an old man—and ever lonely—with the silence of the falling snow.

Time to Cheer
The Underhogs

L et us all rise for a moment, if you will please, on this Sabbath day and
send forth a cheer, loud enough to blow the ears off those who listen,
for the great and grand and glorious underhogs of Wisconsin.

I mean, let's kick it in. We're talking explosion here. We're talking loud,
as in deafening.

"Hold on just one minute, writer fella. You mean underdogs, right?"

Wrongo, Mr. Copy Editor, and all of you nitpickers out there who get
off on finding simple-minded typos. I mean underhogs, as in groundhogs
or woodchucks. I mean the littlest of the little, the plainest of the plain, the
simplest of the simple.

The reason for the cheer, you see, is because the little guy won a round
here the other day. The 90-pound weakling got up off the sand and kicked
back. The guy who couldn't hit the size of his hat slugged one out of the
park with the bases loaded.

The woodchucks of Wisconsin won a reprieve. They got a stay of
execution. They won't need to order a last meal. They won't need to walk
with a kind old padre at daybreak.

Here's what happened:

The State of Wisconsin, for reasons deemed good and sufficient, wanted
to place the woodchuck on what it calls the unprotected list. What that means,
simply, is that anyone so inclined could waste a woodchuck, sometimes
called a groundhog, any time, any place, anywhere for any reason.

Woodchucks are not now, nor have they ever been, high on the list of
prized wild Wisconsin animals. Nobody, in fact, thinks very much about
woodchucks except on February 2, when there is momentary insanity
because of a legend that says the animals can predict the arrival of spring.
It's dumb business perpetuated mostly by television.

The thing is, the woodchuck isn't very pretty. It isn't very smart. Its fur
coat is not coveted by anyone except another woodchuck. There are people
who claim its flesh is tasty but there are many, many more who say they
don't know about that and really don't care to find out.

Anyway, it seemed like a simple enough proposal. And I'd bet a month's
pay that nobody in the Department of Natural Resources expected its plan
for woodchucks to meet real opposition.

But they were wrong. It did.

After a round of public hearings, the state brought the idea to the Board of Natural Resources where perfunctory approval seemed as likely as tomorrow's sunrise.

There the idea ran afoul of Richard Hemp, a board member from Mosinee, who had a thing or three to say about the indiscriminate killing of woodchucks.

Because Hemp interceded on behalf of the underhogs, the full Board voted to table the DNR's proposal for a year during which some additional study will be put into the matter of woodchucks and whether or not they should be shorn of the uncertain protection of the law.

You might have figured out by now that I like what happened with the woodchuck issue. I like to see the little guys win sometimes.

In the great scheme of things, woodchucks are not worth dry spit on a hot day. They have no real value as is measured in terms of most other wild animal species.

But they live and they breathe and they are out there in that part of the state that we like to think is reserved, in part, for wild things.

We spend a bundle of money and a ton of talk on deer and ducks and grouse and pheasants. We value them as if they were chips of gold to be collected and cashed in when the time is right.

We turn ourselves inside out proclaiming our righteous intent to save and conserve and stand on the side of virtue. We let words like ethics and sportsmanship roll off our lips as easily as the leaky residue of wine sucked from a bottle and all in the cause of those wild things we rank highest in the pecking order.

But what the heck about woodchucks? Just because you can't eat them; just because you can't sell them; just because nobody stuffs them and hangs them on the wall; does that mean they should not be considered as something of some value, no matter how insignificant?

Hey! The state will one day win its fight to strip the woodchuck of whatever protection the law gives it. And, really, there is nothing wrong with that. Maybe, even, it is the way it should be.

There is no real reason to expect a great wave of public support for the woodchuck. We probably won't see, for example, formation of organizations like "Woodchucks Unlimited" or "Woodchucks for Tomorrow." There will be no fund-raising banquets or door-to-door collections.

But for now, by golly, the little guy beat the big guy and that does not happen often. It is reason enough to cheer this Sunday morning.

Olympics Have the People Upnorth in an Uproar

Upnorth, Wis. — Things are slow on the outdoor beat these dog days of August.

The fish are hiding out somewhere and hunting season is still several gunshots away. It's too damned hot for affairs of rod or gun, or heart, for that matter.

So what we have here today is an Upnorth postcard....

Hello from Upnorth.

The Olympic spirit has taken over, and the town's three television sets are smoldering. It is especially noticeable in Jackpine Joe's Saloon, headquarters for hunters, fishermen and others here.

Two young guys stopped in the saloon early this week. They had to be athletic types because they wore Nikes and ordered soda. In fact, they drank up Jackpine's entire stock of four cans.

And they talked like real Olympians. Said they were going for the gold.

They did, too, because when Jackpine went to the basement to tap a fresh keg, they took the two gold fillings he kept in the cash drawer for good luck. They had belonged to his grandfather who was said to have spit them out on his deathbed while making one final denunciation of the DNR's deer management policies.

They also got $7.25 in cash. Jackpine said it could have been worse. On a really good day he might have had 15 bucks in there.

They've even got an Olympic flame here. A fire started in a pile of used tires in back of Smoot's Garage. The flame, so far, has withstood four rainstorms and three attacks by the town's volunteer fire department. It burns brightly still.

Upnorth has not been without injury since the great athletic event began in Los Angeles.

Fired to a frenzy by the Olympic walkers, Mattress Mike and Chilblain Charley, the town's two noted fishermen, decided to imitate the walkers while going to Jackpine Joe's for their morning beer.

Mike got a spasm in his lower back and had to crawl the last 40 yards. The locals said it was the first time they ever saw Mike crawl INTO the place. He's in the hospital at Duluth now. Doing well.

They are wearing black armbands here these days in mourning for the Milwaukee Brewers. Local analysts say the team actually died last May. They are hoping for a quick burial now.

The armbands will be saved, however, since the thinking here is that they'll be needed again once the Green Bay Packers start playing for real.

The story about Robin Yount possibly being shifted to the outfield hit this town like a thunderbolt. The analysts at Jackpine Joe's say it would be a good move, particularly if they let Yount continue to play shortstop as well. They bet he could play both positions at the same time as well as they are being played now.

The trials and tribulations of the Milwaukee Bucks have everyone on the edge of their chairs. The matter of matching contracts has a local angle.

Milford Pick, the bus boy at Jackpine's, says he's been offered the same job at better pay by a night spot in Hayward.

> "They've even got an Olympic flame. A fire started in a pile of used tires..."

Milford says the ball is now in Jackpine's court. (Milford is widely known in these parts for knee slappers like that.)

Jackpine says he is waiting for the results of Milford's last examination before deciding whether or not to match the offer. At the rate Milford has been moving lately, it is not certain if the examination was an autopsy or a physical, according to Jackpine.

But it is the Olympics, without question, that holds the center of attention here in Upnorth now.

Just before closing time at Jackpine's the other night, somebody suggested a long jump competition, using the men's john, the pool table and the end of the bar as measuring marks. The winner would receive a gold medal embossed with the likeness of a six pack.

But cooler heads prevailed.

"We're too old to play with fire like that," said Jackpine as he turned out the lights.

That's it, for now, from Upnorth, Wisconsin. 🐦

Death of Summer
Keened by Wind

It was too nice a day for death. In the beginning, there had been bright sunshine and a sky so blue you wanted to reach out to feel the softness of it.

The trees wore crowns of marketable gold. And there was the eternal music of birdsong and the air was warm and rich with dreams. The amber dust of memory billowed all around and life was so good, at the moment, there was need to embrace it with love instead of lust.

But then death came on the creepy feet of a turn in the wind. A bank of clouds, dirty in their darkness, had formed like an assault force just behind the hills to the west. The clouds moved across the sky, chasing the sunshine like hounds hot on the track of Old 'Coon.

It was then that summer died. And the hunter stood on this grassy knoll and watched as it happened.

The season of fun and food and frolic died quickly once the wind got to its throat. And it went out with style and class. There was no kicking and screaming and scratching in the dirt.

Instead, there was a calmness about it. An inevitability. The golden crowns the trees wore so well began to trickle down in rolling sheets, or yellow rain. Limbs, once clothed in debonair dress, were stripped to cold, gray nakedness.

The hunter moved off the grassy knoll but he couldn't leave the scene of death because it was, suddenly, everywhere. His footfall soft and silent that morning, now crunched on the crisp carpet of leaves, ferns, and underbrush.

Sweat had trickled down his back and dampened the collar of his shirt when the day began, but now the wind slashed at him and stabbed down to where the flesh was wet.

So the hunter walked the little forest patch. The shotgun cradled in his arm was suddenly heavy. Why? Where was the lover's embrace it always provided? Why was the steel of its barrel cold as death to the touch when all the times before it felt warm and exciting as a woman's fingertips?

There was no thought of the hunt now. The sky hung low over the tops of the trees, fat and full and heavy as the stomach of a cow with calf. It left no more than a sort of half light in the woods.

Was summer really dead? Was this the end of a love affair which had started in May, was consummated in June, and perpetuated through those lush days of July, August, and September?

Was the woods where he walked nothing more than a casket to hold the bones of a beautiful woman now dead this very day?

No. It couldn't be.

There still were ducks to hunt and partridge to shoot. The sun would come out again even if the air would be cold. And November would bring the big deer hunt and there would be a little shack, then, with an oil lamp and a stove for warmth and the good smell of food and a soft bunk to sleep upon.

So the hunter walked his patch and thought his thoughts and dreamed his dreams.

> **"A bank of clouds, dirty in their darkness, had formed like an assault force..."**

The rain began so softly he didn't notice it until an oak leaf, wet and cold, plastered itself against his cheek. Before his eyes the drops took on substance until, at last, the rain was snow.

He held out his hand. A flake landed on his palm. He squeezed it tightly and when his fingers uncurled it was gone, leaving only moisture behind.

Like that snowflake, another season was gone forever.

Jackpine Joe Renews His Hope in the Brewers

If the days of summer are yet incarcerated somewhere west of the Mississippi, the boys of summer are not, which is why Milwaukee's heart beat so vibrantly Monday and everybody got a headache.

The dreaded Bostons came to town, and the Brewers smoked 'em on opening day of the baseball season, thereby giving rise to such jubilation as to make you wonder if it was a war that was won instead of a ball game.

World hero Robin Yount had barely fielded the final out when the merrymaking began in Area No. 5 of the North Parking Lot at County Stadium.

It was there, amid the uncommonly raucous revelry where I met Jackpine Joe, noted barkeep and sports authority from Upnorth, Wisconsin, for a post-game critique of the action.

"Well, if it ain't the scribbler, master of the three-word sentence," he said as I pushed my way through the crowd, crunching dead aluminum soldiers with every step.

"No rips, Jackpine," I said. "It's been a tough day in the press box. My pen ran dry, somebody spilled my coffee, and the window was so dirty you could barely see the field of friendly strife. What did you think of the game?"

"No wonder you are a fixture on the hook-and-shoot beat," he muttered. "If you are going to talk like that, at least whisper. The game was great."

"How about that pitcher Teddy Higuera?" I asked.

"He had the Bostons killing snakes, didn't he? You see how he went high and tight to Jim Rice in the first inning? Gave a new meaning to 'stick it in his ear.' The kid should own Milwaukee in another year, plus Wisconsin and everything east and west of the Great Divide."

"You are observant," I said. "What do you think about the Bostons going with Bob Stanley on the mound? Pitching, that is."

"I think the problem with Stanley was, being a reliever, he swooned when he saw nobody was on base when he came out to pitch, giving up a triple to Molitor and a single to Yount. He don't think it's a game, you know, until the seventh inning or later. But by then he was long gone."

"Any other impressions of the Red Sox?" I asked.

"Some. Who's their welfare case, Roger Clemens? The one who pleads poverty. He looked good walking out for pre-game introductions. He looked even better walking back to the dugout. I think this year the Bostons will have to be content with being famous for a legume that gives you gas."

"That's a harsh assessment, Jackpine," I said. "What about the Brewers?"

"Maybe this is the year they'll win 'em all," he smiled. "It's one down and only 161 to go."

"Be serious," I begged. "This is heavy stuff we're into here."

"The thing I like best about the Brewers, " Jackpine said, "is that while Molitor and Yount and Gantner will do most of the heavy work, like they did today, the middle of their lineup is exciting.

"You see Rob Deer belt that foul into the left field stands in the eighth?" If they counted hang time in this game, he'd lead the league. And Billy Joe Robidoux? In the first he rips this liner up the middle and there is no way the Bostons' second baseman makes the play. But he does. The guy should be a dip, as in pickpocket.

"And I liked the new kid on first, Greg Brock. Reminds me of Steve Garvey, if you'll pardon the expression."

"Anything else? I asked.

"I thought you scribes said Dale Sveum wears a concrete glove. The kid was positively graceful at short. Marty Marion reborn, as it were."

> **"This year the Bostons will have to be content being famous for a baked legume that gives you gas..."**

"What did you think of Mark Clear and Dan Plesac in relief?"

"Listen, they are how you spell it. Clear blew 'em away in the eighth. And Plesac proved that he is quick. I got a deer rifle that has less velocity than he has.

"Well thanks for the info," I said. "I gotta get back and write this up for the newspaper. You are staying the night?"

"Part of it," Jackpine said. "I want to leave early in the morning so I can get to Ashland for happy minute."

"You mean happy hour," I said.

"No. Happy minute. It's Ashland we're talking about here. For right now, though, I'm going to join the celebration. I ain't seen a party like this since V-J Day. Invite me down when you guys play in the Series."

"We should live so long," I said, and walked into the cheering crowd.

Some Problems With Wolves Are Part of the Package

Well, the wolf's at the door again. In a manner of speaking.

The Department of Natural Resources is all hot and bothered because one of its workers, with a permit, killed a gray wolf that found its way into a deer farm near Hazelhurst, where it had done, we are told, an estimated $40,000 in damage.

The DNR is busy these days, offering public explanations about why the wolf had to be shot dead, an act that, had it been done by a private citizen without a permit, would have been an arrestable offense. Hangable, some say.

The agency evidently believes it needs to talk at length about the episode since it is the main protector of wolves in the state. And protectors don't usually kill the protected without a valid reason.

The wolf, a female, had been inside the 900-acre enclosed deer farm since sometime in the fall of 1998. Officials say a male wolf also made it into the enclosure this spring, but it was live-trapped in April and relocated by DNR personnel.

> **"If that wolf ate $40,000 worth of deer, she must have weighed a ton..."**

The female, though, was too smart for her own good. She avoided all attempts at live capture, and finally, the decision was made to kill her. Even at that, it took more than a week to get close enough to her for a clean shot.

Nobody has ever said that wolves are not smart.

"We were relieved to learn that she was not caring for pups," said Randle Jurewicz, an endangered resources biologist. "But we won't know her exact age or if she'd ever had a litter until pathology reports are completed."

We do not know this for sure, either, since her weight has not been discussed, but if she ate $40,000 worth of deer while in the enclosure, she must have weighed a ton. Since lame, ill or otherwise poor animals are usually not kept in a deer farm, you can kiss goodbye the theory that those are the kind of animals wolves almost always kill.

Since Day 1, I have been an outspoken advocate for, and supporter of, the DNR's wild wolf recovery program. Some cheer that. Many others do not. I don't care one way of the other about that.

What I do care about is the fact Wisconsin's wolf population is now said to number about 200. So the recovery program is working, and that, to me, is good news.

The management population goal is 350. When it reaches 250, the animals will be removed from the endangered species list, which is another concern that can be taken up at the appropriate time.

All of which brings us back to the wolf put down by the state in Hazelhurst. One wolf, more or less, will not make a difference in the great scheme of things. So I shed no tears in that regard.

But appropriate to it, DNR program coordinator Adrian Wydeven offered what I believe to be the key thought here:

"Depredation is an anticipated part of the wolf recovery program."

It better be. You can't have 200 to 300 wolves roaming about without expecting problems. Some livestock will certainly go down. Maybe some dogs. So will a lot of deer, healthy or crippled or both.

A few humans are also likely to be scared out of their long underwear by wolves.

Mothers will weep, fathers will scream, redneck hunters will demand the scalps of each and every one of us who supported the wolf program and farmers will stand with their hands out waiting for cash payments.

They are the ones who believe the only good wolf is a dead wolf.

In the midst all of that, however, out there somewhere, will be those of us who do not want to see the last wolf die.

There yet remains a place for those animals in Wisconsin's slowly diminishing wilderness.

That is good.

If you've ever felt a chill deep inside your guts put there by a wolf's icy green eyes or if the hair on your neck has ever curled at the sad music of their long and lonely lament to spirits in the sky, you already know the right of it.

But certain troubles are the price we'll pay down the road. We've already seen the first of them.

In Memory of...
Wisconsin

The town road hasn't really changed much, I suppose, if you gauge change only with the yardstick of the eye or if you weigh it only upon the scales of the mind.

It still twists like a piece of brown string through cutover timber northeast of Modena, Wisconsin, until it reaches a pond that has no name. The same rolling hills still look down upon it. Its bed is the same one that was made years ago when it was no more than a trail through the woods.

And you can go even further. The same sky still looks down upon it, the same clouds still hover over it, the same trees still cast shadows down toward it.

But that, sadly, is about all that remains the same.

Man, in his infinite wisdom, has improved the road.

To understand the change, you should have known how it once was. Ideally, you should have walked down it at dusk on a winter evening when snow lathered the fields and hills. Ideally, you should have listened for the sounds of silence and should have reached and picked a star or

MEMORY LANE. A scenic country backroad like this one remained vivid in Jay Reed's mind for years after it had been widened, straightened and "improved" to move more traffic.

two from the sky which always seemed that close.

When darkness wrapped itself around the world of the road and when the moon came out, shafts of silver light would slide toward the shadows and a man with a call could whistle up a fox. You could watch the animal glide across the openings where the moon kissed the snow.

And you could hear its footfalls crunching ever so lightly on the crust. And then, like dreams of yesterday, it would disappear.

If all of the game killed off the road over the years could be brought back and stacked in a pile, it would make a magnificent mound of bones and blood, fur and feathers. It was that kind of a place for wildlife.

But there was more. The road was a classroom for nature study. You could always count on seeing some kind of wild game whenever you walked its length. More than one young man knows that a pheasant prefers a ground sprint to open flight because of lessons learned along that road.

They know that deer drop their fawns in May because you could always find one or two of the spotted miracles along the road at that time of year.

But I'll tell you true. That sort of thing won't happen anymore.

Hunters won't kill enough game off the road now to even think about. And no driver need fear damaging his automobile by colliding with some bird or animal. For none will be there. And that is because the road has been improved.

Workmen came. They brought saws and scythes. They hacked down the willows and cut the grass that had choked the sides of the little road. Then they

"The price we paid goes beyond the accounting of dollars and cents..."

burned off what was left until its sloping shoulders were draped in a black shawl of ashes.

They brought in a bulldozer. Its blade ripped the soil, turned it toward the sky. They broadened the road and built it up. They leveled it. And then they covered it all with sterile rock.

Now the road stands as a monument to man's ingenuity to create something out of nothing at minimum dollar cost. The road still twists and turns. Its course is the same. It still slides through the country toward the pond with no name.

But it has been cleared of its obstructions. You can see ahead and to either side with no trouble because there isn't so much as a blade of grass left to block the view.

And it is a sturdy road. Its sides, rock ribbed now, no longer crumble to the breeze and the rain and the snow. It is tough enough to withstand the spring breakup. High water won't cause washouts. No woodchuck will be able to burrow into it, leaving a hole which could erode.

Snow covers it all now; mercifully, I think. The scabs and scars are hidden and you can walk down the road remembering how it once was when willows clogged the shoulders.

The snow lies white and flat like an alabaster carpet and there are no marks upon its surface—no scratches from pheasants or grouse, no paw prints from animals. It is clinically antiseptic.

And that is sad.

Maybe it is important to improve a road. Maybe it is important to make it bigger and higher and wider and stronger than it ever was before.

I hope it's important. Man, I hope it's important. Because the price we paid goes over and beyond the accounting of dollars and cents. They sliced away a part of Wisconsin. It's gone, now, and they can never bring it back.

CHAPTER 5

Vietnam.
A Quiet Return

INTRODUCTION

In 1967 and 1968, Jay Reed covered the Vietnam War for the *Milwaukee Journal*. In 1989 he returned to that country, embarking on a personal odyssey to find out what had happened in the ensuing 22 years. With Reed was photographer Carl Hoyt, himself a veteran, who got his start in photography with the U.S. Army National Guard.

The stories that follow were selected into this book by Jay Reed with good reason. Twice they brought him within a crosshair of winning journalism's most prestigious award, the Pulitzer Prize. He was a finalist in the competition in 1968 and again in 1990.

The stories that follow represent the professional pinnacle of Jay Reed's career, a broad body of work generated over 40 years as a newspaper columnist.

"I have been around the world on various assignments," he wrote in 1999. "I have covered war, a presidential debate, a South American rain forest, a World Series, the Kentucky Derby and more. Twice I damned near won Pulitzer Prizes. "That ain't bad for a poor, unschooled boy from Nelson."

Not bad, indeed.

In Vietnam 22 Years Later, Images of Rice Paddies and War

The man pressed his face hard against the window of the airliner as it swept low on its approach to the airport called Ton Son Nhut.

Then the rice paddies squeezed the trigger of his mind.

The neat squares looked back at him like giant unblinking eyes of green and brown, tranquil in the hush of early afternoon.

But he had seen them, though, so long ago, when they ran red with blood, when they turned lumpy with bloating bodies. They were fearsome places then, too exposed for cover from small arms fire, their dikes frequently laced with deadly punji stakes. Never get caught in a rice paddy, they had said. If you do, you die. It was a truism of war.

The plane inched closer to the ground and his mind did tricks. Suddenly, unaccountably, he felt the hair on the back of his neck bristle and little shivers swept, like waves, along his arms.

In his head he heard the zip of a body bag closing. The whine of incoming artillery ricocheted off his heart.

When the plane touched down, it bounced a little and the jolt brought him back from reverie. Did it all really happen 22 years ago? If it did, and if it was that long ago, then why was the memory of war so real? Then why did he feel the sudden and intense impulse to urinate?

The plane stopped, the passengers pressed toward a doorway, and the man grabbed his carry-on bag and shuffled forward. From the shadowy coolness of the plane he stepped into the hazy, heavy heat of early afternoon.

VIETNAM REVISITED. Jay Reed returned to Vietnam in 1989. In this story he describes the mixed feelings of a U.S. war veteran visiting a former war zone.

On the tarmac he became aware of the once-familiar smells. His shirt turned wet with sweat. But there was this chill deep inside him, and this snapping of nerves. He had, for real, returned to Vietnam. And he smiled, inwardly, at the inevitable question:

"What the hell am I doing here again?"

If I had a dollar for every man who asked that question of himself when he arrived in country during the war, I could give away half the money and still be rich.

Trouble was, the question had no answer then, but that was wartime, when answers to anything were hard to come by. It's different now or, at least, I think it will be.

Readers who go back a ways with the Journal may remember that I was in Vietnam during parts of 1967 and 1986 covering the war for the newspaper.

So what am I doing here — again? The war has been over

> ## "My plan is to tour, by automobile, this country from the Delta to the DMZ..."

for about 14 years if you count the fall of Saigon in 1975.

Now Vietnam is a country with which the United States does no official diplomatic business. We won't even give it normal recognition, as a matter of fact, although that could change down the road.

The war itself was a headache and a heartache for Wisconsin and all of the U.S., a deep-seated divisive pain that still lingers in varying degrees.

Nevertheless, what happened in this country two decades ago was important then and continues to be important now. It reshaped the lives of millions of people; it left an imprint on the way we govern ourselves; it changed the way we, as a nation, think and act.

With that in mind, I am here to get a feel of Vietnam as it is today, more than two decades after I last saw it.

My plan is to tour, by automobile, this country from the Delta to the DMZ. That has been done only once before by Americans since 1975, I am told.

I'm going to visit old battle sites and many of those places where America's military forces were established at bases still familiar to those who were stationed there.

I want to see what is left of it all. I will be going to those combat outposts where the courage and dignity of American servicemen and women burned brightest and longest. And, too, I will see those places where combat turned

273

young men into savages, where the only legacy is shame.

And, along the way, I will seek out those signs that tell of the American presence here. Did we leave anything behind that now, after 20 years, might remind the world that we were here in the first place?

I did the Vietnam tour alone 22 years ago. Not this time. With me in Vietnam is veteran Journal photographer Carl Hoyt. We also will look at Vietnam through the eyes of several other people who have seen this country before from widely varying perspectives.

John W. Raths, a Michigan native who now lives in Florida, was a Marine Corps sniper who fought in the battles of Hue, Khe Sanh and Con Thien. He will be with us.

So will David S. Keen, also of Florida, who was among the original US military advisers sent to Vietnam. Keen will guide us through the action he remembers in the Mekong Delta.

Michael Castellano, of Guilford, Connecticut, a Navy veteran, did not fight in Vietnam. But he has made a half dozen trips to the county since 1985 and has sharp insight into the country and what is happening here.

That is the cast, except for assorted government guides who will join us as we travel Vietnam.

We will touch, taste and feel this nation, measure it as best we can, against how it was in wartime.

We will remember. And we will look ahead. We will jog the memory. We will see many of the places that made history two decades ago.

And we will try, with words and pictures, to look at it all in a way that has not been done before.

That is what I am doing here — again.

Con Thien: A Hill Stands In Deadly Silence

It looks so innocent in the pale hot afternoon sun, this place they call The Hill of Angels.

The softly rounded peak rises half-scarlet, half-blue in the distance, giving it a purple cast you might expect only from robes of royalty.

The highest hump of it gives way quickly to a graceful slope that sweeps downward toward a sea of green growth and a blue river called Ben Hai.

Death used to march toward Con Thien from the north, but now farmers and water buffalo labor there in newly developed rice paddies.

To the east, a tree line looms. Green and lush, it gives shade this tranquil afternoon to women carrying bundles of grass. But once those trees offered cover, of sorts, to U.S. helicopters speeding low and fast toward Con Thein's chopper pad, there to pluck the dead and wounded from battle.

And silhouetted over all against the faded blue

RETURN TO BASE. From the abandoned bunker at a former U.S. combat base, Jay Reed looks over the landscape he knew 22 years before. A local child surveys the scene with him.

horizon, pointing like a crippled finger toward heaven, stands the corroded, crumbled remains of a concrete bunker, a melancholy headstone for the Americans who died there.

To those of us who had seen Con Thien in the late 1960s when it was Vietnam's answer to hell on earth, the scene was almost surrealistic.

Con Thien, one of a series of U.S. combat bases, was the most heavily bombarded American position in the country in 1967. During one period, Con Thien endured 24 separate bombardments, during which more than 3,000 rounds of artillery, rockets and mortars crashed into the garrison.

Now, the hump of high ground, the slope, the tree line, even the bunker, was well within the context provided by misty memory. But something was wrong here.

Why did my nerves snap and my stomach turn tight? Maybe it was the silence. There was, after all, no sound of incoming artillery. When you heard that whine during the war, you had but three seconds before impact.

There was no "whump" of mortars that gave you five to 10 seconds to seek cover. And there wasn't the terrifying whisper of rockets that gave you almost no time at all.

There was none of that now because the war was over, and we were standing in a group in broad daylight, fearful of little more than the effort it would take to walk the mile to inspect the bunker.

Our government guide was not wild about the idea. He wondered why we couldn't simply eyeball the sight from a distance and move on. He said there remained much unexploded ordnance in the fields around the hilltop, many

> **"I had to reach that bunker just as much as I had to take another breath..."**

unexploded mines. He said numerous Vietnamese scavengers had been killed hunting for stuff that could be sold as scrap.

I told him it was necessary to reach the bunker and so, reluctantly, he set off up a narrow path.

About halfway to the bunker, we were joined by a half dozen children of local farmers. We were the first Americans they had ever seen. One spoke to the guide who suggested that we return to our vehicle.

"The child says there are many mines," the guide said. "We should go back."

I told him he could go back if he wanted. I told him I would take the point. I told him I didn't come halfway around the world to stop now. It was an obsession. I had to reach that bunker just as much as I had to take another breath.

It represented all I would ever know about hell. And I wanted to see hell in the daylight. I wanted to see it without fear in my heart. I wanted to see it on the walk instead of on the run. I wanted to see it without my nose bleeding or my hearing gone blank. I wanted—hell, I needed—to get to that bunker.

Buffalo tracks were all over the trail, so I figured that the animals must have already exploded any ordnance there.

Even though we considered the trail to be safe, it's funny how swiftly you can slip into wartime habits. I made sure our party was well spaced along the trail. And with each step I took, I felt the ground through my boots, testing the compactness of the earth. My eyes even searched for tripwires though I knew none would be there.

Along the way you could see the old bomb craters, half filled from the blowing sand and earth of 20 years. And you could see the new digging where hunters scrounged for military brass.

The remains of an old U.S. combat boot, ripped and faded, lay to one side of the trail.

When we reached the bunker, I was alone on that hill with the ghosts of 22 years ago. I was back in the underground bunkers with the mud and the rats and the men who called themselves the walking dead because, in a sense, that's what they were.

It was foggy — it was always foggy — and it was raining — it was always raining — at Con Thien that fall of 1967. The moisture was so intense, so continuous that men developed painful skin rashes. Jungle rot was common.

But the special misery of Con Thien was the incoming artillery. It rained down in deadly patterns that forced men to count it and time the lulls so that you could run from one bunker to the next.

The thunderous noise of it, sometimes combined with our own artillery fire, turned you temporarily deaf so that, when there was a lull, we had to shout at one another to make ourselves heard.

Nobody walked at Con Thien when I was here last. But this time I did, to the helicopter pad on the "safe" side of the hill. I left this place once on a chopper, me and seven dead men. Which is why I knew I had really gone back in time because I smelled those body bags again and I felt the choke build in my throat because I wanted to cry and curse at the same time.

I had it easy in Con Thien because I could go there and leave almost anytime I wanted given only the constraint of whether helicopters could arrive and depart. The fighters, though, had to stay.

There were other bad-news places in Vietnam at the time and I saw many of them. Con Thien always represented to me all that was the best and the worst about war. That is why I made three return trips to the place during my first stay in Vietnam.

If you are too young to remember the war, or if the years have taken away your recollection of the details of it, Con Thien was established by the Marine Corps as a combat base. A small patch of high ground, it was a bulldozed plateau that overlooked one of the principal Vietcong supply routes into

South Vietnam, which was its main strategic value. North Vietnamese and Vietcong forces tried desperately to drive the Americans from the hill.

U.S. forces abandoned Con Thien, called The Hill of Angels, early in 1970.

Maybe you can understand this, or maybe you can't, but there was fear and suffering and pain and heartbreak and isolation and frustration and terrible danger at Con Thien.

But there also were such incredible instances of courage and bravery and charity and dignity and loyalty that it is doubtful you could find them in such abundance in any other circumstance.

I saw so much at Con Thien to be admired, even as I saw so much to be abhorred. Such was the impact of this place on my senses that it was to shape my thinking about the war for a number of years, just as it was to disturb my sleep.

This place never was *Platoon* or *The Deer Hunter*. Con Thien was war, down and dirty. And it was real.

I don't know how long it took to come back from a 22-year trip that afternoon. But I never really did rejoin the group even though I was there physically.

Without its trappings of war, without its gun emplacements and underground bunkers, without its barbed-wire perimeter, Con Thien looks much like any other piece of real estate in this part of Vietnam.

Maybe it was important during the war. It is not important now.

I thought about that a long time as we moved slowly down the safe trail toward our vehicle. I don't know how many Americans or Vietnamese died here. From the vantage point of two decades, however, you have to think that, whatever the number was, it was too many.

I look at the hill called Con Thien and decide it wasn't worth one American life. It couldn't have been.

You see, Americans had the hill all along. The North Vietnamese and Vietcong tried to take it. They hit it with artillery and ground attacks. They hit it and hit it and hit it again.

But they never did take it.

In the end, we walked away from it. We left behind some unexploded mines and ordnance, miles of barbed wire, some nightmares that will never go away and a concrete bunker that still stands, pointing like a crippled finger toward heaven.

Weeds and rust, the ultimate conquerors, own The Hill of Angels now.

And the ghosts of the dead men dance alone. 🐾

His Only Wish...
To Get Home for Deer Season

Jay Reed filed this story from Vietnam in 1967. Albert Watson died Monday, October 30, of that year as a result of his grenade wounds.

There is a bed next to an aqua-colored wall in Ward C-4 of the intensive-care section deep in the bowels of the American Navy hospital ship *Repose.*

That bed is occupied by a Wisconsin serviceman, Lance Corporal Albert Clay Watson, a Marine from Mauston, whose mother, Mrs. M.H. Franke, lives on Route 4.

Watson and I talked the other day — mostly about hunting, for in civilian life there was nothing that Watson liked to do more than hunt deer.

"My buddy and I used to go up to Necedah for deer season," he said. "We'd go and make camp for a weekend and hunt all the time. Got some good deer up there, too."

And he smiled in the sweet memory of it. Only he couldn't smile much because his lips were puffed and the words came out soft and slurred.

He remembered how it was when the leaves would change color, and he whispered about the crispness of them and how they would crunch at a footfall.

"You couldn't sneak up on a deer when it was like that," he said. "And I was always a walker. I didn't care much about staying on a stand waiting for something to come along. I liked to hunt — really hunt."

Albert Clay Watson told me that he wasn't a bow hunter. He said he liked to hunt with a rifle because it felt good. There was something about the weight of the weapon as it hung from his hand. There was something about the sound of it when he squeezed off a shot. There was something about the smell of cordite that drifted slowly into the air around him after firing.

In those moments when he was awake, he remembers now the beauty of the land he left behind.

"I liked fall best," he said. "Maybe it was because of the hunting. But it was pretty then, too. The woods were the only place to be once the weather got cold."

He talked, too, of his school days back in Mauston. And he said he would like to get back home in time for deer season. He may hunt deer again someday. But it will never be the same.

For Albert Clay Watson was wounded in a grenade explosion.

He has multiple shrapnel wounds in his abdomen.

His right arm has been amputated.

So was his right leg.

He was 20 years old September 15.

.

Letter to a Marine Who Died in 1967

Lance Cpl. Albert Watson, Jr.
Lot 35B, West ½
Evergreen Cemetery
Mauston, Wisconsin

Dear Albert:
　　They say dead men can't read letters. Well, maybe not. The thing is, though, I owe you this report because I talked with you 22 years ago, a couple of days before you died of wounds received in the Vietnam War.

You didn't get to see the stories I wrote about you then. You'll recall that we talked a lot about deer hunting and about how you wanted to get back home for the next season.

Anyway, I want to tell you that I have been back to Phu Bai, where you were based with the Third Marine

MODERN STREET SCENE in Ho Chi Minh City—formerly called Saigon—doesn't show any indication of the war once fought over it, or the many on both sides who died for that cause.

Division in 1967, and I got close to the Nong River, where you were pulling guard duty the night a grenade explosion got you.

There's nothing much left of the base at Phu Bai. There's the fence, a ton of rusted barbed wire, some piles of picked-over junk and a couple of concrete bunkers. That's about it.

Otherwise, it has pretty much gone to seed. That's what most of you guys figured should be done with it anyway, right?

I tried my damnedest, Al, to get to the exact place on the Nong River where you attempted to pitch that live grenade back in the direction from which it had come, only to have it explode in your hand before you could get rid of it.

The Marine Corps awarded you the Silver Star for that act. While it cost you your life, it saved the lives of a lot of your buddies. That's why they put this inscription on your headstone back home:

"Greater love hath no man than this—that he lay down his life for his friends."

That says a lot about you, Al, and the way you took the last, long walk. The people back home are proud of you.

But to get back to the Nong River. I never actually reached the spot where it happened. Time constraints had something to do with that. So did strange government regulations that prevent people from going just anywhere in this country. Mainly, though, I wasn't sure I could find the place in daylight.

Two decades of monsoons and wind have no doubt wiped away all signs of what happened there. But the bridge you were guarding that night still stands. And they are growing a lot more rice in the fields away from the river than they were back then.

It all looks so peaceful now. You stand and look over all of it and you find it hard to believe that such awful violence took place there.

And another thing I have learned here on the Nong River and at other battle sites I've visited: None of them looks important now. Certainly not important enough to have cost you your life.

A bridge is nothing more that a bridge, a river nothing more than a river, a piece of high ground nothing more than just that. But in wartime, it is different. And that's why the Marine Corps decided that the bridge over the Nong needed to be guarded and sent you and your buddies there to do it.

I look at it now and it seems like such a waste. I don't know how you look at it, Al, because your view was far different than mine.

How I wish you could talk to us now the way we talked on the hospital ship *Repose* that day in October 1967, just before you died. You could tell us so much.

You could tell us how it is when death comes on the battlefield, if dying gloriously for flag and country is really all it is cracked up to be.

I've wondered about that over the years. We can write about it and we can read about it, but unless you've ever been put down in some grassy hell with half your body blown away and your life seeping slowly out in the mud, it is difficult to adequately address the issue.

After the war, Al, many people, myself included, got hot and bothered about such things as draft-dodging and other things that seemed unpatriotic. One of my biggest complaints had to do with the fact that 18-year-olds could die for their country but couldn't buy a drink of spirits in it. That never made a lot of sense. I have this feeling that the lawmakers figured that getting killed didn't require as much experience or good sense as buying a drink. Most of those people knew nothing of the former and a lot about the latter.

But maybe there is something to that. Getting killed in Vietnam was easy sometimes. You didn't need special training for it. You didn't need special skills for it. All you really had to do was be in the right place at the right time and you were dead. Simple.

In all my life, I believed that there was only one reason to go to Canada. And that was fishing. Well, the Vietnam War created other reasons for young men to go there. And many did, unlike you, who elected to enlist in the Marine Corps. Along with other people, I called those guys many names back then, none of them complimentary.

> **"You should have been getting ready for deer season. Instead, you were getting ready to die..."**

Over the years, though, that has changed. I don't like the thought of it any more now than I did then. But I understand it better. War does strange things, as I am sure you would agree.

I keep thinking about the reasons the government gave for sending you to Vietnam. You were to "win the hearts and minds of the people." You were to "stem the flow of communism." You were to "help the Republic of South Vietnam maintain its independence."

Well, I just hate to tell you this, but not much of any of that happened.

Take Phu Bai, for example. It looks just the same as it did the last time you saw it two decades ago. The buildings look the same and so do the people.

They light their hooches with candles. They cook their food over open fires. They work their fields with oxen or water buffalo. They dry their rice crop on the sides of the roads. Their babies still play in the dirt.

In the center of town, the market still flourishes. It's a sea of cone hats with people squatting under them. Women still carry immense loads on chogie sticks balanced over their shoulders. Next to foot travel, the bike is the most common form of transportation.

That's the Vietnam you knew before you went out and got killed, right?

283

It hasn't changed. Only the government has. It is communist now. And if we ever won the hearts and minds of the people, it really does not show today.

And South Vietnam is no longer independent. In fact there is no South Vietnam. The country has been liberated, as the government people here say.

What all of this means, it seems to me, is that we lost. And you, Al, lost more than most of us.

And when I stood there outside Phu Bai looking in the direction of the Nong River where you were wounded, I got to thinking that I really wasn't there at all.

Actually, I was back in Wisconsin, kneeling beside your grave and remembering how it was when we talked. I went through our entire conversation, Al, and it came to me again how wasteful it was that you had to be in that grave.

Two decades ago, you should have been at home getting ready for deer season. Instead, you were on a hospital ship getting ready to die.

That bothered me then, Al, but it bothers me much more today as I tour this country.

> **"None of the battle sites look important now. Not enough to cost you your life..."**

It is one thing to die in a movie or in a book or on the pages of a newspaper. It is something else to have your life seep away in the blackness of a Vietnamese night near a bridge on a river called Nong.

And all for goals that never really were accomplished.

After 22 years, Al, I understand that more clearly now. And I wanted you to know.

Your friend, Jay Reed.

Return to An Orphanage

Late on a hot, muggy afternoon in June 1969, a 20-year-old U.S. Marine from Milwaukee shot and killed a Vietcong terrorist who was attempting to attack a supply truck with a satchel charge he carried over his back.

The incident took place near the main gate of the Da Nang orphanage in Vietnam, within the shadow of Marble Mountain and on the way to China Beach, by the South China Sea.

The Marine's name was Kelly Forrest.

On that same afternoon inside the orphanage, a 58-year-old French nun and other members of her order were preparing the children for prayers before their evening meal.

When the nun heard the shot, she ordered the children to lie on the floor and remain quiet. It was not an extraordinary happening at the orphanage, for firing of one kind or another was

HEARTFELT GREETINGS from an American friend were passed along from Jay Reed to Sister Marie Angelina, then 78 years old.

commonplace in those years. Yet they had to take precautions every time. After a while, she went outside to see what had happened.

The nun, now 78 years old, remembers the incident clearly.

Her name: Sister Marie Angela.

It had been a long trip from Nha Trang to Dan Nang and, en route, I thought a lot about Kelly Forrest. Now a lobby guard in the Journal Building, he had told me about the incident before I left for Vietnam.

"Please, if you can, see if the orphanage is still there."

I said I would try.

You should know some things about Kelly Forrest. While he was doing duty at the Marine base in Da Nang, he and his buddies helped the nuns and the orphans whenever they could.

They wrote their relatives about the orphanage, and an abundance of food, clothing and medical supplies soon began arriving there for the children.

But if war is sometimes a matter of giving, it can also be a matter of taking. Forrest paid a terrible price, over the years, for killing the terrorist.

"We knew he was hot," Forrest recalled. "We could see the explosives on his back. But after I shot him, we went over to look at him and I saw he was so very young. I had a brother at home about the same age. I had terrible dreams about it after that."

Several years of counseling and the tender understanding of his wife and other relatives has helped him to learn to live with the memory of it.

I thought about that in Da Nang when we set off in search of the orphanage.

We found it, and I stood in the sun in front of the gate and wondered about Kelly Forrest and how it must have been to be 20 years old and have to kill someone who reminds you of your brother.

Just as this line of thinking was getting gutter deep, there appeared a short, slightly stooped woman with sparkling eyes and a voice as soft as sweet violins.

It was my time to meet Sister Marie Angela.

The woman, fluent in English, French and Vietnamese, met our group and immediately took us on a tour of the buildings. No longer an orphanage, it is now a school for Vietnamese street children.

She said she remembered the incident with Forrest although she said she hadn't learned his name at the time.

She remembered the gifts the Marines had arranged to have sent, and she said she continued to remember them in her prayers.

After the tour, she served us lemonade in her study, apologizing because she had no ice to cool it.

And that was it. No politics, no economics. Just pleasant conversation with a pleasant woman who remembers the American presence in Vietnam, especially a young Marine from Milwaukee who had to kill a man when he was 20 years old.

Yesterday, for Sister Marie, is a book from which she is reluctant to read. And the chapter on war seems particularly distasteful.

That's why, as I gently urged her back in time, the little nun always broke away, returning to the present, her convent, and her children dancing, laughing and learning in a place where terrorists no longer threaten and where troubled young Marines exist only in the mists of another time.

Da Nang, like most cities I have visited on this trip, seems no different from the way it was more than two decades ago. Still big, still sprawling, still smelly, still dirty, it seems mostly to have been untouched by either the war or time.

Soviet ships occupy berths at Da Nang Harbor instead of American ships. And Soviet faces appear routinely on the streets instead of American faces.

Otherwise, it all seems unchanged. We were denied a look at the Da Nang airport. We were not told why. I wanted to see it again because it was from there that I flew a couple of combat missions, one with the South Vietnamese air force.

Because I spent a lot of time in the northern part of what was then South Vietnam during the war, it was always necessary to fly to Da Nang. I was familiar with the city and thought that returning to it might be something like "coming home."

It was not. The buildings that housed the media center were gone. So, too, were a couple of restaurants we used to visit. I found no one who could remember, or wanted to, the reporters who worked there. Our government guide would not allow us to see the big airport from which U.S. military planes used to take off for missions in North Vietnam. So I was not disappointed when we headed north.

To get from Da Nang to Hue by automobile, you have to traverse what is known as the Hai Van Pass. During the war it was a stretch of pure hell. The pass, winding around and up mountains provided ideal terrain for Vietcong ambushes.

Military personnel who served in what was called "I Corps" during the war will remember Hai Van Pass.

I never had to cover it by ground during the war, but I did spend a day in a helicopter gunship, one of the four or five craft that would hover over the pass each day to respond to VC attacks.

So this trip through the pass was safe, easy and interesting, offering scenic views. I admit to wincing, once or twice, through some of the hairpin turns and switchbacks, knowing that attacks were launched from those spots during the war.

John Raths, of Homestead, Florida, the leader of our group and a constant companion since leaving Ho Chi Minh City, travels Vietnam with a U.S. Marine Corps cap on his head, a whistle around his neck, a clipboard in his hand and an American flag sticking out of his shirt pocket.

A combat veteran of the war, Raths has made numerous trips to

287

Vietnam since 1985 and is planning more. As a partner in Indochina Communications Services, he coordinates the activities of U.S. veterans wishing to return to Vietnam.

Raths grew quiet once we entered Hue, the city where Vietnam's royalty used to live. Hue, once said to be the most beautiful city in Vietnam, suffered widespread damage during the Tet Offensive in 1968 when North Vietnamese forces occupied the city. The scars of war are still obvious after two decades.

It took nearly three weeks after the Tet Offensive to drive communist forces out of Hue. Raths was a sniper with the Third Marine Division and took part in that battle.

Still reluctant to talk about details, Raths told of firing his rifle so often that the noise of it made his nose bleed. He told how the rifle barrel became so hot from repeated firing that it couldn't be touched.

He took us to the bridge where he was knocked into the water by enemy gunfire and was rescued by a patrol boat. He showed us the locations of two mass graves where the VC dumped the bodies of more than 1,000 Vietnamese civilians they killed.

And he showed us the landing zone across the Perfume River where his Marine detachment entered the battle.

But his eyes softened and, after a while, his voice choked and so we asked no more questions.

We toured the streets of Hue where the most intense of the fighting took place. Even after 20 years, nearly every house is pockmarked from bullets and scratched where shell fragments dug in.

The Citadel and the old Imperial Palace, two of the city's most cherished and historic buildings, were both badly damaged. A plan to renovate them is in progress but has not yet started.

When the battle for Hue was over, enemy losses were estimated at more than 5,000 killed. American losses totaled 21 killed and 1,345 wounded. And, like so many battles in Vietnam, it was unclear who had emerged the real victor.

As our tour ended, I knew at least one thing: The real loser was the city. It suffered the unique agony of having lost its beauty, its charm and its reputation for peace and tranquility in a battle as fierce as any in the long Vietnam War. Hue isn't beautiful anymore. Bullet holes and shattered buildings have seen to that.

Indeed, it seems much the same as the rest of the country, sad, sullen and in a state of neglect.

Like Raths, I, too, was silent with sadness as we prepared to leave.

A Deafening Sound of Death Hovers Over My Lai

It takes some doing, especially for an American, to reach this place where a village once stood, this place that has become synonymous with senseless death in an unpopular war.

You have to cross the bridge over the Tra Khuc River and turn off Highway 1 onto a single lane, a deeply rutted road where, for 12 kilometers, you dodge dogs, ducks, chickens, children, oxen, bikes and water buffalo. It takes the better part of an hour.

That is the easy part.

Because once you reach this place that is the Vietnamese version of the killing fields, you have to scale, or otherwise negotiate, a monumental wall of shame. American shame.

That is the hard part.

It hurts so much that you want to hang your head. You want to turn away. You want to blink back the tears that burn in your eyes.

STONE MONUMENTS memorialize the dead of My Lai, marking the exact spots where people fell. Jay Reed wept at the sight.

You want to shake off the pain that is breaking your heart. You want to shriek to the skies and to all who will listen that you are sorry for what happened here.

You want to take it all back. You want the memory of it to go away. You want to tell someone, anyone, that Americans are good people, that we are not killers of old men and women and babies.

You want someone to believe that My Lai was a mistake, a terrible mistake of war.

And, more than anything else, you want the dead to come back to life. You want the babies to laugh and play again. You want the old men to sit in the sun and you want the old women to chatter and smile on their way to market. You want things to be the same again.

But My Lai was. And My Lai is. It remains an ugly blemish on the complexion of a nation, and the American visitor to this place of death becomes, instantly, and uncommonly, aware of it.

When U.S. soldiers came to My Lai and killed everything and everyone in sight, the event cast a new and sinister light on what was already perceived to be an evil war.

They killed in clusters, the soldiers did, and by ones and twos. More than 170 went down in one place along a ditch where their blood turned the stinking water to shades of muddy red.

The way they tell it here now is that the final toll was 504 people, mostly old men and women and children.

The story of the My Lai massacre was big news in America for a while. It weighed a ton on the public conscience. It was thought to be a crime, this killing of old people and babies. Yet only one person, Lieutenant William Calley, was ever convicted for it.

Two decades after the fact, the matter is all but forgotten except for those history books that chronicle it and those military texts that refer to it.

What these texts say is that on March 15, 1968, a company of American soldiers conducted an assault on the village of My Lai. Their target was the 48th Vietcong Battalion, a local force of about 250 men that posed a threat to the nearby city of Quang Ngai. The company had previously suffered casualties from mines, booby traps and snipers near My Lai.

The soldiers entered the village shooting at any Vietnamese they saw. Army reports, hidden for more than a year, said 175 Vietnamese were killed. Vietnamese officials put the death toll at 504.

The incident came to be known as the My Lai massacre.

It was, and is, a national embarrassment buried, just as surely and as deeply as the victims of My Lai.

But for Americans who visit here, the sounds that come from the nearby graves are silently deafening. They grab at the heart, twisting and tearing at it with skeletal fingers that leave bony imprints on the soul.

The area where most of the killings took place is no more than a five-acre tract, maybe less. You walk down what was once the village's main street counting, as you go, the clearly defined humps where 24 hooches once stood, all that My Lai ever was.

It is not all that well kept. Weeds reach up to mid calf. The ground is spongy with water and spotted with the dung of grazing water buffalo.

But when you cross the wooden bridge that spans the little creek, you see the first of a score or more of gray, stone markers that cover those places where the people fell. Each displays the names and ages of the victims.

Do Thi Hep was 70 years old when the Americans killed her. Do Cu was four years old and Pham Cu was one. Do Cu Bay was 10.

Unaccountably, the stone is cold to the touch despite the heavy heat of midday.

Your eyes sweep the plot and you see the gray markers standing in tragic profusion midst the weeds and the hedges, calling cards of death.

You walk to the ditch on the outer perimeter of the plot to the maker that shows where 170 people died. You look at the trickle of brown water where it rushes between two rocks and you wonder why there is no sound to it.

Only then do you realize that there is no sound at all in this place of death. No sound. You hear no bird songs even thought they flit in flocks about the trees. The water buffalo at work in nearby rice paddies grunt and groan as they slosh through the mud, but you can't hear it.

"You want to say that Americans are good people, not killers of old men, women and babies..."

Even the afternoon wind that bends the grasses and moves the tree branches is silent.

You hear only the beating of your own heart and the sound of your own breath coming in gasps as you try to pull forces within yourself sufficiently together so that you might cope with the memory of those events that took place here.

You feel the moisture build on the palms of your hands and you wobble ever so slightly as your knees weaken and your legs tremble. Sweat pours down your neck and the heat seems stifling.

You kneel before the first marker and try to figure out what threat four-year-old Do Cu or one-year-old Pham Cu might have been to the American soldiers.

And what about Pham Thi Trinh, who was 10 years old that day and who survived the killing by hiding inside a clothes cupboard? She saw her parents, six brothers and sisters, grandmother and aunt and uncle killed by the Americans.

Trinh, now a government employee in Da Nang, still finds it difficult to discuss the massacre with Americans.

At the end of the plot marking the outer edge of the village that once was, the Vietnam government has erected a billboard-size mural depicting the villagers in their final death agony.

It is part ugly, part beautiful and delicately informative in a heart-crushing way. It is self-explanatory for any nationality.

Away from the stone markers and the mural and the other monuments to death, there is a building housing photographs and papers and other memorabilia of My Lai.

Inside, a young woman, Miss Thao, leads us on a brief tour. Through an interpreter, she tells us the story of My Lai, pretty much the way we had come to know it. Her voice is soft and her luminous eyes shine brightly as she recounts the grisly details.

She stares directly at us as she speaks, and some of us find it necessary to break the eye contact and stare at the floor.

Feelings of guilt are sometimes difficult to understand. I can't speak for the others, but I know I felt shame grinding at my gut. And I felt sorrow. Genuine sorrow for the Vietnamese and for the Americans who didn't need this and deserved better.

When the soldiers killed that day, they turned My Lai into a monument, a most inglorious one for America. And they did it by going beyond the ordinary meaning of search and destroy.

I know it is dangerous to make judgment on any military man's actions in wartime until you have walked a mile in his combat boots.

And I know the Vietnam War was of such fiber that while old men and women and children did not actually pull the triggers that caused American deaths, they frequently aided and abetted those who did.

If My Lai is a scornful blight on America's military reputation, I know there are a thousand other incidents that stand as bright, shining examples of courage and bravery and dignity.

When the lecture is over, Miss Thao thanks us for our visit. She says she thinks it must be difficult for Americans to do that. I tell her it is, indeed, difficult. I tell her I'm sorry for what happened here. It sounds weak.

She nods, eyes still penetrating, still luminously bright. Do they brim with tears? Or do they gleam with hate? I can't tell.

From the shadowy heat of the building I turn once more to the place where the village once stood. It is wrapped in a death shroud. You can't see it, but you can feel it.

The silence, the deadly silence of it, pounds at my being like drums of eternity.

I wear a cloak of sadness now and I wrap it tightly about and turn my back, for the last time, on My Lai.

Fittingly, then, it begins to rain.

My Name is War

Jay Reed filed this dispatch from Vietnam during the war. It was published after he returned home early in 1968.

Know me now and know me well, for I'll be around as long as the hearts of men throb with greed and the need for power.

And, above all, know me by my right name, which is War.

I'm clean and dirty, ugly and beautiful, courageous and cowardly, gentle and brutal. My heart is black and my soul is corrupt, but mostly I'm made of such simple things as sights and sounds and smells and emotions.

I'm a Vietnamese child whimpering in the night for a mother I'll never see again. I'm a shoeshine boy selling dirty pictures on the side. I'm a letter from home, a bloody bayonet, a leech that will suck until there is nothing left to take, a stick of gum, a pair of dry socks.

Know me for what I am and rejoice that I am not to be your bedfellow this night.

For I am the salty taste of sweat, the dry taste of fear. I am the pain that rots in your stomach when you know that death might come with the next step or the next. I am the saliva that balls up in your throat and chokes back your breath when the firing begins.

And I am the soft night, the warm night, the icy green of a million stars. I am the sound of the sea splashing in gentle rhapsody against a tuning bar of soft sand.

But do not be lulled.

For I am the whine of an artillery shell, the thump of a mortar, the roar of a bomb. I am a shriek that rips from the throat of a man whose arm has just been blown off. And I am the sobs of a boy who has come to realize he walked through a corner of hell—and lived.

There's more too, you know.

I am the growl of a bulldozer, the pounding of a hammer, a truck loaded with brown, cardboard cartons. I'm traffic, incredibly snarled. I'm a convoy, a barge, a motorbike, a pedicab. I'm a helicopter, a vintage airplane, a sleek jet worth more money that you will ever make in three lifetimes.

I'm a can of C rations heated over a little fire hidden so the smoke won't show. I'm powdered eggs and canned milk and chocolate candy melted into one sticky, brown lump. I'm a hundred one-room shacks with tin roofs standing in a row under the blazing sun.

And I'm a little brown man knee-deep in garbage sifting it for bits of meat and greens. And I'm an old man, sleeping on the sidewalk. Flies crawl over me. But I don't feel them.

I am the music of the universe, the song of eternity. I am a hill called Con Thien where the spirits of a hundred dead men dance each night in the brilliant glow of artillery fire. I am the olive-drab pouch that holds all the remains of what once was life. And I am a broken heart.

Men may protest the fact that I exist. They may march and beat their chests and send agonizing shrieks toward the sky at what they call the injustice of it all. And maybe they are right or maybe they are wrong.

But I do exist and I am as real as tomorrow's sunrise. It just may be that those who agonize the longest and loudest over my being have no real knowledge of what I am.

> **"Rejoice that I am not to be your bedfellow this night..."**

For if I breed corruption and agony and death, I am also the womb in which is conceived courage and bravery and honor and love. I may be the arm that reaches out to kill but I am also the hand extended to help.

If there is no right and just compensation for the tears shed upon some grassy grave, neither is the limit to the price of pride and dignity.

So know me now and know me well. Know me for what I am. The pain I render is unrelenting. The scars I leave are deep.

My name is War.

Be glad I do not hold your hand this night.

Years After the War, Combatants Meet Again

Two decades ago, had we met on a dark Vietnamese night, he would have killed us. Or tried to.

He would have shot us down or sliced our throats or bled us to death with punji stakes.

And then, killing accomplished, he would have cut off our ears, or worse, because that is what Vietcong warriors did in those days, if the spirit moved.

But that was yesterday.

Now peace, of sorts, is full upon this part of Vietnam that borders the rice-rich Mekong Delta and there is no fight left in Ngo Anh Dao, former Vietcong squad leader, former killer of Americans, former guerilla warrior and, now, a full-fledged, bona fide, 24-karat hero of the Socialist Republic of Vietnam.

At 65, Dao is a leader of this village of Can Tho by virtue of his combat record. If the Vietcong awarded campaign ribbons for battle-field accomplishment, his

ENEMIES NO MORE. Two decades after the war, Jay Reed and David Keen sat across the table from Ngo Anh Dao, once a Vietcong military officer and now a revered war hero of his nation. The former combatants shared memories freely.

chest would be full of them. Other village elders look up to him. Children worship him. His advice and counsel are sought and prized.

So score one, a big one, for Dao.

David S. Keen of Stuart, Florida is a successful businessman now, but from 1962 through 1964, he was a military adviser to the army of the Republic of South Vietnam stationed here in Can Tho, and in the Delta, as a communications and cryptography expert.

Keen fought the Vietcong in this spongy, water-soaked land of rice paddies and jungle they used to call Ambush Alley. That combat left an indelible mark upon him.

Even today, Keen is uncomfortable sitting or standing near open doorways. In public places he sits, whenever possible, with his back to a wall, where he can observe those things going on about him without worrying about what is happening behind.

Bridges still make him nervous because they were favorite ambush targets, and he avoids, when possible, darkened streets and narrow alleys.

"You can say," he says, "that I still live defensively." But Keen also understands the enormity of his tour of duty. "You can also say," he says, "that I lived through a rough draft of history."

So score one for David Keen.

It is entirely possible, although neither can be sure, that Keen and Dao shot at each other during the war. They do know that they each took part in the battle of Ap Bac in 1963, when the VC inflicted a serious defeat upon South Vietnamese and U.S. forces.

Keen and I, along with Journal photographer Carl D. Hoyt and Michael Castellano, of Guilford, Connecticut, visited Dao's village during our trip through Vietnam. We met with him and some other village officials plus 50 or so residents attracted by the rare appearance of Americans.

There was a stiff formality about it all. We were taken to a building, a sort of village hall, where Dao and two officials sat on one side of a table with Keen, Castellano and me directly across.

Dao did most of the talking. He had much to talk about. Through an interpreter, but looking directly into our eyes, the old man told us some of his battlefield exploits, dwelling on the Vietcong victories.

We traded stories and, after a while, some of the stiffness, some of the cool formality melted away until it was nearly like old soldiers reliving the past.

At the end, Dao said:

"I no longer hate Americans. In fact, I don't think I ever did really hate you. You must remember we were fighting in defense of our homeland.

He said he was glad we took the time to visit his village. He said he hoped that we would return to America with good thoughts of Vietnam.

I spoke for our party.

I said that we had come to Vietnam in peace, that we were honored to visit his village and converse with him, that we wished him good health, prosperity and a long life. Then we shook hands.

And that was that.

Except for this:

I thought about the old Vietcong guerilla for a long time after that. And I thought about our conversation. I remember trying to read his eyes. He had sat ramrod straight throughout at the edge of his chair. His hands painted invisible pictures in the air as he talked, but his face was without expression. And his eyes gave no clue, either.

He said the hate was gone from his heart, if, indeed, it had ever been there, and I wondered whether that was really true. Did he really mean the many good things he had said about Americans or was he just being polite in the way winners can be polite?

Later, we visited a Vietcong cemetery and I found the grave of Truong Ban La, a guerrilla fighter who was killed in 1963. Another grave held what was left of Le Van Nam, who was killed in 1968. The first was a significant year for David Keen, the other a significant year in Vietnam for me.

I remembered what we had seen at Cu Chi in another area near the Mekong Delta the day before, the elaborate tunnel system the Vietcong used to elude American forces. And I remember the obvious pride expressed by the tour guides who told us how the VC had

"I no longer hate Americans. In fact, I don't think I ever did really hate you..."

operated there during the war at the expense of American dead.

I had the feeling that they enjoyed the telling of it too much, especially to an audience of Americans.

And I remembered the place at Cu Chi where some young people played volleyball on a muddy court in front of several burned-out American tanks and crumpled helicopters, bullet holes in them clearly marked.

With all of that spilling around in my head and my heart, I made a judgment of which I am neither proud nor ashamed. It is just the way things are within one person.

In the interest of common courtesy, I had been a hypocrite in our meeting with the old Vietcong fighter. And I had used hypocritical language.

If the old man could say in truth that he no longer hated Americans, I could not say that about the Vietcong. Even after 22 years and a nearly complete change of attitude about the Vietnam War, I knew I still hated the old man and all those like him.

Now maybe he felt the same way. I have this thought that he did. I have this thought that he hated the guts of the Americans who came back to the scene of defeat without showing or voicing humiliation.

297

Maybe the old man could forgive and forget. He had said as much. But I knew I couldn't. Usually, when I walk through a cemetery, any cemetery, I get an almost overwhelming feeling of sadness.

But not at the place where the VC were buried. There was no feeling at all. Maybe it was American guns or bombs that had put them in that place where they could be called martyrs by those who survived and won.

But dead VC or martyrs, whichever you call them, you had to know they'd taken Americans down with them. But I knew that my heart wasn't large enough to accept it any other way.

I could not forgive or forget.

But that's just me.

David Keen is different. I believe he meant it when he told the old Vietcong squad leader that he was honored to meet him. I believe he meant it when he said he was sorry for the way the American government ignored the Vietnamese people after the war.

And I believe Keen meant it when he talked about his deep and abiding love for the Vietnamese people.

"I lived with them. I got to know them. I shared their food with them. I learned to speak at least some of their language. I think we should do something for the destruction we caused in this country."

He seems determined, now, to make amends in his own way. He brought a trunk full of clothing with him to Vietnam for distribution to those who needed it most.

And he is making plans for a return trip when he can bring medical supplies and other items.

He admits that it is a small thing. But he is intent on doing his part to make things at least a little better for a country and people that once tried to kill him.

I am envious of him. He has found a way to forgive but not forget.

And so on this strange, sometimes beguiling, often remorseful odyssey through Vietnam's past and present, we learn some things about ourselves.

In Praise of the Grunts

Jay Reed filed this story from Con Thien, Vietnam, in 1967.

This may be your finest hour, for you are about to meet a "grunt."

Doff your cap, if you will; wave a flag; choke back a sob in your throat; wipe away a tear from your eye, for this is the man who is fighting your war.

He is the one up front, the one who is sticking his nose in the mud each day, every day. He is the one who sees the enemy at 25 yards. He is the one who knows what it feels like to be shot at close range by small arms.

He is the one who dies a thousand times when the night is dark and the moon is gone. And he is the one who dies once and forever when an enemy rifle belches flame.

If you have ever slogged through a sticky rice paddy or waded a stream carrying 60 rounds of ammunition, a canteen and a pack with enough field rations and clothing to last a week, you'd know why they call him a grunt. It's fairly obvious.

But look at him well and know him, for he is really something. He wears, in

LETTERS FROM HOME. Tough as a grunt may be, he lives for happy news from back home, and mail creates that important connection.

dirty dignity, a helmet and a flak jacket and a faded field uniform.

His pockets are full and his boots are mud-caked and his eyes never stand still; they move and squint and twitch. He is nervous, aware of every sound. For he operates in a never-never world where the difference between death and one more tomorrow often depends upon what he sees or does not see, what he hears or does not hear.

The grunt is the man who lives as close to war as it's possible to get.

He likes the Air Force because planes give him a measure of protection. He likes the artillery because they can knock the bejabbers out of an enemy platoon. He cares about supply outfits.

He lives first for the day when his tour will be up and he can get out of this country. He lives next for an R and R (rest and rehabilitation). He'd like to get his hands on a can of cold beer because it would drive the heat from his throat and ease the corroding pain in his gut. He'd like to feel the softness of a woman.

But he is a grunt and if he can live through today there will be tomorrow. And if he can live through enough tomorrows there will be the R and R, the cold beer, the feel of the woman, the end of his tour.

The grunt, as he stands in dirty, muddy majesty, is as fine a young fighting man as the United States has ever produced. He is young, tough, intelligent and he knows how to kill.

> **"The grunt is the man who lives as close to war as it's possible to get..."**

But there is something of the builder in these young men. They speak, sometimes, of what must be done in South Vietnam to make it right and workable. They speak, sometimes, of government and how it must work. And, if you are lucky, you may get a grunt to speak his mind about war.

He may tell you many things in language rarely printable. But it may or may not be surprising to learn that for the most part, he understands why he is here and he believes in the purposes that put him here.

And that is something, because if you take a grunt out of his muddy, water-filled bunker, remove his helmet, his flak jacket, his field uniform, take away his rifle, clean him up and dress him in a sport shirt, slacks and loafers, you've got the kid who was playing halfback on last year's high school football team.

He is a national asset to be cherished.

Once Lusty Saigon
Is a Morose, Frowning Shell of a City

August, 1967

The American sips a beer and sucks a cigarette in a dimly lit bar in Tokyo's infamous Ginza district. The Japanese woman at his side wants to keep their somewhat thin conversation alive, so she asks:

"Where you go from here, Joe?"

The American, whose name is not Joe, looks at her.

"I'm leaving tomorrow. For Saigon."

It startles the woman. Her face shadows. A sudden frown sends tired little lines racing around her eyes and mouth. She exclaims:

"Ooooh, Saigon!"

Her voice is richly resonant with all the danger, excitement, mystery and intrigue wartime Saigon then represented.

The American would never forget the sound of it.

Ooooh, Saigon! What have they done to you?

Yes, what have they done to that lovely, lusty, gracious, vibrantly exciting, darkly dangerous, always intriguing city we called "the Paris of the East?"

For one thing, they've changed your name. It's Ho Chi Minh City now. That's for the late communist leader whose forces "liberated" this city, united North and South Vietnam and were the clear winners of that war of which

A BUSY DAY in Ho Chi Minh City, 1989. Street vendors, bicyclists and "cyclos" (pedicabs) clog this avenue in the city formerly called Saigon.

the United States was a part. But Ho Chi Minh City? It's clumsy. The words stumble off the tongue. They stick somewhere in the area of the lips. They stagger in the speaking.

They named a snake-thin jungle supply trail after Ho Chi Minh during the war and that seemed appropriate. This, though, does not. But winners of war, like thousand pound gorillas, can do just about anything they want.

The name change has not played all that well in the city except for government people, buildings, agencies and government-operated hotels. Most businesses and shops still use Saigon as their location, and nearly everyone older than 30 still calls the city by its old name. Maybe it's loyalty. Maybe it's defiance. Or, maybe it is simply that old habits are hard to break.

Ouooh, Saigon!

Thousands of Americans, military personnel and civilians, were stationed in or near Saigon or, at least, visited the city or passed through it during the war.

The city they knew then is not the same one I visit now.

They've managed to squeeze the life out of Saigon. It is listless now, sullen, morose. It is a city that frowns. It is a city that limps. Instead of a bright Ao Dai, Vietnam's traditional party dress, Ho Chi Minh City wears black pajamas and dirty, gray shirts.

And it suffers from neglect. Except for a few new government

> **"Imagine a city of four million people without taxicabs. That's Ho Chi Minh City..."**

buildings, some shrines to Ho Chi Minh himself and a couple of downtown hotels that have been given an exterior face lift, this city needs a new coat of paint. It is dull. It is drab. Rust and rot are kings here.

During the war, maybe because of it, Saigon laughed and danced and lusted its way through. It was one of the most exciting and busiest cities in the world then. Bangkok, Thailand, was a cow town in comparison. Now that is reversed.

Oooooh, Saigon!

Ho Chi Minh City runs on pedal power these days. It is a city of bikes and trucks. Except for a few government vehicles, there is virtually no auto traffic.

Imagine a city of four million people without taxicabs. That's Ho Chi Minh City. The streets are all but deserted. A few lights blink through and break up the distant darkness. There are no sounds. No traffic. No music. No people. It is 10 p.m. on a Saturday night.

Ooooh, Saigon!

Ho Chi Minh City and a man named Huang:

During the war he was South Vietnam's chief civil engineer. He worked closely with the South Vietnamese army and with American military officials. He had power, position and wealth. He made, by his own estimation, about $70,000 a year.

But his side lost the war. And he endured the indignities of a communist "re-education camp."

Now he is a cyclo driver in Ho Chi Minh City. He is denied the choicest locations to work. He feels he is lucky when he makes $4 American a month.

He is an old man now. And he is tired. He is as faded and frayed as the St. Louis Cardinals baseball cap he wears in memory of better days.

Huang weeps easily.

I know about that because he was my cyclo driver the other night and I could feel his hot tears on my shoulder as he pedaled me up Nguyen Binh Chieu St. to the Que Huong Hotel. I wanted to cry with him.

Oooooh, Saigon!

———————————

Ho Chi Minh City and a man named Phan Xnam Anh:

Born in Da Nang, he was a Vietcong sympathizer during the war. When the fighting ended, he was a student at the University of Saigon.

He grasped the new government policy and became a firm supporter of the new Socialist Republic of Vietnam.

He speaks of the "liberation" of Vietnam and Saigon. He speaks of the "people's victory." He calls the Tet Offensive "the people's uprising."

Today he wears crisp, white shirts and sharp blue trousers. He carries a clipboard and a brief case. He appears to live well although he will not tell me how much he makes in his job with Vietnam Tourism. The benefits, though, are obvious. He rides in new, air-conditioned vans and automobiles from his agency. He has the power to give orders. He has the clout to expect compliance. He is a pleasant, helpful young man who speaks fine, clear English. He is full of stories about the history of his county. He attempts to answer all our questions. When he can't, or won't, his usual answer is:

"Our authorities have no information on that."

Much of what I do here in this country and much of what I see depends upon his approval. He is one of the government guides assigned to us.

His side won the war.

Ooooh, Saigon!

The old U.S. Embassy building in downtown Ho Chi Minh City looks much as it did during the war except that neglect has chipped away at it, too, over the years. It stands on one of the gracious tree-lined streets just off the center of the city.

The embassy building may be remembered for many things but two stand out in the mind:

One has to do with the attack upon it during the Tet Offensive in 1968 when it was defended by a handful of guards.

The other involves dramatic photographs taken as the last Americans were evacuated from the top of the building on the day of the fall of Saigon in 1975.

Government officials now are eager to take the inquiring American visitors to see the building because they regard it as one of the outstanding symbols of the "liberation."

We are not allowed inside but are given the freedom to walk around the compound. Some signs of those final days remain although the outside wall has been repaired where tanks crashed through it.

Chickens scratch through the weeds and a half dozen vendors operate on the street outside.

The building now houses the offices of Vietnam Petro-Chemical. But our guide thinks it will soon become home to a U.S. mission, which he believes will be established as a first step in developing diplomatic relations between the two countries.

Ooooh, Saigon!

One of the most important collections of buildings in Saigon during the war was the headquarters complex of the U.S. Military Assistance Command — Vietnam, dubbed MAC-V. It was from this complex that most of the military decisions regarding the war were issued.

The buildings and compound are currently being used by the Ho Chi Minh City police, but our guide would not, or could not, explain how.

The U.S. Navy headquarters at Saigon harbor during the war was one of the busiest military complexes in the country. We are allowed to drive past it, but no stopping and no photographs.

We could see a half dozen Soviet ships in the harbor and no personnel who appeared to be Soviets.

Soviets, in fact, are everywhere in Ho Chi Minh City.

Most of the better downtown hotels are filled with them. When street people see a Caucasian man or woman, they immediately think that he or she is a Soviet citizen.

At the Rex Hotel, where public dances are held three times a week, the orchestras are scrupulous in playing both Russian and English music in exactly the same proportion. A Vietnamese friend told me that policy annoys the dancers who have a strict preference for American rock 'n' roll.

Ooooh, Saigon!

We are packed for our trip to the airport. Our bags are at the curb, waiting to be loaded. A woman, Vietnamese, maybe 40 years old, approaches. She is dirty, dressed poorly.

She neither begs for money nor tries to sell us anything. She says, in near perfect English that she remembers the Americans. She had a job, she says, at the MAC-V headquarters.

"Even with the war, it was wonderful to be alive then," she says.

We board our van, and the woman holds her hands outstretched toward the American flag we display.

"Don't forget us," she pleads, "please remember us."

The van pulls away. I look back. The woman is crying.

Ooooh, Saigon!

The U.S. Shadow Has Faded From View

O n the highest of the mini-mountains that ring Vung Tau, a seaport city on the South China Sea, there stands in alabaster splendor a nearly three-story-high statue of Jesus Christ, arms open wide as if to embrace the ships that come from beyond the distant horizon.

It was erected by American troops as a lasting symbol of the United States' presence in Vietnam.

It is an imposing sight, this religious figure. Close inspection shows, however, that its right side was once used as a target by some trigger-happy gunner, for its skin is scarred by .50-caliber rounds. And its brick base is breaking up.

In one of the openings where the bricks have fallen away, a lizard as long as your arm sleeps peacefully in the sun.

And beside it is a huge, rusty French cannon, its firing pit still wide and deep.

Our government guide remarks:

THE HOLEY MAN. Shot full of bullet holes, this statue of Jesus Christ was erected by Americans in the 1960s.

"See. The French left us a cannon that no longer shoots. And you Americans left us a statue that is full of holes."

It is a gentle rip at two countries most often identified with Vietnam's immediate military past.

After 17 days and nearly 2,000 miles of touring Vietnam from the rice paddies of the Mekong Delta to the bleak, memory-laden former combat areas of the north, it is possible to report that precious little remains here to show for America's long involvement in the Vietnam War.

306

We hear, frequently, of the "French Influence" in Vietnam. And, indeed, it is here. But it is architectural in nature. The French built a lot of houses — villas, actually. Many still stand, especially in resort communities such as Dalat.

Those buildings, plus ceiling fans, a couple of restaurants, some bad memories and a rusty cannon here in Vung Tau, seem to account for the French legacy.

It is more difficult to obtain a reading on "The American Influence" if, indeed, there is one.

Americans constructed a lot of buildings, too. But most didn't last the 14 years that have gone by since our departure from the country.

At a place called Cam Ranh Bay, American money and American skill constructed one of the largest, finest deep-water ports in all the Far East.

Presumably it still stands, or most of it, because our government guide tells us that it is used now by Vietnamese and Soviet ships. We are not allowed to see it.

The big U.S. military bases and airfields have succumbed to neglect and diligent scavengers. A rubber plantation, for example, now covers the encampment at Long Binh.

The airstrip at Phu Cat is used sometimes by Vietnamese aircraft, but mostly it has gone to seed. There is military activity at our big

TANKS FOR THE MEMORIES. Vietnamese youngsters now play on war relics like this destroyed battle tank.

base at Ben Hoa, which is why we were not allowed to inspect it.

Ton Son Nhut Airport, once one of the busiest in the world due to American military aircraft, is, in comparison, all but deserted now except for commercial use by Thai Airways, Air France and some Soviet aircraft.

The only remaining sign that America ever used the place at all is a faded yellow building, now collapsed, with a large red cross still visible amid the debris. That building once housed the largest medical evacuation hospital in all of Vietnam.

It is garbage now.

Ho Chi Minh City, once know as Saigon, had a definite American imprint during the war. That is gone. Erased. Some of it by design, some by neglect and some by the simple passage of time.

Even if the American shadow is slowly fading from the face of Vietnam, it continues to show itself every now and then, if in insignificant ways.

Journal photographer Carl Hoyt sips a local beer called Tiger in the lounge at our hotel in Hue. He finishes the beer and orders another.

The waitress says:

"Fini Tiger. How about American?"

Hoyt tells her that is fine. So she returns with a fresh can. The brand?

"Old Milwaukee."

And there is this:

During the war, any bridge that amounted to anything was blown up by one side or the other. Some several times. The country is still in the process of replacing them.

We pass one bridge construction site and spot a piece of heavy machinery. Markings on it clearly indicate it was manufactured by: Harnischfeger of Milwaukee. Who else?

> **"Precious little remains here to show for America's long involvement in the Vietnam War..."**

But David S. Keen, of Stuart, Florida, one of our companions on this trip and among the first of the American military advisers sent to Vietnam early in the war, thinks it is a mistake to seek out material evidence of the American presence here.

"We didn't leave buildings," he says. "We didn't contribute to this country's literature or to its social structure. But we did leave behind ideas. Ideas about freedom, ideas about liberty, ideas about the ability to do what you want, when you want within a framework of rules equal to everyone. That's our legacy to Vietnam."

He may be right. We saw an abundance of evidence that many Vietnamese yearn for the freedom, the liberty, they enjoyed when the Americans were here. The sight of the American flag, which our party almost always displayed, was greeted with uncommon excitement. So it is possible that the American idea still lives in this communist country.

The problem with that is that the number of Vietnamese who were actively involved with Americans and who, through osmosis, absorbed American ideas, dwindles each year. Some have left the country, some were killed, some have died and many, particularly educators, have been pushed so far back in the social structure that their voices are rarely heard.

There is a line of thought that holds that the current communist government is simply waiting for the "American generation" of Vietnamese to die. Then it will have a complete hold on the populace.

Why, then, is the Vietnamese government encouraging American tourists to visit the country? Shouldn't there be fear that increasing contact with Americans might "contaminate" the people?

For one thing, Vietnam desperately needs American dollars. They see the tourist trade as the best means for obtaining them. And the way travel is structured here, the tourist actually has little contact with people other than those the government wants them to have contact with.

The question now is this: How many Americans will want to come here?

My sense is not many, except for some veterans who might want to visit old battle sites, as I did, and perhaps a few world travelers who have seen it all except for this.

My guess is that not a whole lot of Americans will jump at the chance to visit this country. Here's why:

Vietnam is really not a very nice place to visit. Its climate, for the most part, is disagreeable. It is hot. It is wet. It is dirty. It is crowded. The finest hotels the country has to offer right now would rank no better than third-rate anywhere else. And that is a kind assessment.

Travel is difficult and highly restricted. There aren't 50 miles of good road in the entire country.

Tourist officials say that is going to change. Plans are in the works to make the country more attractive, to provide better food, better services with less regulation. The government, with the help of Chinese and Japanese money, is looking at new resort hotels with casino gambling as major attractions of the future.

It could happen. Certainly not everything about the country is negative.

The Vietnam coast along the South China Sea has some of the most beautiful beaches in the world. Developers with money, imagination and a free hand from the government could create resort complexes of uncommon desirability.

But for now, for those Americans who think they might like to come here, let it be said that if you hope to find some sign, some indication of our wartime presence here, you will be disappointed. Our legacy to Vietnam, if you go beyond the children fathered and deserted by Americans and those servicemen still listed as missing in action consists of this:

More barbed wire than the country could ever use.

The junk of war. Shell casings and tank tracks and truck fenders and old wheels and runway matting. Anything of use has already been used. The rest is piled in heaps waiting to disappear.

A few concrete bunkers. Rice grows around them. Water buffalo rub their backs on them. Children play in them.

And that's about it, except for the statue of Christ overlooking Vung Tau. And that's full of bullet holes.

Somehow, and sadly, that seems appropriate.

Because in more than a decade of political and military involvement, the United States spent almost $200 billion to fight the war. Over that period, more than three million American men and women served in Southeast Asia.

Of that number, nearly 304,000 were wounded and 58,000 were killed. When American forces withdrew from Vietnam, 1,284 servicemen were listed as missing in action. Some bodies have since been returned.

Of the total killed or missing, 1,158 were from Wisconsin.

There is no count of the number of Americans whose minds were forever scarred by the war. Nearly 100,000 Americans left Vietnam with acute physical disabilities ranging from amputated limbs to shattered spines to blindness.

Thousands more returned addicted to drugs and alcohol.

Together, that price tag is almost incomprehensible.

And I saw nothing in Vietnam, two decades later, that seemed worth it.